ANGELS OF ACEH

For dear Immaculée

With my deepest respect,
affection & admiration,

[signature]

SOPHIE YORK
5. 7. 10
mscyork@optusnet.com.au

This book is written to honour those who died in the tsunami which hit on Boxing Day 2004; to salute those who were injured and bore their suffering so bravely; and to thank the CASTA team who went in the name of our country Australia, to help in Banda Aceh, Indonesia.

For my boys, who will one day be men. And for their father, who showed them what is possible.

'Do what you can for others and not for yourself'
Liam Dunkin, January 2005

ANGELS OF ACEH

The compelling story of
Operation Tsunami Assist

Sophie York

ALLEN&UNWIN

First published in 2005

Allen & Unwin
83 Alexander Street
Crows Nest NSW 2065
Australia
Phone: (61 2) 8425 0100
Fax: (61 2) 9906 2218
Email: info@allenandunwin.com
Web: www.allenandunwin.com

National Library of Australia
Cataloguing-in-Publication entry:

York, Sophie.
    Angels of Aceh: the compelling story of Operation Tsunami Assist.

    ISBN 978 1 74114 746 9.
    1. Indian Ocean Tsunami, 2004. 2. Natural disasters –
    Social aspects – Indonesia – Aceh. 3. Disaster medicine –
    Indonesia – Aceh. 4. Emergency medical personnel –
    Indonesia – Aceh. 5. Aceh (Indonesia) – Social conditions.
    I. Title.

362.18095981

Set in 12.5/14.5 Cochin by Midland Typesetters, Australia
Printed in Australia by The SOS Print + Media Group

10 9 8 7 6 5 4 3 2

All photos courtesy of the CASTA Team.

Contents

For whom the bell tolls

No man is an Iland,
intire of it selfe,
everyman is a peece of the Continent,
a part of the maine;
if a Clod bee washed away by the Sea,
Europe is the lesse,
as well as if a Promontorie were,
as well as if a Mannor of thy friends or of thine owne were;
any man's death diminishes me,
because I am involved in Mankinde;
And therefore never send to
know for whom the bell tolls;
It tolls for thee.

John Donne (1572–1631)

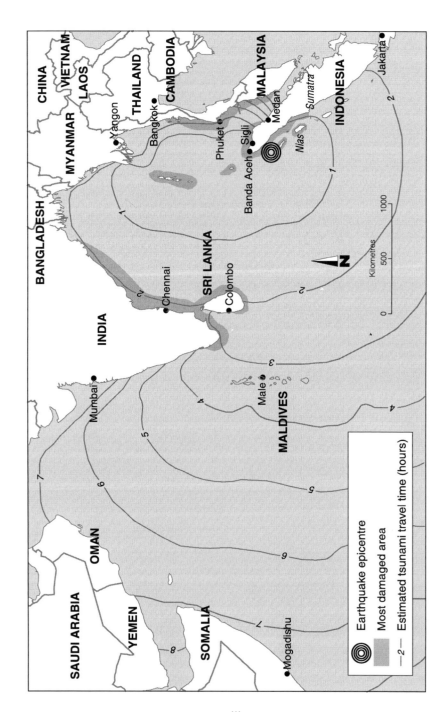

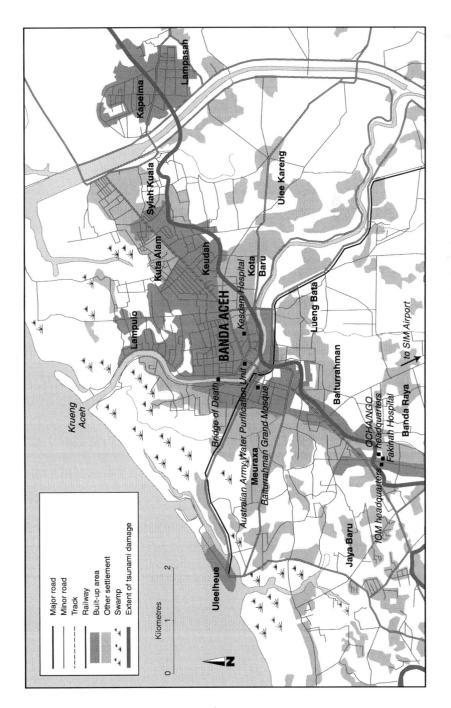

chapter one

The Call

The telephone rang at 10.20 p.m. It was either my family or an emergency. My husband Paul answered it. 'Let me talk to the boss, I'll call you back in ten minutes.'

Paul Dunkin hung up the telephone in his study alcove and sat on the couch, facing me. We looked at each other. He knew what I would say, but he had to hear it from me. We knew each other well. Twenty-three years together does that for you. You know exactly what the other is thinking.

'You have to go,' I said finally. 'They need your skills. And even if you cannot do anaesthetics, just help in any capacity you can. Set up systems, fix things. Repair stuff.'

We talked briefly and Paul called back David Scott, anaesthetist in Lismore and consultant to the government on anaesthetic matters.

'Ask not for whom the bell tolls,' I thought, as I listened intently to the call.

We started packing. He had to be at RAAF Base Richmond first thing in the morning.

It had been a lovely day at Stu Lloyd's. It was Tuesday 28 December 2004. They had barbecued steaks and some sausages for the kids while the chitchat meandered from topic to topic. Stu poured some of his rich eggnog, to curious sips and acclaim. It was a sunny day on Sydney's North Shore. Children jumped happily on the trampoline. The dog played with the toddlers. Stu's eclectic music taste blared inside. Everyone was, as is typical in Sydney's clement summer weather, either on the front verandah or out in the backyard.

The tsunami incident inevitably came up. I commented on the newspaper headlines from Monday which had said that as many as 5000 had been killed. 'No, it is closer to 14 000, Soph,' my husband gently updated me. People sighed. 'No, it is 24 000,' said Roger, the host's brother. I gasped. It was too much for the brain. And nobody could do anything. It was shaping up to be one of these over-whelmingly tragic events which you just absorb, feel gutted by and ultimately cannot do anything about. It was bigger than anything anyone had ever imagined or read about. I hugged my baby, fifteen-week-old Pierce. I had seen a televised story from Thailand where a baby had been ripped from its parent's arms. It was unthinkable to lose a child.

I was not to know yet that my life, the life of my husband and children, and some of the accepted dynamics in the world, would be changed forever by this wave of water called a tsunami. When enough droplets of water join together, they can change everything in their path.

Paul Dunkin was 39. He was the type who looked the same for the twenty years between 25 and 45. Rugged and Australian, there was not a sniff of slightly feminine Leonardo DiCaprio good looks about him.

His eyes were what grabbed your attention. Blue, intense, and fringed by unfairly long dark lashes. And then there was that roguish smile. He hadn't been nicknamed 'Maximus' by nurses in the past for nothing. Think Russell Crowe rather than Jude Law.

Paul was not sentimental, except perhaps about me and our four sons. His style, which befitted an anaesthetist, was no-nonsense, practical and dizzyingly time-efficient. He was the president of a group of anaesthetists. He had started the group a few months ago, three weeks before I had a new baby, and while working on renovation plans to make room for the new arrival. Setting up the anaesthetic practice had meant meetings, telephone calls, solicitors, the drafting of a raft of documents. He was working full-time in a number of different hospitals, which included some weekends and nights on call, and he was also studying a Post-Graduate Diploma in Perioperative and Critical Care Echocardiography. He got through it all somehow, without drama. And spent time with his children and wife, too.

Paul was a good anaesthetist. It was just one of those things observed and remarked upon by his colleagues. Real praise was always good to hear, everyone needs it occasionally. It made you want to continue to live up to it too. Over the years he had performed anaesthetics on a host of people, for a host of conditions, from the double-lung transplant on a well-known Australian CEO and the kidney-stone surgery for an Australian governor, to the eye surgery on a comparative 'nobody'. But to Paul, no person was a nobody. People were people, to Paul. The eye surgery would make that person see. The work was intense, but it came with its own rewards.

Early the next morning, Wednesday, 29 December, Paul re-packed his bags, throwing out half of my selections, and loaded the luggage into the back of the car. As he drove to RAAF Base Richmond, he rang everyone he could think of to re-arrange his work so that the operation lists were covered. Visiting Medical Officers (VMOs) like him often work at a number of hospitals. He called his fellow anaesthetist and friend Nigel Symons to see if he could cover for him. 'Be careful Paul', said Nigel. 'Stay safe.' He spoke to Anne Pike at the Seventh Day Adventist Hospital, Greg O'Sullivan at St Vincent's. They immediately took care of his lists. They each said warmly, 'Good on you, Paul, for going.' It was gratifying to hear. He didn't particularly feel like a hero. The unknown was scary, but sometimes the known can be worse. Some of the affected areas were suffering severe aftershocks, some had disease outbreaks, others were war zones. Piles of dead people. He didn't want to think about those things yet. Plenty of time to meditate on the plane. Brace himself.

Reminding himself of the malaria risk, he looked for a roadside pharmacy.

It was strange. Here he was, driving out to Richmond with no idea of what his specific mission was or where on the planet he was heading. He just knew he had to help and that he had his wife's full support. He did not want to imagine how she was going to cope with four little boys on her own while she was still breastfeeding Pierce, born fifteen weeks earlier and still not sleeping through. Soph's going to be doing it tough, he thought. Twenty-two month old Francis was fun, but a bit of a handful. He had begun the terrible twos early. Darcy, four, was improving in his behaviour as he began to articulate his requirements, but he and Liam had their moments. Like young puppies, they could all bounce off the walls sometimes. They were great kids—really cheery, loving and capable. Thank heaven for that at a time like this. But his family was healthy and alive. They would be fine. He had to think positively.

Paul pulled up at a pharmacy, handed over his prescription and, while he waited for it to be filled, mentioned the tsunami, its victims and his destination. The concerned and generous proprietor loaded him up with travel items, gratis. Paul was deeply touched and told me about it on the mobile. I decided to compose a letter about this unexpected kindness from a complete stranger, and emailed it to the *Sydney Morning Herald*. It was printed the next day, Thursday, 30 January, amid a steadily growing host of Letters to the Editor on the horror.

On Monday, 27 December, David Scott had emailed his entire professional database at 3.25 p.m. He had been at home in Lismore, New South Wales, and had watched some early news reports. The tsunami story was unfolding on radio and television by the hour and in the daily newspapers. David was a Wing Commander in the Air Force Reserves and an anaesthetist at Lismore Hospital, and he was also the chair of the Consultative Group to the Australian Defence Force (ADF) on Anaesthetics. Issues which came up were discussed by the group, usually by email, and the feedback provided to the ADF. It could relate to anything in anaesthesia, from the purchase of a new monitoring machine, to the use of a particular drug or technique. As chair of this group, David thought he should get some anaesthetists on standby and that he was the best person to put the word out, post-haste. This sounded like something medical types should get involved in, and fast.

From the news reports, things were looking desperate and they would not have time to lose if they were to do some good. Critical injuries become fatal if left untreated. Surgery, and therefore anaesthetics, would be needed.

He called Air Commodore Tony Austin, director-general of the ADF Health Services to let him know what he had in mind. Tony was the highest-ranking medical officer in the permanent forces. Head Honcho. It was a tri-service position — Army, Navy and Air Force all deferred to him. David asked, 'Do you need me to get a group on standby, Tony?' They knew each other well. 'That would be great, David. Thanks. I will be in touch.' They spoke briefly and quickly.

At this stage, too, the Commonwealth Department of Foreign Affairs and Trade (DFAT) was across the issue, and was liaising with the prime minister's office and the Health Services Wing (HSW), the Air Force's medical department.

Health Services Wing called David at 10 a.m. on 28 December, wanting the names of two specialists for an advance mission to the devastated areas. The two chosen would be needed to do a reconnaissance, (a 'recce'). This was an advance mission to survey what the damage was, what resources were available at a local level, and what medical and other supplies and personnel were needed to be sent in. These specialists would be responsible for establishing Aero-Medical Evacuation services (AME) in the region. Wing Commander Bill Griggs from Adelaide and Squadron Leader Allan MacKillop from the Gold Coast were chosen. They left immediately.

Griggs had sussed this kind of thing out before. He had even assessed Christopher Skase for the government. But the stakes here were altogether different.

Tony wanted a shortlist of anaesthetists. It had to be top-heavy with specialists who had experience in particularly austere conditions, those who had shown in the past they could hack it emotionally, professionally, and could work very, very hard. The type who could face adverse factors of every variety and not fall in a heap. Think Rwanda, Somalia, Bougainville, East Timor. The faint-hearted and prima donnas were not going to be needed on this mission.

David Scott's email to his professional database on the Monday had been short and to the point; you were either available or you weren't. His initial contact asked recipients for the number of days they could spare (at least seven would be needed), contact details, and their nearest airport. At this stage the mainstream news were reporting the big picture details of the disaster but the real and technical scope of the disaster was still undetermined. Communications (or comms in military speak) had been knocked out in some places, and in others the survivors were still in shock. The appropriate response Australia would make was yet to be clarified. MacKillop and Griggs would gather relevant information and report back from sites as fast as they could. The challenge of this task, when many places were in complete chaos, could not be underestimated.

The defence medical community is a close-knit one, and the anaesthetists are even closer, but David wasn't holding out much hope. It had happened on Boxing Day; everyone was on holidays with their families. The message was hardly an attractive one in the scheme of things. David saw that Paul Dunkin, a Lieutenant Commander in the Naval Reserves, was on the list of recipients of his email. Paul would be a non-starter this time, he thought to himself. David recalled Paul telling him, 'Won't be able to play soldiers for a while, mate, we have a new baby on the way. Our fourth. Soph needs me.'

David and Paul's paths had crossed a number of times over the past years. David had been the Director of Training at Lismore Hospital where Paul had undertaken a stage of his anaesthetic training. They had been deployed together to the Solomons on HMAS *Manoora* in 2003. Australia had sent the Navy to support the 2000-strong Australian Federal Police force there. Paul had been involved in a dramatic episode involving a heavily pregnant islander who had been convulsing with eclampsia, and seemed to be dying. The medical team had choppered her to hospital from a field, from among a wide-eyed village crowd. Paul had kept a cool head in a crisis and both mother and baby survived. David smiled to himself at the memory. She had given her baby a rather unusual second name for an islander—Paul.

It would have been good to have had him along again. Shame about the timing. So David was surprised when, at 6.36 p.m. that Monday, Paul responded and said he might be available to go, if needed.

David was pleased at the overall response. His inbox was filling, and the available list was growing. Thank goodness for the internet—you could notify a stack of people simultaneously. The only drawback was the reply delay. Meanwhile, he gathered some of his things together, handed over stuff to Rachel his wife and chatted to her and his young son and daughter, James and Suzannah, watched the news and waited for the next instructions from headquarters.

He had fifteen people answer with a 'yes' by 6 p.m. on the Monday. By 1.00 p.m. Tuesday, the next day, he had 30 volunteers. All who could respond had said yes. David telephoned through the names to the director-general, Tony Austin.

The answer came back. Four had been chosen: Paul Dunkin, Paul Luckin, Brian Pezzutti and David Scott. David hit the phone to confirm that these four could definitely join the mission.

Paul arrived at RAAF Base Richmond at 9 a.m. on the Wednesday, 29 December. When he arrived at the front gate, he was told he needed to obtain a pass. But when he went to the pass office, he was told that this requirement had been waived for the mercy mission. So he went back to the gate and was allowed through. Ahhh, military admin! It was all coming back. He hadn't been out of the permanent Navy—back in the civvie world and the Reserves —long enough to forget.

He parked in the secure parking and strode purposefully over to the air movements building. He was the first to arrive and stood in the warehouse watching the loading of the aircraft. Air Force, CareFlight, New South Wales Fire Brigade and Ambulance personnel had obviously been working around the clock to load up the plane with provisions. Pallet after pallet went in. Mike Flynn, former commodore of the Royal Australian Navy and past work colleague of Paul's, walked up and shook his hand.

'Glad to have you on board, Paul!' he said. 'I was very happy when I saw your name on the list!' Mike was to be the team leader.

Paul smiled. Brothers in arms, now brothers in alms, that's how it was. There was a bond forged by the suffering you endured in the services. Well, not really, but you shared camaraderie under training, you knew the pitfalls of administration, the agony of dealing with large bureaucracies, the tedium involved in paperwork, the necessity of working with hierarchies . . . and you also knew how to get on with the job despite all these frustrations. The armed forces gave you skills that you sometimes only appreciated after you'd left. Not everyone could make a proper speech, prepare a methodical lesson, organise a function, drive a warship, fly a jet. It wasn't only about shiny shoes and parades. It was about being instantly able to discern what was necessary, in any situation, and quickly. It was about being adaptable. Managing change. Improvising.

Mike Flynn was in his fifties. He was the New South Wales State Health Services Functional Area Coordinator for Disasters and was in the Navy Reserves. He had been the Fleet Medical Officer in the permanent Navy. And a pilot. He had been a classic good-looking fighter-jock in his younger days. He had flown both fixed-wing and choppers. CT4s, Maachis, and then Skyhawks. Wessex, Iroquois and the UK Gazelles. He was close to six foot and of normal solid build, clean-shaven with well-groomed brown hair, cut short, back and sides. Mike had a reliable, affable personality with a pleasantly relaxed manner. He was savant, well-read and a deep thinker. A closet scientist and philosopher. His life experiences had made him wise, but not jaded at all. Married to Caroline, they had three children—a daughter and two sons—who were all now grown up and making their own marks.

Mike was vague on detail, preferring to leave that to others, his concern was the big picture. His speaking style was professorial. Why use two clipped words when ten eloquent ones would sound so much better, that was Mike. Although far from a military movie cliché, he was highly competent and had a good handle on what was required and how to achieve goals. His Navy background was going to be a bonus here. His leadership skills would be crucial. You cannot take 28 highly intelligent people out of their comfort zones to where there will be numerous competing ideas on how to do things and hope to dictate to them unless you can command their respect. Expect mutiny otherwise.

Today his clothes were rumpled and his eyes red-rimmed. His pen was behind his ear; his hands held paper. He had obviously not slept, preparing for this mission.

Other members of the team began to arrive. Some came from Perth. One was from Melbourne. A few from Brisbane. They milled around for hours, as the plane-loading went on. Watching the cricket on TV and twitchily chatting. It was the Fourth Test. In Melbourne, against the Pakis. There was a brew bay and bikkies. Bags to be re-packed and fiddled with. Mobiles, texting. The time dragged. Hurry up and wait.

The media were also there, wandering around. They latched on to Paul and David, and a young blonde woman TV reporter interviewed them briefly with a television crew in attendance. Caught their smiles and reassurances to their families and, before the cameras cut away, Paul's worried look.

Some of those waiting were given their immunisation shots. Dr Jeremy McAnulty, the director of the Communicable Diseases Branch of New South Wales Public Health, briefed everyone on health in a tsunami-affected zone, 'Don't eat anything you haven't cooked or peeled yourself,' he said. 'Throw it away.' They were to drink only bottled water, take doxycycline daily for malaria, wash their hands whenever possible, keep their fingers out of their mouths and eyes; dress to cover their skin. Dr McAnulty outlined the disease risks—the mosquito-borne ones: malaria; dengue fever; Japanese encephalitis. Then there was cholera, typhoid, hepatitis A, salmonella, dysentery, all contracted via contaminated food and water. Hepatitis B, HIV—blood-borne diseases. The list seemed endless.

Paul was up to date with his shots, having been to the Solomons. Going there in 2003 was one of the reasons he probably made the short-list, he thought.

Finally, Mike called them all together. They knew why they were there. There had been a major earthquake to the south-west of Sumatra on Boxing Day, 26 December 2004. It was a 9.0 on the Richter scale, one of the largest in forty years. The seismic movement had triggered tsunamis in the Indian–South East Asian region, causing thousands of fatalities and injuries. Eleven countries were affected: Bangladesh, India, Indonesia, Kenya, Malaysia, Maldives, Myanmar, Somalia, Sri Lanka, Thailand and Tanzania; some more than others.

They were to learn more about tsunamis later. Right now Mike was discussing Alpha and Bravo Team. Each team comprised fourteen personnel. Paul Dunkin and Paul Luckin were to be the anaesthetists on Bravo Team under Dr Paul Shumack.

As the names of the two teams were read out (*see Appendix 1*), everyone looked around at each other, sizing up who was who, in which list. Nobody was in uniform. Everyone looked tired, as though they had been packing until all hours and sleeping restlessly. Funny that. One name made heads swivel—René Zellweger. But it was not the Hollywood actress, it was a male surgeon from Perth.

Mike continued with his briefing. Logistical support was to be provided by the New South Wales Fire Brigade. The medical team was to be totally self-sufficient for the unspecified period of time, assessed at this stage to be approximately a fortnight. Four teams—Alpha, Bravo, Charlie and Delta—had been put together by the New South Wales Health Department, acting in accordance with the Commonwealth Government Overseas Disaster Response Plan (AUSASSISTPLAN), in co-ordination with the Commonwealth Department of Health and Ageing (DoHA). Emergency Management Australia (EMA) managed the plan for the Australian Agency for International Development (AusAID). EMA had been set up after Cyclone Tracy.

A committee had been established in response to the Bali bombing to ensure that health responses in an emergency were coordinated—the Australian Health Disaster Management and Policy Committee (ADHMPC, the so-called 'Alphabet Committee' due to its letter-abundant acronym). EMA played an active part in the AHDMPC.

Although it had not been determined yet, Charlie was to end up in the Maldives, Delta in Sri Lanka.

Mike moved to the practical issues of medical supplies and equipment. The Commonwealth did not keep disaster response stocks on hand, the states did. These were medical supplies for treating victims of a disaster. The event could be a bushfire, a train crash, an earthquake, or perhaps a tsunami. Team coordination and supplies would be provided by New South Wales. The obtaining of the crucial items was a job in itself. The clinical pharmacist at Westmead Hospital had stayed up all night on Tuesday, filling a cache with drugs, while nursing staff had put together the surgical supplies such as syringes, plasma-like fluids, dressings and disposable scalpels. The list was endless. Down at the fire station at Greenacre, firemen had been feverishly packing tents, sleeping bags, mozzie-nets, portable toilets and showers, torches, bottles of water and ration packs of food.

New South Wales Health was requested to provide teams that would give acute medical support for a fourteen-day period. Dr David Cooper, director of New South Wales Health and Ambulance Service Counter Disaster Unit, and his deputy George Smith were busily matching what was required with the people and the resources. The names selected from David Scott's replies had gone to Canberra and, through the EMA network, were now part of the response equation. The mission was to go in and set up the support station and coordinate medical configurations for incoming longer-term support. It was called 'Operation Tsunami Assist'.

They walked out to the waiting plane. Itching to go.

Hurry up and wait again. Paul could barely stand it. He was on the hot tarmac, waiting to get to a disaster zone and quick as a flash nothing was happening.

When he was a child, Paul's mother was smart enough to realise she had a clever, slightly hyperactive son who was best-behaved when he had an engrossing project. She gave him wood pieces and nails and he would happily bang away with a hammer, constructing something, anything, for hours.

Short of wood pieces and a hammer now, he started writing on the lid of the RAAF in-flight ration box. This was a small cardboard box containing a meal for the flight. They each had one. He started a tote right there on the runway, taking names and bets on the wheels-up time. His great-grandmother had been an SP bookie. It was a great way to get to know people's names, too. Mike Flynn looked at Paul smiling, 'Are you going to be our light entertainment for the trip, Paul?' Someone had to have that vital role. Mike then laughed, tossed Paul his own ration box and disappeared off to the terminal with a 'Put me down for 5 p.m.,' over his shoulder.

Some of the team were optimistic, others not so. Ray Southon bet it would be 4.27 p.m., Paul Shumack 4.38. Mike got it on the nose, at 5 p.m. His prize was dinner, with some still left in his own ration box, kindly left uneaten by the others. Not a bad thing for Mike's leadership, coming first at the outset.

chapter two

Operation Tsunami Assist

'You're welcome to come up the front and see the 1970s
workspace,' said the young pilot. He had walked down
the plane, past the densely packed supplies, to talk to the
medical teams as they sat in their aircraft seats. He was
typically trim, athletic and baby-faced. Everything the Air
Force would dream of for its recruiting brochure. Not one
of those moustached silver-templed pilots from the
commercial airlines. Think *Top Gun*, not *Flying High*. They
were in a 707, a four-engined Boeing jet circa 1970. It was
state of the art back then when all the airlines flew them.
John Travolta now flies one, in a retro statement.

Paul had The Seekers playing in his head. Both pilots
were younger than the aircraft, which had daggy décor,
but was more comfortable than a Herc.

They had been warned not to take photographs at
RAAF Base Richmond, as it was a military base. It was
a legitimate request for security reasons, but Paul now
wondered light-heartedly whether it was to keep this
museum-piece under wraps.

Paul pulled the elastic seat pocket towards him and pulled out of it a Qantas in-flight magazine, an early 2003 edition. An interesting find in an air force jet, probably a kind donation from the commercial airline, he speculated, flicking through it idly and catching a glimpse of the world before the tsunami. There was something in it about the Dixie Chicks. He remembered it had been a big year both personally and professionally, he had qualified in cardiac anaesthetics and his son Francis had been born.

Paul stretched out his legs. The late night and early start were starting to catch up with him and the apprehension he had first felt at Richmond hadn't left him yet. The Air Force 'hosties' walked past with garbage bags. 'Pop your stuff in here,' they requested politely. There was to be no clinking of drinks trolleys on this flight.

Their supplies filled the front two-thirds of the 707. The team was jammed up the back in the last five rows, behind a partition. They had no illusions about the mission now. They had seen what was loaded onboard—bottles of water, body bags.

The changeover to a different world was happening incrementally. The plane, the old magazine, the food, the lack of baggage-handlers, the absence of drinks trolleys. The separation from their normal comfortable lives was happening gradually. Despite this the destination was still going to be a culture shock for some in the team.

People chatted and moved around, as much as the remaining space allowed. Some slept. Others pondered life and used the time to prepare themselves mentally. Some tapped into themselves spiritually. For some, all of the above. Bravo's leader Paul Shumack, Alpha's anaesthetist Brian Pezzutti and the two firemen slept. Old hands at this, they knew to grab the zeds while you could.

Ken Harrison sat and plotted a plan for the deployment. How it was all going to work. They were going to be there for about a fortnight. The logistics were his responsibility. He was an anaesthetist by profession, but on this mission he had the supplies and health of the team to take care of.

It was all so weird.

They were a motley crew, from Australia. Most did not know each other. Most had never worked together. Now these men and women were going to work, live, talk, eat together. Sleep side-by-side. Share powerful emotions. Nobody had full knowledge of what to expect. Each wanted to contribute, and nobody wanted to be the weakest link. Mike told them a *Sydney Morning Herald* was circulating and that it contained useful information about the tsunami. I had packed it into Paul's bag as he raced out the door that morning. It was looking pretty tattered now. People talked about rumours they had heard, that a whole island had been washed away, taking all of its inhabitants. That 55 000 people had died, across all the countries affected.

It had all been a bit strange at Richmond. They knew only that they were headed to provide tsunami relief and that they were stopping in Darwin. They had no clue beyond that of their destination. They knew the aircraft would have to top up its tanks in Darwin and take on enough to do a return trip because there was no betting on there being fuel in a tsunami-affected region.

Being the festive season, there was also the concern that there might be nobody at Darwin to refuel the plane. The silly season is when Australians chill out. Maybe nobody would be around, apart from the odd person doing security checks. The flight was not a normal or rostered one. It was hardly 'in the program'. So much was unknown. So many decisions being made and updated. Everything changed, sometimes by the time the speaker had finished his or her sentence. Only the charter was the same. It was simple. Get there, do your bit.

Mike Flynn was to say later, 'You only get the call for The Big One once in your lifetime.' This was it.

They were told not to take uniforms or their military identification cards. Some had turned up with their uniforms, unsure until that point whether the mission was military or civilian. The reasons for making it civilian were still not quite clear yet. They would be, eventually.

In Darwin, they learned of their next destination — Jakarta. And by the time they landed at Jakarta military airport it was night, 1 a.m. Sydney time, but who knew what the local time was. All Paul knew was that it was late.

Paul got off the plane with his small blue daypack, and milled around with the team nearby. The airport was a military airfield. There was no terminal and it was quite dark except for the occasional searing flood-light up high. There were a few people around, but not many. It was shadowy with not much happening except for every ten or fifteen minutes when a plane would land near them, loudly, and then there would be a burst of activity.

Paul realised he'd left his Navy issue bag, his 'bluey', which held his undies and toilet bag on the plane. He inwardly cursed himself. The plane looked like it was closed. Nothing was being moved off it because the decision as to what was the best craft to use to get to wherever they were going had not been decided upon. It couldn't be, at this stage. Not until more was known about their destination. The 707 needed heavylift machinery to unload. A Herc didn't. There were no guarantees that there would be machinery available when they reached the disaster zone.

He stood on the tarmac looking out for the bus that was going to take them into Jakarta, which eventually appeared near the wing of the plane. At that moment, Mike Flynn tapped Paul on the shoulder. 'Isn't your brother-in-law in the military? Is that him over there?'

'What? No, he wouldn't be up here.'

Paul looked over, following Mike's gaze and saw my brother, Bernard York, standing on the tarmac. Bernard was a lieutenant commander in the Royal Australian Navy. Good-looking, olive-skinned with a big gummy smile, doe-eyes, thick, shiny brown hair and short classic naval haircut. Courteous, kind and always ready to listen; girls wanted to mother him. Expressive hands and earnest expressions as he spoke.

With wide grins and a bit of incredulity at how life arranges things, Paul and Bernard exchanged news. Bernard was the godfather to our eldest son Liam and was very close to me. Sophie will worry twice as much, knowing that Bernard is here, Paul thought to himself. When news of the tsunami broke, Bernard had been posted to Jakarta to augment the embassy staff. The staff were busy. The Bali bombing had made everyone on edge about travel to Indonesia and there had been recent warnings, reminding them not to frequent places where expats tended to gather, and not to stay in certain hotels. The Australian embassy in Jakarta had been bombed itself, not so long ago. It was hard not to take it personally.

None of this was on anyone's mind right now. The tsunami response had eclipsed everything else. People were suffering. The irony of having your safety at risk, when you had come to help, escaped them for now. They were too tired to absorb it. Bernard was pre-occupied and couldn't talk for long. He was a supply officer and he was working out the logistics. Essentially, he was traffic-copping incoming aid provisions, supplies, non-government organisations (NGOs) and refugees, who were landing in from all over the place. The Indonesians were wisely vetting everyone, including aid workers who were arriving as a pit-stop to elsewhere, in order to prevent the needy areas becoming even more stressed by the arrival of well-meaning but under-resourced groups.

Major Supri was a gracious officer from the Indonesian military (the TNI) who was fluent in English, and helped Bernard enormously, especially in the coordination of aid from Indonesian warehouses into waiting RAAF aircraft bound for the disaster zones. Over the next few days, an AusAID representative and personnel from RNZAF and the RAAF would take over the coordination of the aid effort and aircraft tasking, which required liaison between the TNI and the ADF Joint Task Force set up in Medan.

Paul joined the rest of the medical team, who were boarding two hot, stinking, short-length buses. They stopped at boom-gate after boom-gate to exit the airfield, with endless discussions taking place between the bus drivers and the uniformed figures manning each one. It was dark and the traffic was thick on their way to the hotel. Paul was feeling irritated and gritty. He looked forward to relaxing after the long day.

The hotel was in a one-way street that was designed to thwart terrorists. The guards swept mirrors under every arriving vehicle, searching for explosives. There was no friendly check-in process, it was more like going through security at an airport. Bags through X-rays, hand-held detectors sweeping over your body. Jeepers.

Sherryn Bates, the hotel's marketing manager and fellow Australian, met them in the foyer. She had stayed up late to greet them and she warmly welcomed them all. She was forty-ish, brunette, well-spoken and stylish. Nothing was too much trouble for her. The embassy had organised the medical teams' stay. After writing down their names, the teams went off to hit the hay.

Paul noticed that some kind team member had brought along his bluey, he was relieved and thankful. His grimy clothes could be changed after all. Everyone retired for the night, believing they were exhausted. They were soon to discover what true exhaustion was in the days to come.

Paul was disturbed at 4 a.m. by Dallas, a nurse at the Sydney Adventist Hospital in Sydney. The TV in the nurses' tea-room was tuned to the *Today* show. Over her Vegemite toast and before the morning shift started, she had seen Paul interviewed at Richmond. She phoned immediately, concerned but proud of him. She heard his groggy voice. 'Go you good thing!' she said. Something like that. Paul mumbled a response. He remembered the call later that morning when he was woken by Bernard knocking on the door.

Breakfast was croissants, perfect eggs, luscious fruit, freshly squeezed orange juice and strong, fragrant coffee. Sherryn had outdone herself. This was the last real meal before ration packs. Beef bacon, of course, reminding the team that they were in a Muslim country.

Paul breakfasted with Bill Griggs and Allan MacKillop. Bill Griggs had been Paul's instructor on Emergency Medicine courses back in Paul's Navy days. Big build, had once had more hair, affable. He was known as Dr William Griggs, AM, Director Trauma Services, Royal Adelaide Hospital in his civilian life, and was a Wing Commander in the RAAF Reserves. Whenever the country had a problem, the government called on Bill Griggs to look into it. He had been to countless disaster and war zones, and numerous sensitive matters that he simply couldn't talk about.

MacKillop had also been an instructor on the courses, but this was the first time Paul had met him personally. Paul was surprised to see the men in uniform. The message at Richmond had been that the initial Australian aid effort was civilian. The two men in camouflage battle fatigues looked incongruous in this five-star hotel. It was all part of an unfolding story.

Griggs looked tired, but MacKillop looked dreadful as he recounted some of what he had seen on their 'recce'. Paul was worried about him, as MacKillop was very drawn and agitated. Slightly wild-eyed. The strange, slightly apprehensive feeling Paul had felt at Richmond came back. His stomach knotted a bit more. These guys were old hands at disaster areas and were clearly carrying some weighty psychological burden. It spooked the team. Not that they needed a wake-up call. They already knew it was not an adventure they were going on, it was something else altogether.

There was nowhere to go, yet. Bernard, who was now at the airfield, rang Mike Flynn: 'There's no point in coming out here, Sir,' he said. 'You have no clearance to depart. Banda Aceh is too congested with aid aircraft landing, for the moment.' Mike called the team together for a briefing in the foyer of the hotel. 'We're going to Banda Aceh,' he said. Paul had never heard of the place. He had heard of a war in Aceh from the news and from a visit to Jakarta in 1999, and thought it was probably a city or something. Mike kept talking—important details, logistical matters, mission update, expectations. Paul could barely hear him, the distractingly jolly music in the foyer was drowning out the key words. He asked the reception staff to turn it down and they obliged immediately.

Mike brought them up to speed with their destination. Banda Aceh was the capital of the province Aceh (Nanggroe Aceh Darussalam), on the north-western tip of the Indonesian island of Sumatra. Banda Aceh had had a population of about 250 000 before the tsunami struck. The population of Aceh province had been estimated at just over four million in recent years. The population of Indonesia was just under 240 million in 2004. Already they knew that the western coastal areas of Aceh had been levelled by the tsunami.

James Branley, an infectious disease physician on the Bravo team, had earlier thought he had heard Mike Flynn say 'We are going to Madang' and had dutifully filled out his destination documents with Madang, Papua New Guinea. It seemed smart, James had surmised, it was probably a neutral place from where they would launch operations. The others enjoyed James' rationalisation greatly, especially as they discussed landing arrangements for Medan, Indonesia. The safety of landing at Banda Aceh, Indonesia, at this stage was in question and so Medan was being considered. They learned the airfield could take the 707, but heavy-lifting equipment would be needed, as there were 17 tonnes of densely-packed pallets to be unloaded from the plane's high doorways.

Mike Flynn then announced that the Australian medical teams of Alpha and Bravo would combine to become the Combined Australian Surgical Team (CASTA) Aceh. As the CASTA members formally introduced themselves to each other, Paul was characteristically upfront. 'I have never been into a disaster zone,' he admitted to the others, 'you'll have to bear with me. If anyone is going to "lose it" first, it might be the most inexperienced.' René Zellweger, a surgeon of considerable experience, looked at Paul thoughtfully. Not many people hid their light under the bushell like that. He heard Paul saying, 'I will carry boxes, fix things. I will do anything you find useful.' This was a highly trained medical specialist making this offer. René knew then that the team would be good, with attitudes like this. Others spoke up about where they had been — East Timor, Bougainville, Somalia, Rwanda, Bali.

For Marjorie Raggett, Lisa Dillon and a few others this was their first deployment. Marjorie and Lisa were emergency nurses from Westmead Hospital in Sydney. They were equally as upfront as Paul. Now was not the time to pretend to be a know-it-all. Being wet behind the ears might be temporarily embarrassing, but the others on the team needed to know, as it would mean the difference between life or death in a critical situation. Experienced people might have a better idea of what to do, to take over a task or at least lead the way.

'There is a phrase you're going to hear more than any other,' said Paul Shumack, the leader of the Bravo team, part of the newly combined CASTA, looking around at their attentive faces. He cleared his throat, to speak a little louder. Some had moved closer.

'Shmackers', as he was nicknamed from quite early on in the operation, put them in the picture. He was scarecrow-thin, medium height, with salt and pepper hair, moustache and glasses. Very secure and laid-back, he didn't take himself too seriously, and had a ready humour. He worked as a consultant physician in occupational medicine at Amberley Airforce Base in Queensland. He was expert at assessing and working towards preventing health problems caused by hazards such as radiation, solvents, fuels, and inhaled particles. He had been in the RAAF for twenty years and the Specialist Reserve for another sixteen. He was a Group Captain. Married to Christine ('Sam'), he had three adult children.

Shmackers was an extraordinary man. Apart from being an accomplished physician and PhD, he had given much of his private life in the last fifteen years to serving the cause of Variety Club, Australia's largest children's charity. The charity stages a state-wide old car bash each year to raise money for disadvantaged and disabled children, and a nation-wide bash through the Australian outback, every four years. He now chaired the appeal in Queensland. Shmackers was also an inveterate tinkerer. There was nothing he couldn't repair or build from scratch, a very handy skill to have if you were going somewhere rendered a backwater by war or disaster. As a veteran from war zones, including East Timor and Iraq, he knew what was required in demanding situations.

'The phrase you're going to hear most is "Get over it". Frustration is part and parcel of a disaster. Supplies are always short. You're going to have to get on and do your job, in the most professional way, with half of what you're used to, and that's if you're lucky. You'll probably find you are getting by using your imagination and inventiveness most of the time. You'll find even washing your face, going to the loo, becomes a challenge. Remain flexible, adaptable. Things can change at a moment's notice, and there is nothing you can do about it. Nothing.' He stopped. Letting the team absorb what he'd just said.

'You'll just have to get over it. You will wait, you will hurry, then you will have to wait again. At some stage, each and every one of you will have had a gutful. You will have had it up to here.' He placed the flattened back of his hand vertically under his chin. 'And do you know what? You will just have to *get over it*. Good luck!' He finished, with a broad smile. 'We are all in this together, don't forget that.' He was right. Shmackers was a plain-speaking man and he knew what he was talking about. 'Get over it' was to become their catch-cry.

chapter three

The Gate Opens

Bernard York was assisting Flight Sergeant Michelle Maclachlan at Jakarta's military airport, Halim Perdanakusuma Air Base, with the embassy's task of being the intermediary between the Australian and Indonesian governments. The Indonesians were being very accommodating, showing their appreciation for the assistance. However, nobody wanted to abuse this latitude. If a soldier had forgotten his passport, you had to find a way to smooth it. Promise to have it couriered over as soon as possible. All rules of international transit could not be completely cast to the wind, notwithstanding an almighty disaster. It would be churlish to expect that, simply because you had arrived to help.

Initially Bernard and Michelle simply had a small exercise book where they made entries and did their best to keep track of aircraft movements, cargo and passenger details. Michelle's mobile phone rang incessantly and Bernard's first job on arrival had been to field her myriad messages.

Bernard had been approached by a group of scientologists who wanted to be flown to Banda Aceh. He was being told by their liaison officer, 'We know the Indonesian General So-and-So.' Bernard sighed inwardly. He, as politely and as quickly as he could, indicated to the go-between that in a disaster there are priorities. Medicine and water were considered higher priorities than other things, even important ones such as general counselling services. Such protocols are always hard to enforce. The flights were few. They were also fully laden. Personnel being cleared for departure in the early stages had to be fully self-sufficient so as not to cause further liability to the suffering areas.

James Branley stepped in and convinced anyone still in any doubt that they were not needed as critically as the life-saving teams, who had their own supplies. James wondered privately whether, given all the language barriers, this group was being mistaken for 'seismologists'.

The scientologists were briefed about the hostile natural environment prevailing at Banda Aceh due to its having borne the brunt of the tsunami, about the possibilities of rampant disease and aftershocks, until they were eventually reconciled with the fact that their services were better utilised where most of the refugees were being taken, which was Medan. They thanked the team.

Bernard was no stranger to diplomatic relations. He had been to sea numerous times on warships to different countries. There had been exciting moments, but the tsunami response was something else again. He was helping a nation recover from a terrible trauma. It was exhilarating, and it was humbling.

The highlight of Bernard's posting was to come later, when refugees from the tsunami-affected areas arrived in Jakarta. On touchdown they would shake his hand and say thank you, thank you. They had escaped hell and they thanked him with heartfelt voices for their rescue. He would always remember them.

Knowledge of the rough conditions on the ground had filtered through to the team. Having left their usual military kits at home as instructed and realising that there would be no issuing of gear, some of the team had needed to buy supplies. Before heading out to Halim Air Base, Paul had gone on a shopping expedition with the two surgeons, René Zellweger and Peter Sharwood, and the other anaesthetist Paul Luckin.

Paul Dunkin had met Luckin ten years before at a naval medical symposium. Luckin was in the Navy Reserves. He was a tall, slim, dark-haired anaesthetist with impressive posture, and reminded Dunkin of the perennially well-groomed Pierce Brosnan. Luckin had worked in South Africa, medevac-ing people out of the snow in the Drakensberg. He had left before the system he worked within drove him crazy. The night nursing staff used to turn off the patients' drips, go to sleep, and fill out the charts pre-emptively, as though the drips were on all night. Patients missed out on medication, pain relief, antibiotics, saline for tissue repair and care generally. If they survived until morning, the drip went back on. Their recovery was slow and painful under such a regimen, and no wonder.

Sometimes they died during the night and their charts, which had been pre-filled in, showed them as having vital signs for hours after they had died. Luckin had some exposure to non-ideal medical scenarios, serious cultural differences and urgent situations. There was no saying what would prevail in Banda Aceh.

Paul Dunkin, Paul Luckin, René Zellweger and Peter Sharwood had rushed back to the hotel from their supply shopping, only to have to then wait out at Halim Air Base. While they waited they loaded a heavy tow bar into the plane, to assist in manoeuvring it out of the way once it had landed at Banda Aceh airfield. Anything they could do to facilitate their departure, they did—enthusiastically.

Waiting always seemed interminable, and never more so than now. To while away the time, the team grabbed a stick and a ball and started a game of backyard cricket with the locals.

The pilot called Bernard from the cockpit.

'Can you use your influence to get us a slot to land in Banda Aceh?'

'Leave it with me,' said Bernard.

The air flight space around Banda Aceh was still too congested and no landing slots were being given. The impact of the heavy weight of the plane on the small airfield's runway was also being debated, as was its manoeuvrability, which also didn't help the cause for flying in. A backdrop to these discussions was the fact that the import of the immense tsunami tragedy—and the impact of the international response—was still sinking in with the Indonesian authorities. They had responded positively to Australia's offer of help, a response which had been the trigger event at Australian government level for the formation of the team, but Banda Aceh was presently still in the heart of a tightly controlled war zone. Permission to land was not being given without vetting for good reason.

Finally, they took off after they had received approval to land at the other end. Paul found himself sitting next to James Branley. James was in his early forties, good-looking and genial, with a well-developed sense of humour. He and

Paul had spotted each other at RAAF Base Richmond, 'I know you,' they had both said to each other. After the twenty questions to work out how, it became clear. James looked very similar to his brother, who was an eye surgeon for whom Paul had done some anaesthetics. This did not explain how James knew Paul, except that Paul had the kind of face everyone thinks they know already. They chatted very little about what they were in for. It was not what anyone wanted to dwell on just yet. They were all keeping their thoughts on that private—they just wanted to keep their spirits buoyed, because there was a big task ahead.

At one stage, James commented to Paul about his holiday plans for after Banda Aceh. 'We will be going north after this,' he said. 'My wife and I holiday at a beach just near Forster.'

Paul replied conversationally, 'So do we.'

Thinking this would trump him, James went on. 'Yes, and we'll be taking our four boys.'

Paul answered, amazed. 'So will we.'

It turned out they both holidayed on precisely the same stretch of coast and their four boys were within the same age range. They did not know it yet, but this little coincidence would turn out to be quite providential.

They were also learning about others in the team. Sudhakar Rao, a surgeon from Western Australia, had three boys; Jeremy McAnulty, a New South Wales doctor who had briefed them at Richmond, also had three. Between these four doctors, they had fourteen young lads. It was too good to be true—they were all going to have to get together in the future.

As the plane approached Banda Aceh, they peered out through the windows, some took photos. Voices were hushed, aghast. They saw a beautiful sunset and a landscape lit up with pink. Pink light reflected in water. Large puddles of water, in places where there shouldn't have been puddles at all. There should have been houses and signs of life. This was a city of over 200 000 people. There should have been bright lights, colours, buildings, streets with streetlamps, a patchwork quilt of properties. Instead, there were only a few dim car headlights and a wasteland which stretched for miles and miles along the coast. And a couple of miles inland too.

This scarred landscape was Banda Aceh.

As the plane flew in to land at Sultan Iskandar Muda Airport, Paul saw the lines of people along the road. There were thousands of them. People had congregated around the airfield, carrying plastic bags or suitcases tied with string. Their remaining earthly possessions. Wide-eyed, quiet, dazed. These were the uninjured, homeless locals. It was a disturbing introduction for the team.

It was almost night-time and there was work to be done. Boxes and boxes were being unloaded by a conga line of enthusiastic people—doctors, nurses, firemen (fireys), public health officers and aircrew. Paul went up to Scott Bevan from Channel Nine and introduced himself. He told Scott that his network had interviewed Paul's family that day. Bevan was busy trying to get Mike Flynn to do an interview. But the Channel Nine television crew soon worked it out—because there was a lot to be done here, nobody could take time out to talk to them. In a short time, the television crew were rolling their sleeves up and unloading with the team.

It was hard work, but nobody shirked. Everyone worked to his or her fullest extent. Paul kicked his knees up and broke into a jog carrying some over-sized boxes. He couldn't help being a clown, he liked to keep the people around him smiling. There was a lot to be sombre about, as they had been given enough information and seen enough to have heavy hearts already. Everyone would need to be upbeat to last the distance.

The team stacked the boxes by the runway and covered them to protect them from the weather, which was blowy and unpredictable. Someone was put on watch, as they had to keep an eye on their stuff—the food, drugs, surgical supplies, camping equipment and personal gear. Some of the local people wandered close to the boxes, curious. The team did not know it then, but these people had not eaten in days.

Some of the Acehnese started boarding a heavylift plane that would take them down to Jakarta, all sitting on the floor like cargo. They were leaving their . . . what exactly? These people had no homes anymore. Some had no families either. They were leaving a nightmare.

Sudhakar Rao was asked to provide the flight safety briefing. Sudhakar had been born in Malaysia, he had then lived in India until he was two, before returning to Malaysia and living there from age two to thirteen. He could speak passable Bahasa, the official Indonesian language, which was similar to Malay. Although the Acehnese had their own language, most understood Bahasa. Sudhakar felt his life had become slightly surreal overnight. Here he was, the director of Trauma at Perth Hospital, giving safety instructions to a planeload of wide-eyed refugees, on a Boeing 707, in the middle of the night, in a foreign language, in a disaster zone. Sudhakar was not a novice to trauma—the Royal Perth was the largest trauma hospital in Western Australia—but this was his first deployment to a disaster zone. He had had theoretical training in disaster management but had never been in the military. When he got the call on the day after Boxing Day, Sudhakar felt strongly that he had to go.

Sudhakar and his wife Narelle had three little boys, Luke aged seven, James aged five and Andrew aged four. Narelle was a physician whose parents had provided assistance work for fifteen years in Papua New Guinea, where she had grown up. She supported Sudhakar going to Indonesia because the idea of going to another country and helping out was not far-fetched to her, even though news reports indicated that most of the areas were still dangerous. On the afternoon when Sudhakar left Perth young Luke said solemnly to his dad, 'Don't walk outside when you get there, Dad. Don't step on a landmine.' Luke had been watching the news, and the reports were of disturbed landmines in Sri Lanka, one of the tsunami-affected areas. At that stage, they had no idea where Sudhakar would be sent. Narelle and Sudhakar prepared their wills and photographed the boys with their dad. He organised cover at work—not easy in the Christmas holiday period—and packed. Narelle put in chocolates for any children he might care for. He went into work to do a last check on his patients and had a tetanus shot.

The family had their 'last supper' at the Mekong Restaurant in Mount Lawley, Perth, where they lived. His parents, both in their eighties, insisted on coming to the airport. They were proud of their son. And terrified for him. Narelle's dad, Barry, drove her and Sudhakar to the airport. Her mother minded the boys. Andrew, the youngest, burst into tears. There was so much that was unknown. This in itself can be frightening. Even the adults felt the strain, as much as they attempted not to show it. They tried to be reassuring, but children somehow always know.

Darkness was falling rapidly, making tents and toilets a priority.

Bruce Cameron, an officer in the New South Wales Fire Brigade, had confidently told everyone their tents would be ready soon. He and Greg 'Watto' Watson, another fireman, fiddled in the dark with tens of thousands of dollars of new kit, with which they were barely familiar, trying to put up tents which had all these nifty little attributes, such as windows, before the exhausted team arrived ready to hit the hay. No pressure at all. The team would never know that the kit was unfamiliar nor that it was tricky putting it all together; the capable fireys had their pride.

Watto was a senior fireman with the New South Wales Fire Brigade. Tall, slim, he was your quintessential Aussie bloke. Laughter lines, a dry sense of humour and no bullshit about him. He smeared his sunblock good-naturedly all over his virtually hairless head, to the amusement of the team. He was eager to help and good at doing most practical things. He was married to Kerrieanne, a father of three girls, two in their twenties and one in her teens, and had a new grandchild, little Emily, and of course, his dog, Annie. He would later tell the team, with a twinkle in his eye, that being outnumbered by the girls in the house meant he would continue to volunteer for deployments.

He worked in the rescue section. His deputy manager had tipped him off about the tsunami and a likely Australian response, then called him at home one night at about 9 p.m. and told him to pack as he would be leaving at 6 a.m. the next day. Watto never thought twice about it.

Major emergency response was the specialty of his section. The section had been involved in fighting the horrific Canberra fires of early 2003. There were countless other disasters he'd participated in, including the Thredbo landslide and the Glenbrook and Waterfall train crashes. The job of a fireman is often portrayed in the movies as simply spraying water on a fire but some of Watto's colleagues had been involved in rescue work at the Turkish earthquake in 1999, when 17 000 died, and the one in Taiwan, also in 1999. The firemen had brought with them some tangible resources but, most importantly of all, Aussie know-how. The specific skills they had to offer were the ability to establish a water supply, to make a building safe with support structures, to provide wiring for whatever electrical supplies had been knocked out, and much more. They were the ubiquitous Mr Fix-its.

The tsunami was different from others in one respect — its immensity was unprecedented. Watto was no stranger to sadness and death. He had learned that you deal with it by being the most practical and the least needy. The needs of those in trouble were what came first. And if you couldn't help those people directly, then you got in and supported those who were helping in the heart of it and needed backup. Yet, when he joined the Australian medical team, Watto knew they were all initially wondering why on earth two firemen — Watto himself and Bruce — were coming along to the aftermath of a giant water wave. There was no fire, quite the opposite. He felt that they were thinking, 'Fireys on the medical team, what the . . .?', but were too polite to vocalise it. The medical team would learn how useful fireys could be — their experience in the management of people and wreckage after a crisis proved invaluable.

Now they were at the airfield in the dark, able to see with torches the fireys had distributed — and the tents were up. The East Timor veterans went and showered; they knew the deal. You had to take any opportunity to clean yourself, or eat, or rest, as you never knew if and when the next opportunity would present itself.

Annette Holian, an orthopaedic surgeon from Melbourne, felt sweaty and dirty after all the travel and unloading. She heard there was a toilet and shower block across the airfield. As she and a couple of anaesthetists made their way over there, she ran into a few of the female nurses. They warned her, 'Don't go in there!' She went in anyway.

The toilets were three squats. The 'shower' was an oblong area surrounded by a low corrugated-iron wall with rocks underfoot. In the darkness she could make out above the low wall the bare torsos of about a dozen men. They were dipping water from a couple of 44-gallon drums, which were lying on their sides, cut in half and full of water, and tipping it over their tired bodies. Her male colleagues picked up on her hesitation. 'Come in, come in,' they cried gallantly. 'You can stand between us!'

She seemed to be the only woman and there were a dozen foreign national men bathing in this one open area. She thought she would wait for the numbers to dwindle, but they didn't. More and more men kept arriving as their day's work came to an end. Courage, Annette thought, trying to bolster herself, it must be done. You are not sleeping in a filthy state. Conditions may well be this way for the entire duration of the mission. This might be as good as it gets. Get over it. Get used to it early.

'Tell me they have their undies on!' she asked her colleagues cautiously.

'No. No undies in here!' they laughed.

Right, she thought. I can wait no longer. I did not come all this way to be a princess. It's only the exposure of my white flesh in the dark, with distant airport lighting, to a dozen men I may never see again. She checked herself—in an Islamic country, could a woman possibly be stoned for this? Hygiene was important to good health. Health was a priority for her assignment here. And Aussies loved showering—being fresh and clean. Get on with it, she thought.

She braced herself and stepped into the washing area. Her colleagues were right. All the men were naked. She resolved to keep her own underwear on and calmly hung up her washbag and whipped off her T-shirt and trousers, tossing them over the top of the surrounding wall to keep them dryish. She waited her turn of the dipper. Dip and tip. Ahh, bliss! Another dozen dipper loads to freshen the spirit.

She enjoyed the cooling effect on her skin, marvelling at the fact that she was standing near-to-nude on an airfield in a foreign country, in a cubicle with undressed men she had never met. Some experiences you just couldn't predict.

She soaped up and reached for the dipper again to wash it off and rinse out her hair. The dipper was suddenly not there. Annette stood, waiting, with soap running from her stark white arms and belly. She felt naked and exposed, despite her underwear. A man nearby kindly offered to throw water over her hair rather than give up his dipper. She accepted, leaning forward, to make the job easier for him. He tipped the water over her head and she was again refreshed by the combination of cool water and light breeze. She waited for the dipper to rise again, and again. Surreal. A delightful wash from an unknown man in extraordinary surroundings.

She had to brave the toilet now. Three old blue doors, side-by-side. Full length, she noted. Privacy! Really brave and all-knowing now, she entered a just-vacated door. With her torch on the ground to help locate the puddles around the squat, she carefully took one shoe off, and eased one of her legs out of her trousers, gripping the gathered far end of the trouser leg firmly, making sure it stayed well out of the puddles. She squatted confidently and looked up. Straight into the eyes of a stranger, a man standing to urinate in the next squat. The side walls of the toilets were low, but she hadn't noticed this until now. Once upon a time she would have been mortified if this had happened. Now it was almost normal. She still cringed with embarrassment. Thank goodness it was dark, she thought. Torch off. It was too late to reconsider, too late not to do the business. There was some rough paper in a basket nearby and a dipper to flush with before she gingerly returned her leg to her trousers and her foot to her shoe.

Annette had survived the shower and the toilet. Smiling to herself, in the darkness, she rejoined one of the anaesthetists outside and strolled back to the tent, as if she had just had a warm private shower in a modern caravan park shower block.

It's amazing where life can take you, she thought. You just need to accept the ride and keep going.

Paul had been trying to get through to me. The occasional SMS message would get through, usually during Muslim prayer time, when the congestion eased. He sent me a message: 'We R here safe! Things R worse than expected. Luv U.'

When they landed, there had not been a drop of fresh water to drink, nor a place to sleep. They had had to set it all up themselves, and they had done so.

So ended their first day in Banda Aceh.

chapter four

The Real Work Begins

On 31 December 2004, Team CASTA all woke at 6 a.m., packed up their tents and ate their first ration-pack breakfast. Today was going to be a big one and they needed their strength. One of the first things the fireys and paramedic Jeff Gilchrist did was set up a latrine and familiarise the team with its unique workings. While the men were happy 'to take a leak' anywhere, the women were not as keen—there were men working in nearby rice paddies and the toilets were squats and not the most private—especially in daylight. Consequently the women were not tending to drink the copious amounts of water the warm weather and constant moving required.

Paul called me, getting through just as he reached the head of the latrine queue. He couldn't talk for long. He just wanted to hear my voice, and hear that our boys were okay. And let me know that he was not in any danger.

Wing Commander Greg Norman was the Officer-in-Charge of the RAAF Hospital at Richmond and was serving his final days in the Air Force when he was sent to

Indonesia. He had scouted Banda Aceh with Bill Griggs and Allan MacKillop on their recce mission two days earlier, with a couple of other service personnel. They had cursorily inspected Banda Aceh's main public hospital, Zainal Abidin, and assessed it as unusable. It had borne the full brunt of the tsunami and was full of mud and dead bodies. The clean-up there was going to be a major project on its own.

As they drove around Banda Aceh, they saw bodies all over the roads, which were being bulldozed into freshly dug pits. On their way back to the airfield, the men had seen that many of these piles had been lit so the bodies could be cremated. The smell and the smoke filled the air. The three of them chose not to dwell on these scenes and impressions, but these were forever etched into their memories. At one place they had seen a pile of little bodies, with skinny arms and legs. Children.

Wing Commander Greg Norman was calling the team together for a briefing. 'Basically,' he said to the gathered team, 'the first 2 kilometres of coastline have been picked up and dumped on the next 2 kilometres.' He went on to describe a graphic scene of cats, dogs, human bodies and rubble. He prepared the teams for what they might see, telling them what he had seen on his earlier recce. 'I saw a mass grave and was told by the locals it contained some 8000 bodies,' he said. 'The locals have been bulldozing bodies into a large hole in the ground. The risk of disease is high, and the heat makes the decaying bodies perfect incubators for bacteria.' Identification of victims — normally an intricate process involving dental records, DNA sampling and analysis of personal effects — had apparently been abandoned. The sheer numbers of dead made it impossible. Bodies were simply being counted, for the record.

Greg then explained that there was a local private hospital called Rumah Sakit Teungku Fakinah (Fakinah) which had been secured by the Indonesian Police. It had been closed since the tsunami. It was small — about 50 patient beds — but it would be suitable for the team to set up in. There was also a large public hospital with 300 beds called Rumah Sakit Kesdam (Kesdam), where Norman and some Army medics were going to work, probably in the Emergency Department.

While CASTA waited, an Australian surfer who was married to a local Indonesian woman came and introduced himself. Breathless, he described the tsunami approaching, and how he put his wife and children into the car and headed for the hills. When he and his family returned from the high ground, the village was gone. He wanted to help them and he had rounded up some local youths to help with loading the trucks.

Meanwhile, Watto had had a slightly discomforting introduction to Banda Aceh. He had been helping to finish unloading the plane the night before with the precious lone forklift — he was licensed in forklifts of course — and had been noticed by the Indonesian military (TNI). The next day a couple of soldiers approached him and asked him to unload a generator for them off a truck. He was happy to help, once everyone had broken through the language barrier. Once he had unloaded it for them, the machine-gun wielding soldiers indicated they wanted to have it taken back to their camp. 'No worries,' he indicated, while trying to look and sound as nonchalant as possible. 'Where would you like it to be taken?' They set off for their camp down the road from the airfield. One soldier sat next to him, the other rode a motorbike in front, both still heavily armed. They beeped their way through traffic, scattering pedestrians (mostly dazed refugees) in all directions. As they drove along in this interesting motorcade, an Australian Army ute pulled up alongside them.

'Worried I'd steal off with your forklift?' Watto teased. 'No, worried someone might be stealing *you*,' the Australian soldiers answered. They had observed an unarmed Watto disappearing with the TNI strangers and wanted to make sure it was on mutually agreeable terms. One of the Aussie soldiers jumped onto the forklift with Watto, while the ute accompanied them the rest of the way.

They drove to the TNI military camp, some 4 kilometres from the airfield. Watto unpacked the generator, set it up and also dropped off the TNI soldiers, who asked if he and his Army colleagues would have their photograph taken with about twenty of them—fully booted and spurred for battle—out the front of their camp. They were all smiles and very friendly, so the Australians happily did as asked, and then went back to the airfield.

Mike Flynn, firey Bruce Cameron, Dr Ken Harrison, paramedic Adrian Humphrey and Greg Norman went on ahead to Fakinah to get it ready. They rode in a military four-wheel-drive light truck (UNIMOG) which the Australian Army had been using to tow the trailer carrying their water purification plant. A Herc had arrived overnight bringing the Army's water plant and the UNIMOG. The vehicle was also loaded with grey space-cases.

Mike Flynn and the others clambered above all the space-cases. The gear that they had brought from Australia was mainly packed into these and this was the first truckload of them. As the vehicle moved off, Greg Norman shouted over the noise of the engine, telling the men to duck as there were many low branches and sagging power lines draped between bent poles. The men flattened their bodies as much as they could. Mike Flynn was worried, but he kept it to himself. The team's safety was his concern, as he was their leader, but he knew there was no other option other than for this small group to travel like this, without seatbelts in a crowded vehicle. He had good reason to worry. Suddenly Greg yelled out, as a large branch snagged him, almost taking him straight off the top of the UNIMOG. Greg's head was bleeding where the skin of his forehead had been split open by the branch.

On the way, Mike wordlessly gestured at something down in the gutter. Bruce looked and saw a sight nobody should ever see — a bloated, naked male corpse, with its foot half ripped off, revealing exposed bones and tendons. A mangy dog was feasting hungrily on the ankle, then it began licking and salivating noisily through its teeth as it turned its attention to one of the legs. Bruce was completely shocked. It offended his sense of human dignity. This was someone's father or brother. Where was his family? Why was he there, abandoned in this disgusting state? It was a brutal introduction to the horror of the tsunami. The reality of it had not hit home yet. Bruce did not know it, but by tomorrow all Bruce and the others had thought was 'normal', would change.

The remainder of the CASTA team got moving out at the airfield. Seventeen tonnes had to be manually loaded onto trucks which had been arranged largely through the diplomacy of René Zellweger. With Shmacker's approval, René had approached the driver of a nearby truck at the airfield and a deal had been done. Yes, he could provide transport but, in exchange, the medical team would have to help at Kesdam Hospital also. The Australians did not know the driver, but they needed the truck and he was indicating their skills were needed at yet another hospital. They were in no position to argue the toss, and they knew that questions are not always answered in disaster situations. You have to roll with what is happening. They agreed. They would work it out somehow. They were there to build bridges, to get something established for later teams and the arrangement merely added impetus to what probably would have eventuated anyway. Greg Norman and a handful of Army medics had already made a plan to work at Kesdam. Some of the CASTA team could undoubtedly be made useful there too.

They found an additional Indonesian truck, and the Army UNIMOG was going to return for more loads.

Paul crawled over the top of the medical team's supplies into the front part of the tray of the second truck. Every nook and cranny was occupied. The driver of the second truck was reluctant to drive them initially but, after a persuasive talk with paramedic Jeff Gilchrist, he finally agreed. As the truck driver started the engine, Paul leaned his hand out through a gap in the side of the truck and he and Jeff high-fived each other. For Jeff, it was a turning-point in his relationship with the team. He had felt, like Watto, that there might have been a question mark over his usefulness in this operation, as he was not a doctor or a nurse. Again the team members were beginning to realise how different roles were just as important and vital.

It was a scary truck ride, with the truck driver constantly blowing his horn and scattering traffic. Paul was not particularly fazed as he'd been to Indonesia before, but some of the others were stunned. Near-misses, swerving, close-call head-ons, drivers pulling out at the last minute with no care for their safety—it was hair-raising.

From time to time they passed what looked like the odd dead body lying on the edge of the road. From their earlier observation, efforts were being made to remove them, restore normality to the streetscapes, but the sheer numbers obviously outweighed the efforts.

Paul noticed piles of rubble along the route, and saw several large burial sites being dug out by cranes. Mass graves. In spite of the heat, he felt goosebumps. Mass graves were on television, not by a roadside in your reality. There was a strong smell of decay in the air.

They arrived at last at Fakinah hospital, which was a white two-storey building in the shape of a square that enclosed a large internal quadrangle. There were open balconies, painted white with a brown wooden criss-cross pattern, running all the way round the second storey. The front of the hospital had a dark brown portico over a semi-circular driveway and a decorative white fence across the front.

On the top floor, the team found a large lecture room and decided to unload the boxes in there. It was incongruously adorned with pink streamers, making the team joke, during their team-building unloading activity, about it being a 'safe-from-tsunami' zone.

Bruce Cameron had checked out the Fakinah hospital building earlier. It was dirty. He had found blood, faeces, bits of human tissue. It appeared to have been used as a temporary morgue. However, he was more interested in the integrity of the building. His training in fire rescue made this second nature; fires compromised the structural integrity of buildings, so did earthquakes. When gas pipes broke, explosions and fires followed. He knew what to look for. As senior rescue instructor with the New South

Wales Fire Brigades Rescue Section, he not only operated but often instructed in the art. Bruce's specialty was Urban Search and Rescue (USAR). USAR was an organisation made up of the Fire Brigade, Police and Ambulance Service. Their purpose was to recover as many people as possible from such locations as the rubble of an earthquake, a bombing or a building site collapse. For urban disaster, the equipment included drills which would go through concrete, plus special thermal imaging cameras, seismic listening devices, microphones and air fans—all on long leads which could be fed through the hole which had been drilled. They could then bring air to the trapped and listen for sounds of life. September 11 would have attracted a USAR response. The international body was INSARAG (International Search and Rescue Advisory Group), under the UN umbrella. It worked out international standards and multi-nation cooperation and coordination, when the local resources were overwhelmed or exhausted. It had been set up after the 1988 Armenian earthquake. And in 2002, with UN General Resolution 57/150, 58 nations got behind the idea and agreed to strengthen it. New South Wales and Queensland were registered with the UN for INSARAG purposes.

However, the fireys had not come to Banda Aceh to sift through rubble because even though there had been a massive earthquake, very shortly afterwards the tsunami would have drowned those surviving in the wreckage. The tsunami had moved the disaster goalposts. Now the fireys' brief was to feed, water and shelter the doctors and nurses, to ensure they could provide medical care. Bruce had already met some of the Indonesian military. They had worked out he was involved in rescue work by his uniform. He was not armed, but they felt they could identify with him. 'We do rescue too, and shoot terrorist,' they told him proudly, in halting English.

The medical team could not stay at Fakinah if the building was in dangerous shape. Tents would be safer, even if they were hotter and more awkward. Bruce looked at the walls and corners of the building. He could see cracks in the concrete which had come away in the corners in some places, exposing the steel reinforcement bars. There were a few broken windows, and the pipes leading to the water well were broken. There were some piles of rubble where presumably part of the building had been. The hospital was obviously built more sturdily than other buildings near it, as it was one of the few still standing.

Bruce found a spot on the balcony wall outside where they planned to create the dormitory and measured the width of the cracks with an engineer's ruler, marking the date next to them with a texta. The fissures were up to 3 millimetres across. This was to become his daily habit over the deployment. It would become a journal which would show what was happening with the building. If the cracks became too large, the team would have to evacuate. For now, it seemed safe enough. To make sure that the team had an escape route in case of the building collapsing into a stairwell, he threw a rope ladder over the balcony. As he did so it occurred to him, rather ironically, how thrilled his son Bradley would be if he were there. Bruce was a clean-cut, fit and young-looking 42, married to Alison, with two children — Bradley and Molly. Bradley loved to tie knots and go camping. The idea of a handmade rope ladder to climb down from a building was too exciting for words. The danger would not be the main consideration.

Ken Harrison, the team's medical logistics expert, had already assessed with Bruce that the top storey would be safer in the event of another earthquake, or aftershocks. There would be less of the building to collapse on the team. Bruce and Ken had the team stack the grey space-cases in a simple block formation all the way up to the ceiling. Normally a roof caves in as flat as a pancake but they hoped that, with the stacking plan they had implemented, any cave-in would create two tent-shaped spaces on either side where the team members could lie. Basically, it would create a void with the top of the cases acting as a ridgeline. The team was extensively briefed on what to do if the roof collapsed, and how to best prepare themselves. It all seemed fairly theoretical at this stage. They were not to know yet how important such safety measures would be.

It was another trying, physically demanding session of hours and hours of unloading and carrying. The boxes had to go up flights of stairs, which were narrow and slightly slippery. You had to watch your step as you puffed up them with the hard-edged weight of the boxes. The CASTA team found that they had an ever-diminishing band of helpers. There was no aircrew out here to help with the unloading. Greg Norman and his band of medics kindly pitched in. It was a huge job.

Jeff Gilchrist and Shmackers stayed at the airfield until the last box was loaded, to guard the supplies. The trucks returned from Fakinah and Jeff and Shmackers oversaw and assisted with the loading of remaining supplies into them. They also managed to find a much larger truck to take what remained of the boxes. They didn't leave the airfield until about 4 p.m. It had been an incredibly long day, but neither ever breathed a word of complaint about being left behind.

Jeff was in his fifties, moustached, and was very tall and slim. He was not a normal ambulance officer, but a SCAT paramedic. SCAT stands for Special Casualty Access Team.

It had once been the case that rescue workers would work valiantly to try to recover trapped and injured people, only to have them die of their injuries and exposure during the hours it took to free them. In 1984 a twelve-year-old girl had fallen over a cliff at Bondi and died during the time it took to bring her back up. Her death had prompted changes in the approach to rescue work.

SCAT paramedics now crawled under trains to trapped people, climbed down manholes, edged themselves into collapsed buildings and down lift-wells, onto fire-ravaged boats and down caved-in mines, and into swollen creeks. They carried treatment packs on their backs. It was about getting access and giving treatment, until rescue could be carried out safely.

Jeff and a colleague had once stayed all night with a patient who had fallen over the cliff at Dover Heights in New South Wales. They abseiled down. Waves crashed against them and took their gear—and almost their patient—from their place on a high ledge. They hung in there, in the dark and cold, maintaining the health and spirits of the patient. Police rescue services hauled them up when daylight came.

Jeff breathed life back into badly injured patients. He re-established airways and gave oxygen, adrenalin, morphine, fluids, you name it. He attached splints, neck-braces, bandages, compresses. He wrapped freezing people who would otherwise die of hypothermia. Most importantly, he encouraged them to hang in there. He had helped rescue Stuart Diver, the sole survivor of those trapped in the Thredbo landslide. SCAT paramedics never knew what they would find. It was harrowing work.

Jeff trained with the Fire Brigade USAR unit. These SCAT paramedics did not involve themselves in the rescue or the police operations. They were there to perform the medical side of it. They might accompany police to siege situations, where there were gunmen and standoff situations. If anyone was shot, Jeff could attend to them. He had to be fit, courageous—and not become a liability himself.

Jeff was a manager in the field of Counter Disaster Planning and father of three girls, Danielle, Sarah and Rebecca. His partner Fiona was the senior co-ordinator for a call centre which took Emergency 000 calls. She fully understood and supported his life. Her own was full-on, it was all about life and death.

Jeff's role in Banda Aceh was vital. He knew that he had to look after the welfare of the team. His training had taught him that if people's mental states were good, then they could function and do what they most needed to do. If they faltered, you gave them a role. You might ask them to look out for someone else. People would psychologically gain confidence from that and approach their other tasks positively, which they had previously found daunting. Human psychology in stressful situations was complex. You had to find a way to harness the very vestiges of their spirit. As he had already shown in his dealings with the truck driver, Jeff's interpersonal skills would be crucial.

It was stinking hot out at Fakinah hospital, and the work was getting harder to do. Paul's T-shirt had a large wet patch at the back. He wished he had a hairless body and was skinny. And that a breeze might start up. Paul staggered up and down the stairs, with box after box, sweating profusely. They all did. There was no point in slacking off and nobody did. You knew you had to keep going until the job was done. Some people drank water constantly, they were the smart ones. It was the only way to keep up your endurance in the heat. Everyone was helping themselves to the bottles of water that were sitting on the pallets. There was no other water. The team were using bottled water for drinking, washing their hands, shaving, and for cooking instant noodles.

The team packed away lecture room chairs, swept floors, moved things to make room for their supplies. The boxes and grey space-cases were stacked up to the ceiling at a point a third of the way along the empty lecture room to demarcate the women's sleeping quarters, and to hold up and reinforce the ceiling, which appeared to have been damaged in the earthquake which had triggered the tsunami.

Paul finally took a break and went to set up his bed. There were to be seventeen of the men in one area of the lecture room. Four of the men—CareFlight doctors Ken Harrison and Alan Garner, SCAT paramedic Adrian Humphrey and firey Bruce Cameron—would have to pack up their stretchers each day, as they were in a thorough-fare. The remaining space was for the seven women. Paul was stringing up his mozzie net and chatting to Peter Sharwood, one of the surgeons, who was setting up his own stretcher. Suddenly, a spitting, snarling cat with no tail fell through the roof, almost causing it to collapse. Paul and Peter leapt up in fright as the cat loudly hissed and spat at them, claws out, and then disappeared. They had been jumpy to begin with, now they were completely unnerved. The creepy tail-less cat remained unexplained, its symbolic significance only being made clear to them later. It was just another small segment in a series of unusual things happening all around them.

The cat had caused part of the roof to cave in until the electrical wiring stopped it, but broken pieces of ceiling continued to fall on everybody. Watto and Bruce Cameron were on the scene immediately to help repair the roof. Sleep would be hard enough with the heat and mozzies without roof fragments intermittently raining down on them. Nails, which had previously been used to hold up some pictures, were removed from the wall, and used as stop-gap repairs. They felt bad not knowing anything about the pictures they took down from the walls, which had writing of some kind on them. Everyone in the CASTA team was very conscious of being in someone else's hospital, someone else's country.

Everyone learned very quickly not to touch your mouth, your eyes, your nose. Diarrhoea, or even conjunctivitis, was the last thing you wanted. Prevention was better than cure. It was sometimes hard to remember this when you had sweat trickling down your face, or insects sticking to you, or a strand of hair becoming annoying. The anti-bacterial wipes I had stuffed into Paul's bag were used each time before eating. Paul remembered with gratitude that his wife had put her foot down over a few items he had thought would be unnecessary.

Liz Cloughessy, one of the nurses, set up a storeroom downstairs for some of the supplies. She intuitively knew that giving the Indonesian police 'ownership' of the supplies was the best way to ensure nothing was stolen. She was right. In return for this trust, they safeguarded them with their lives. When she initially mentioned her concerns to the police chief, he responded proudly, 'Oh no, if anyone tries to take anything, we will shoot them!' Liz smiled weakly. Liz instituted a system of accounting for the supplies with everything taken or used being written down by them in a book. The police enjoyed reminding her to use her system.

Liz was warm, sensible and very amenable to a hug. She had reddish-brown short hair with striking blonde patches in it, which made her extremely discernible from a distance. She was the type to organise, fuss and be consistently bright, warm and involved. A clinical nurse consultant from Westmead, Sydney, she had originally been designated as an emergency nurse in Alpha Team, but CASTA's Alpha and Bravo teams were now combined into the one team (although occasionally they would still refer to themselves as being from one or the other, because it was easier) and the role Liz assumed in Banda Aceh was not the one for which she had been originally designated. She took on a broader one when she saw that there was a need for someone to look after all the tasks for which there had been no designation. She looked after the team's welfare, she liaised with the police and the TNI, she looked out for the other nurses, she comforted patients and she even washed clothes by hand for Mike Flynn.

Liz had been a nurse for 30 years. She formed the Emergency Nurses Association in 1982, which had become the Australian College of Emergency Nursing, and she lectured in EMST (Early Management of Severe Trauma). She had been the nurse commander on the scene at reception when Australia took in the Kosovars; she had looked after the displaced community when bushfires raged through Sussex Inlet, she was on duty at the Waterfall train derailment and the Rugby World Cup. Her children Melee and Tharon were immensely proud of her.

She was the chief nurse for the Sydney Olympics and the Paralympics. There had been huge responsibilities inherent in her role with the hospital in the Olympic Village, which provided 20 000 occasions of service, and the Paralympic almost 10 000. Liz ended up sleeping there. Her supportive husband Steve had seen the writing on the wall with that one and brought in a fold-up bed for her, from Clark Rubber.

With Liz around, Paul felt like his mum was there with them. Liz bonded with the patients, making them feel that they were real people who qualified for first-class medical care (all being relative, of course), and showed them that the Australians genuinely cared about them. She bossed the fully armed police around, stopping them from smoking near oxygen cylinders. They smiled and it broke down barriers. They would laughingly ask permission whenever they saw her: 'Smoke? Yes? Okay?!'

Liz Cloughessy and Lisa Dillon, another nurse from Westmead, together with Terry Jongen and Karyn Boxshall, nurses from Western Australia, set up a ward. They decided to ditch the hospital's existing bed mattresses. Although these were unaffected by tsunami water, these were impregnated with blood and pus and various body fluids, and they had also started to grow mould in the heat. Exactly what you didn't want people with open wounds and in a weakened state to lie on.

The patients would have to lie on the metal bed bases and where there were not enough of them, on the floor. The body bags were going to come in handy as 'white underlays'. These bags were from Australia and were made of white PVC plastic. They were preferable to the rank, blood-soaked rags which accompanied some of the tsunami patients. Fortunately, from a morale perspective, the patients did not realise that the underlays were body-bags—their own country used black ones.

Meanwhile, Marj Raggett, Ray Southon, Rosie Clifton and Rhonda Cowderoy, all theatre nurses (for this deployment), were turning filth into a passable surgical environment, with the help of the paramedics Adrian Humphrey and Jeff Gilchrist. First they had to wash down the theatres and all the equipment, from operating tables to buckets, scrub trays and trolleys for instruments and dressings. Some of these had stale blood and pus on them, traces which were obviously months old. The theatre staff asked everyone for any spare disposable polystyrene plates from their evening meal kits, so they could be used for laying theatre instruments out on. Ray cleaned the steriliser, refilled it with water and began the process of boiling the precious few instruments.

The team continued to work. It had already been a long day, but there was still a lot to do. Ken Harrison was calling the shots. It was he who had decided that the upstairs lecture room was relatively safe from cave-in in the event of another significant earthquake. Carrying boxes upstairs was back-breaking work. But because it was in a dead-end—at the end of the balcony—it was also fairly safe from theft. Harrison was being foreman to the team, who were beginning to call themselves the 'Storemen and Doctors Union'. 'Form a line, three feet apart,' he would call out. 'We're moving it all upstairs. Let's move it!'

Slave driver, Rhonda thought. He's certainly got the whip out, thought Paul. The team hated what Ken was doing, riding them so hard when it was intensely hot and they were achingly tired. But the work had to be done and he was being their coach. He did it well, and they loved him for it.

Ken was the team doctor, as well as the logistician, and he was going to be insisting on certain things to maintain the team's health in this foreign environment. Each member would have to take doxycycline for malaria, and they would all have to use mosquito nets while sleeping, and continually use insect repellent sprays. They would have to wear long sleeves and trousers from before dusk, despite the heat. There were many risks for the team, and Ken was constantly thinking of them all and how it was all going to be managed. Diseases, earth tremors, dehydration, psychological impacts, civil war hostilities—the list went on endlessly. One of the first things he planned to do was arrange a medevac arrangement with any incoming American ship for any member of the team who became ill or injured and needed more than what could be given onsite.

One of the fireys, Bruce Cameron, became ill from working too hard in the heat and suffered dehydration. He felt very unwell and had to lie down. It was a wake-up call for Bruce. You had to look after yourself first, if you were to help anyone else.

Fakinah Hospital had not been affected by the tsunami. You could see the 'shore-line' or tide mark, a cricket ball's throw down the street. The wall of mud and debris had stopped 50 metres short of the hospital. Although not hit by the water, it had ended up empty as a result of the tsunami. The staff had left to attend to families, neighbours, friends or relatives (or were possibly killed in the tsunami themselves).

A day after the tsunami had hit there had been rumours that another wave was coming, which might reach the hospital this time. Terrified, any remaining staff had taken fright and left. Since nobody was there to care for them, the patients had then left. The procedures being undertaken before all this occurred were general low-grade surgery, such as knee operations, urology, hernias. Paul and Watto could see the type of work normally done at Fakinah from looking at the surgical instruments, which were locked in a glass cabinet. The owner subsequently closed the hospital. He re-opened it in the days following the tsunami, when Jakarta sent help for the injured who were queuing. Indonesian doctors and nurses from the capital arrived first, the day before the Australian team, but they had not yet performed any operations. The first operation they performed was on the night the Australians moved into Fakinah. They allowed the new arrivals to watch.

By about eight that night, the Australian medical team were allowed to begin work. Brian Pezzutti anaesthetised and Marj Raggett, theatre sister, assisted. Sudhakar Rao operated on a groin wound in an elderly man who later died of tetanus, and Annette Holian performed a debridement (the cutting away of rotten tissue, to prevent it spreading into the rest of the layers of flesh and into the bone). It was on a grossly infected wound on the top of a man's foot, where most of his skin was missing, and it required urgent surgery. She had been told it was a break in the tendon leading to the big toe, which was of a less urgent surgical nature, but on examination it turned out not to be. It wasn't clear whether the diagnosis was wrong, or whether the information related to a different patient. This case flagged an early warning for the team that they would need to be extremely careful, due to language barriers, to accurately identify patient injuries.

Most of the newly arrived Australian team wandered down at some stage over the next three hours to watch both Indonesian and Australian teams at work. They wanted to do something—anything—to make sure it all got under way satisfactorily. The participants themselves tried not to cause a scene when they observed the aseptic techniques and the minimal sterilisation process in place. It was an eye-opener. The correct equipment would have to be found. Softly, softly, it was all going to happen properly.

'Happy New Year, everyone!' the onlookers joked to each other as they drifted back to their makeshift dormitory, shattered with fatigue.

Annette, Brian and Marj followed a while later, peeling their gloves off and stretching their aching shoulders. The theatre lights were switched off as they quietly slipped upstairs to their waiting stretchers. They had been in Banda Aceh for 30 hours.

chapter five

Keeping the Home
Fires Burning

It was New Year's Eve and Linda and Jon, Paul's sister and her partner, had come over to keep me company. It was going to be a quiet one, in contrast to the last few days, which had passed in a whirlwind.

Two days earlier, I had gone shopping at Macquarie Centre with toddler Francis, baby Pierce and four-year-old Darcy. We had met up with my brother Colin because I had finally decided to buy a video camera, after years of somehow thinking they were a luxury. I had changed my mind because I didn't want Paul to miss out on one minute of little Pierce's development. Paul had been away with the Navy for all our children's 'rolling-over' milestones, that one before they start crawling. He was away for five months when our eldest Liam was a baby, a few months for Darcy, weeks for Francis and now, after we had congratulated ourselves that he would be around to witness young Pierce, the call had come. Although this would be his shortest deployment, the indicators suggested it would be his most intense, and unique for its own reasons.

I was hot and the kids were yowling. The shops were crowded and noisy, and I'd been lucky to get a park. The post-Christmas shopping sales. I normally never went to them, now I knew why. I struggled with the pram straps of the double stroller—they were too tight because the wrong-sized baby had been put in the wrong side of it last time. You only worked that one out once you had plonked the kid in it. Too hard to move them again, and too tired to remember which side was whose. Sweat broke out on my forehead, and my fringe started to stick to my face. When, for the third time, a car driver asked, as I leaned over the stroller, 'Are you leaving?', I ground my teeth. Broken sleep takes away your light-heartedness.

Colin and I bought the camera, keeping to the bare minimum that politeness allowed the explanation by the shop assistant of how to work it and details of the fabulous competition you could enter after buying it. Pierce whimpered, Francis grabbed things off the shelves. 'Let me out of here,' I thought. Pierce had worked himself into a full-throated roar, so I decided to breastfeed him in the back of the Kombi before leaving the car park. It really was hot. And cramped. The air was stifling. Darcy chatted endlessly, Francis squawked, the two fought happily and fiddled with the controls of the car. Colin discussed matters.

There were a dozen things I needed to do. First of all, I had wanted to get out of this carpark because I had told my sister Armelle I would visit. I then wanted to see Lisa Hill, my close friend, drop off some things, and then get back on the Pacific Highway before the peak-hour traffic sludge engulfed us. I wanted to be home before the kids' 'crisis hour'.

My mobile phone started going off, electronically jangling out the tune of the opera *Carmen*. Colin handed it

The CASTA team in Banda Aceh. L to R (standing):Peter Sharwood, Paul Dunkin, Ken Harrison, René Zellweger, Sudhakar Rao, David Scott, Rhonda Cowderoy, Mike Flynn, Annette Holian, Rosie Clifton, Paul Luckin, Karyn Boxshall, Jeff Gilchrist, Terry Jongen, Liz Cloughessy, Brian Pezzutti,Greg Watson, Ray Southon, Lisa Dillon, James Branley, Paul Van Buynder, Paul Shumack, Jeremy McAnulty, Bruce Cameron. Sitting: Alan Garner, Norm Gray, Marj Raggett. (Not in photo: Adrian Humphrey)

Above: Fishing boats were swept up the river with force, becoming badly damaged and stranded in odd places. Many Acehnese lost their livelihoods through the destruction of such boats. **Below:** Vessels and the splintered remnants of many lives, crushed against what became known as the Bridge of Death.

Above: Clean-up efforts evident in the city centre. Debris piles lined every street. Masks had to be worn to escape the smell of death.

Below: This hand, caught beneath the rubble, reached into Paul's soul.

Above: L to R: Lisa Dillon, Norm Gray, Watto, Karyn Boxshall, Alan Garner, Liz Cloughessy and James Branley visiting the trashed coast of Aceh.

Below: The devastated Acehnese coastal area. The team would never forget the sight of this wasteland and all the lost lives it represented.

to me amid the mayhem. Someone called Majella. She had met Paul at RAAF Base Richmond—Could she interview the family today.

'Tomorrow?' I pleaded. 'Now is not a good time.'

No, they needed the interview then and there as it was featuring first thing in the morning. Australians wanted to see the families of people who went off to disasters. It was all-important stuff. Did I mind? Paul had said I wouldn't!

Reluctantly relenting I drove hurriedly to where I agreed to meet the TV crew, at Bales Park, stopping only briefly at my sister Armelle's house nearby. Raced in, grabbed a hairbrush and some makeup. The miracle of makeup. Had to hide a thousand lost hours of rest. They didn't call it beauty sleep for nothing. Your face always gave it away.

Majella and the Channel Nine crew turned up in leisurely fashion, filmed the children, asked them what daddy was doing. Ten-year-old Liam said that a tsunami had attacked a city. Toddler Francis ran around. Baby Pierce dribbled. Four-year-old Darcy said there was a giant wave which swept it all away, and that his daddy was a doctor who would 'make it all better'. If only it were so simple.

They asked me how I would cope while Paul was away. Many of the interview's initial questions were focussed on this topic. I was staggered. How would *I* cope? At least I was alive and well. The tsunami had destroyed people's lives, taking children, limbs, homes. Now was not the time for navel-gazing about my own situation. Finally, Majella asked whether it would be tough on Paul, looking after children when he had kids of his own. I said it might, in fact, make him even more caring, because he was already a very good father and loved his children.

Watching the TV the next morning, we saw that the program had ended with the piece about Paul caring for others. Thankfully, the questions and answers about how I would cope were not included. The thought of us portrayed as a well-fed, nicely clothed, cheery family being 'needy' might have been construed as in shockingly poor taste when set against the backdrop of the tsunami. Instead, you could see how the children missed their dad and the commentary accompanying the visuals of them playing in the park maintained that theme. But the sobering note, as Majella pointed out in a compassionate voiceover, was that they had every reason to hope and expect Paul would return safely, unlike some of the children in the tsunami-affected areas.

The day the program was shown, Thursday, 30 December I felt so frustrated by my inability to help that I decided to write to the prime minister. I didn't know if this was a normal decision to make. What was normal?

I was one of twelve children. Six of each. My father had often been away when I was very young. He had been a marine engineer with the Royal Australian Navy. My mother, multi-lingual, a teacher and an artist, had had an insanely tough job raising twelve children. My father had missed some of the births due to overseas deployments. When he was ashore he always pitched in at home, especially once he had finished his sea-time for good. My father worked hard, in the guts of the warships, wearing overalls which were blackened by the soot from the oil-burning engine-rooms of the vessels of those days. He sweated and toiled around the boiler-room and the hot, cramped machinery spaces.

Naval officers had not been paid particularly well, but my mother whirred through the night on the sewing machine and clicked away determinedly on knitting needles, to ensure we always had a school uniform and a smart outfit to wear. We moved house constantly. It had all been about boxes and boxes. And new schools, new communities, new friends.

My mother had a backbone of steel. I realised that now I had four of my own. I was not about to complain about my lot to anyone in my family—four was considered more than manageable. My parents were still in love after forty plus years of marriage and the twelve siblings were all important parts of each others' lives and dreams.

I was now a mother of boys, a barrister and sometime writer. And wife to a doctor who was in Banda Aceh, in the wake of a tsunami. And I was contemplating writing to the prime minister. There was nothing normal about any of it. But it had to be done.

That evening, after I had put the children to bed, I ignored the kitchen mess and started typing a letter to Prime Minister John Howard asking him to take this opportunity to re-build the tsunami-affected regions. I reminded him that normally we might not be allowed such latitude or interference, but these were extraordinary times. It could be couched as an anti-terrorist measure if that was considered necessary to make Australia's involvement more palatable. Poverty, neglect and extremism were probably linked in any event. The reality was that it would be the ultimate humanitarian act, no other reasons were needed.

I copied in Alexander Downer, the Minister of Foreign Affairs. This letter could either put a cat amongst the pigeons, or it could be ignored. I thought about how Germany and Japan had been re-built by the allies after World War II. This was slightly different but you made friends when you helped out. When you showed you cared. Nations might change governments, but the people would surely remember.

Darwin had been flattened by Cyclone Tracy in 1975. It had also been a Christmas-time disaster. It was re-built, in what looks today like a snapshot of 1970s architecture. What would be re-built in Indonesia after this obliteration? It could be a snapshot of Australian generosity—homes built safely for the areas, with plumbing, roads and all the benefits of First World town-planning.

I ran the idea of the letter past a few friends. Too far-fetched, would never work, nice idea but good luck. You are writing to whom? Nobody writes to the PM. Nobody normal. And he doesn't get his ideas from real people either. Haven't you seen *Yes, Minister*?

I posted and faxed the letter anyway. You never knew.

But now it was New Year's Eve. Linda was heavily pregnant with her first child. By the time she and Jon arrived, I had fed the children and parked them in front of the television to watch the nine o'clock fireworks. It seemed so incongruous, such elaborate celebrations in Sydney when there had been such massive loss of life in nearby countries.

Leo Schofield had appeared on camera during the week saying the partying had been paid for already and would go ahead. Mercifully, the fireworks were turned into a fundraiser.

chapter six

A New Year for All

At about the end of the very first hour of the brand new year, the medical team were jerked awake in their stretchers. One or two of them dazedly fled half-asleep out the door as an earth tremor shuddered and roared. The walls heaved, the roof moved, building fragments fell and the ground rumbled ominously. The mozzie nets shook, and loose items jangled. Bags slid around the room. Some of the team members lay there, frozen with shock, unable to think, let alone move. Had they come all this way simply to die, crushed in their beds? Paul slept through the entire thing, lost in the dreamless sleep of the exhausted.

The team whispered to each other, not wanting to wake others, such as the loudly slumbering Paul. They discussed the integrity of the building, the likelihood of another quake, the possibility of being pulverised in the rubble.

They finally lapsed back into sleep, fitfully dreaming of lonely faces at the airport, scarred landscapes, festering wounds, bodies by the roadside.

Everyone woke again at about 6.30 a.m. and ate breakfast on the narrow balcony—muesli from a ration pack, moistened with water or with anything liquid, like hot coffee or fruit juice, rather than fresh milk (because there was none). Paul and the team thought the urn was the most important piece of kit they had brought. Hot coffee made you feel human. A heart-starter. There was no microwave, so the urn could heat meals too. The fireys had given everyone a blue plastic plate, bowl and cup and a stainless steel cutlery set, all in a calico drawstring bag.

The fireys had set up a small kitchenette arrangement, called a brew bay, near the entrance of the women's room. It consisted of the urn, condensed milk, a plastic spoon pile, and a roll of paper towel, hanging handily across a length of niftily knotted string. There were also Kimberley Clark ISO anti-bacterial wipes in a pull-out container and some detergent. You helped yourself to everything, and you washed up your own bowl and spoon in a sink. There was no room service and catering staff had been left off the team.

The first day of the new year was grey and overcast, muggy, and a light rain was falling. Paul sent me an SMS: 'We were in bed by 9 and not a drop to welcome in the NY! The real stuff starts 2day. Thinking of u all the time. PD.' Later on he was able to get through to talk to me. It was brief, but it was always good to hear his voice. I told him how we were going. Paul needed to know that we were all fine. And I duly told him that, every time.

My brother Ollie in Washington DC had emailed that day. 'Soph, I know you are busy, but promise you will keep a diary (bullet form is fine) of what Paul tells you of what he is doing, has seen, felt, etc, etc—this is history.' Ollie's request reminded me of a passage from Lewis Carroll's *Through the Looking Glass*, 'The horror of that moment,' the

King went on, 'I shall never, *never* forget!' 'You will though,' the Queen said, 'if you don't make a memorandum of it.' I asked Paul if he could keep a diary at his end, while I furiously scribbled, getting down everything he said, even while we spoke. Paul sounded hesitant, even as he promised. You had to face things if you wrote them down. Explore feelings.

René Zellweger and Peter Sharwood and two of the anaesthetists, Paul Luckin and David Scott, jumped in the back of a truck with some supplies and some of the original Bravo Team, and headed for Kesdam, the TNI-controlled military hospital. The tentative deal cut with the truck driver at the airfield had been fortuitous. Mike Flynn had cased it out as an appropriate place where the team could be used.

The Australian team remaining at Fakinah were all called to a morning briefing with the top military personnel and an Indonesian professor, Aryono Pusponegro, who had spent some time at Liverpool Hospital in Australia. He had come up from Jakarta and was put in charge of the surgery coordination in Aceh province. Mike Flynn gestured to the team at the start of the meeting that they should stand for the professor. Mike opened the meeting with a few words of Bahasa, thanking their hosts for the welcome.

Lieutenant-Colonel Harianto was introduced and he made it clear to Mike Flynn and the team that he was in charge of Fakinah Hospital. This served as a sharp reminder that, despite the fact that they were there to help, at short notice and in what were trying conditions, they were still visitors in another country. It was sobering, and in some respects added another layer of stress. The medical team was going to have to be very careful. There were many sensitivities. The team was from a Christian country, and Aceh province was predominantly fundamentalist Muslim. The police were in charge of Fakinah Hospital, the TNI in charge of Kesdam Hospital. Those who came up from Jakarta were from the government. The Indonesian government was represented militarily by TNI, who had been in conflict with the armed resistance group, Gerakan Aceh Merdeka (GAM—Free Aceh Movement) since 1976. There had been approximately 12 000 people killed during the last three decades as a result of the clash between the resistance and the military.

Aceh was where Arab traders first introduced Islam to the Indonesian archipelago, around the eleventh century. From here Islam subsequently spread to the rest of South-East Asia. That is why the province is sometimes known as *Serambi Mekah* (the Window to Mecca or, as some call it, the Verandah of Mecca). It was an independent Islamic sultanate for over 300 years, up until 1873, when Aceh vigorously resisted the Dutch who came and colonised the East Indies. The Dutch declared war on Aceh and eventually prevailed in 1904, after a long, drawn-out struggle involving high casualties. Acehnese guerilla resistance fighting continued until 1942, when the Japanese invaded the East Indies during World War II and conquered the Dutch colonial forces. From 1945, when Indonesia gained independence, Aceh fought to become an independent Islamic state. In 1959, Indonesia granted Aceh special territory status giving them cultural and religious autonomy, but the issues of foreign control and a military presence remained unresolved.

As a result, GAM separatists had been active since 1976. Their emphasis was on freedom and independence, and they were very devout Muslims which was a key feature of the Acehnese identity.

The Acehnese are determined people. Their history shows that.

Their province had been under martial law since 2003. Nobody was allowed in or out without permission from the Indonesian government; it was all very tense. And here were the Aussies, with little idea of the details of past animosities, all stocked up and ready to swing into action. Crikey, they were walking on eggshells.

The post-tsunami period might ultimately provide some impetus for peace but right now both sides were in shock and it was far too early for anyone to take up the political opportunities the mass death and disaster afforded. The Indonesians had sent help for their countrymen, despite being at civil war with them days earlier.

It was a deadly serious business, from every perspective. The team would have to liaise very diplomatically with local authorities and all relevant entities to do what they needed to do. Everything hinged on that.

Annette Holian, an orthopaedic surgeon from Melbourne, had no problem with being taken seriously. She hadn't attained the still-rare achievement of being a woman orthopaedic surgeon because she was a shrinking violet. She knew she was in a Muslim country and the traditions in relation to women professionals might well be different. She also knew that some countries and faiths had different ideas about standards of medical treatment. She listened as Professor Pusponegro spoke to the group and contemplated the consequences of what he was saying.

Suddenly a rooster started crowing in the middle of the meeting. Her mobile telephone was squawking loudly in her bag. Everyone looked at her. Some grinned; it broke the tension. Paul thought the timing was perfect. He SMSed her: 'You goose!' She rummaged around and quickly turned it off. The meeting resumed.

The team was informed that the TNI had lost about 1000 personnel in the tsunami. The police force, numbering about 3000, had been decimated. Of 300 Acehnese health personnel, only about seventeen had survived. The survivors were traumatised and incapacitated by grief; many had lost family members, others their homes.

Paul was listening intently to the briefing when suddenly he and the rest of the team were instinctively scrambling for their lives out the door. He had no idea how he got there, but he was out the door and into the middle of the courtyard before he realised it. The whole building shook violently. All the windows and walls were moving. His mind was filled with sheer terror. Paul had never experienced anything like it in his life. Awake, that is. In the Navy, while you're at sea you expect movement. You develop sea-legs and it is not perplexing. When you are on land, with four walls around you, twenty tonnes of roof-tiles above you and solid concrete beneath you, and you are sitting down for the first time in hours, fully engrossed in a fascinating briefing, the last thing you are prepared for is an earthquake.

It was to be one of the smallest quakes he would experience while he was in Aceh.

Everyone from the briefing stood in the courtyard, away from the building, until they were sure the tremors had stopped. Their fingers shaking, even some of the non-smokers accepted a cigarette when the pack went around. One of the Indonesian police fainted. He was terrified and his blood drained into his feet. Nurses Liz Cloughessy and Ray Southon rushed to help him. The assistance they provided caused a group of the police to insist on helping with the stacking and sorting of supplies.

Of course, Paul's mind adapted, which is what happens. Your coping mechanism adjusts until even the strangest occurrences seem normal. After experiencing a number of these tremors, Paul acquired a highly attuned sensory alert system, so that he eventually felt like Radar in *MASH*, and was often the first to ask, 'Did you feel that?' to his colleagues as a quake began. They had to evacuate each time. If the roof or walls had collapsed, they would have been crushed. Rhonda Cowderoy, one of the theatre nurses, noticed that when the rumble first started, geckoes would run down the walls frantically, cats would start miaowing and dogs could be heard barking in the distance. It was an eerie warning.

Technically, these were aftershocks. However, they were quite significant quakes, and a couple were said to be larger than the famed Newcastle quake in New South Wales back in 1989. It came back to Paul now. He had been lying on bitumen in Sydney, repairing a car from underneath, when that one had happened—the car had rocked on its jack, but fortunately stayed put.

After the briefing had concluded, the team was shown over the hospital by their hosts. Even though it was the middle of the day, the corridors were dark. The team was then shown the Emergency Department (the ED) and what work was being done there. There a lot of activity going on and cries from children in pain as they were being examined and treated. Brian Pezzutti walked over to see the array of surgical instruments being used, with an eye to what might be borrowed at some later stage for use in surgery. He found a tray of needles, syringes, forceps and needle-holders and made a note of them for later requests. As he returned to the group, he walked past a black plastic garbage bag on the floor and suddenly he cried out. He'd been stabbed by a hypodermic needle. He pulled his trouser leg up and saw a nasty scratch low on his leg, above ankle-height. The group stopped in its tracks. Everyone gathered round to see what had happened. The needle was sticking out from the bag by about 5 centimetres—it was thick, of the hollow type used for injections rather than the fine type used for suturing. Being hollow made it potentially dangerous—there could be blood in it. They put the bag safely into a bin, and Brian went off and had the wound cleaned and swabbed with Betadine by Dr James Branley. Brian was quite calm, partly due to his personality, and partly due to the fact that he also mentally judged the risk of infection from anything drastic as low—Aceh was a devout Muslim province, so the possibility of HIV infection was small. Brian's military service had kept him up-to-date with all his immunisations. Notwithstanding this reassurance, it was a wake-up call for the Australian team. They were in a different medical environment, with different protocols. There was always a risk, even of straightforward infection, from any wound by any cause; this was an environment where many people had bacteria-laden wounds, were coughing constantly, the cleaning regime was inadequate, and the heat and damp helped germs proliferate.

To prevent any recurrence of this episode, Paul and some of the others made makeshift sharps' bins out of plastic food containers, in which used syringes and needles could be disposed of.

Channel Nine's *A Current Affair* crew visited the hospital in the middle of all this chaos. The crew were famished, so the medical team gave them some food, which they appreciated. The TV people were aware of their multiple responsibilities. They had an obligation to get news out, because the world needed to know of the desperate plight of these people, but they also knew that there were medical-in-confidence issues, respect for the privacy of patients, and cultural sensitivities to be considered. There was also enough melodrama happening in real life to need no embellishment by them. They could have filmed the team in private moments when they shed tears or vented frustrations, but they didn't. Instead, they concentrated on showing the patients arriving, being cared for, the level of innovation and improvisation taking place and the 'can-do' attitude of the Australian team. The TV crew shared the same attitude.

They assisted whenever and wherever they could. A few days earlier they had helped unload the plane, now they helped lift patients. They showed consideration for the Indonesian people, the Acehnese patients, and, when asked not to film, because it might be distracting or breach medical ethics, they didn't. When a power failure occurred, they held torches aloft so the operation in progress could continue.

Paul started seeing the media through different eyes. They were telling the world about this place which was in extreme need, and they were helping out in their own ways, and in any way they could. He vowed to himself to cooperate if they needed him. After all, they were all in this together, they all had a job to do. Cut off from television, radio, newspaper and the internet, Paul did not know at the time what a powerful impact the press coverage was having on Australians, and the world. It would trigger an amazingly compassionate and generous response. The call for him to help came later that day. A call on his mobile came from Katie Jensen of the *Today* show in Sydney. Could he be interviewed live on Monday morning at 4 a.m. his time? No problem, he had answered as he resolutely arched his creaking shoulders.

The work that day was still quite full on. There was more stacking of stores and more cleaning to be done. The combination of the smell and the heat was overpowering. Like Bruce the day before, Paul began to feel unwell. He felt woozy and thought he was experiencing earth tremors. Luckily he had the sense to lie down before he fell down.

The team had been working in a very physically demanding, team-building activity for two days without a proper break. Now from time to time team members would check on how their stricken colleague was faring, to the point where Paul began feeling embarrassed. It was comforting, of course, but Paul couldn't wait to get up again. After drinking lots of water mixed with a bit of salt and sugar and some time spent horizontal, he began to feel much improved.

Paul, Watto and Bruce went on a tour of inspection, checking the effect of the aftershocks on the building. A good idea of the lay of the land was important knowledge. There were also many things they needed and finding resources in the hospital was paramount. The integrity of the building was a consideration. They saw cracks in walls, and some doors did not close properly due to the ruined alignment of the building. They had previously heard the dubiously reassuring mantra, 'It's not the 9.0 earthquake which gets you, it's the 6.5 aftershock that follows which brings the building down.'

Watto described their scouting expedition to Paul as 'security rounds'. 'We're just burglars in uniform, mate!' he said with a grin. 'Two weeks with us and you'll learn what it takes crims two years to learn in the "joint"!' (a slang reference to gaol). The reality was that they really did have to check regularly on earthquake damage, and also had to find much-needed surgical instruments, medical supplies and anything else that would help, such as anaesthetic equipment and electrical powerboards. They still felt somewhat restrained by their desire to be courteous and unintrusive, but the urge of necessity was eroding this rapidly now.

There was a locked room just down the corridor from the dormitory, which had high windows. Paul and Watto lifted Bruce up towards the windows, passing him through an open window so he could get inside and open the room's double doors. Once inside, they found a huge, clunky set of jingly keys on a chair. It was too good to be true. They were now able to gain access to the other rooms along the corridor. One of these became a designated time-out room for the team, another was later used for the loudest snorers to sleep in. A third room, which appeared to have been the CEO's room, had an ablutions ensuite with the usual squat toilet and dipper-in-water arrangement. No showers, but some of the women would commandeer this room with delight.

The three men saw further signs of the quake damage in the outside office. Achievement trophies lay on their sides, some were smashed. Furniture was sitting at odd angles. This area became the office area for the team. Ken Harrison put the chargers for the radios in here and Paul Van Buynder from public health made it his quiet place for tapping out records of public health developments on his laptop. Paul Dunkin found a stack of blank CDs for Ken to download photographs and material on, some power cords and other odds and ends.

The pièce de résistance of the tour was the discovery of precious blood-pressure cuffs, in what appeared to be a midwives' training room—complete with silicon body parts —for teaching birthing and breastfeeding techniques. Taking blood pressure is a vital part of medicine and it is a critical part of anaesthetics. This was an exhilarating find, because checking blood pressure manually takes time and interferes with the performance of other tasks because you have to pump the cuff up by hand and use a stethoscope to detect the pressure. Paul managed to rig these cuffs up to a machine and take automatic recordings. It was almost perfect!

Patients were suddenly turning up in droves, either arriving on their own or with the help of friends and relatives. The word had got out that not only was a hospital open, but it was free of charge, as the Indonesian government had agreed to provide free health care to those people affected by the tsunami. The government also agreed to indemnify the hospital owner against any damage done by the Australians while they were present. This had a powerful effect on the attitude of the owner, who became more relaxed about the team staying and working there.

UNICEF representatives arrived at Fakinah and asked the team for some supplies to distribute. Anything was better than nothing—could they spare something? The team had been given tarpaulins, empty water containers (collapsible jerry cans) and water purifying tablets for distribution where needed. They were not part of the medical cache, but were a gift of aid from the Australian people. These were gratefully received. Public Health doctor Jeremy McAnulty went out with the UNICEF reps to the IDP (Indigenous Displaced Persons) camps, to help. The tarpaulins made great shelters and, if you ran out of body bags, you could use these for that purpose too. There was no road down to Meuloboh, so Jeremy and the UNICEF men drove to the villages they could get to. There was often nothing left standing, but from the rubble you could see there had been dwellings. People were digging graves everywhere you looked. They had set up makeshift living arrangements, gravitating together into camps. Kids were cheerily playing, able to laugh despite being surrounded by surreality and horror. Oxfam were conducting Wat/San (water and sanitation) and health assessments.

At Fakinah, Adrian Humphrey was working in the wards and in Emergency. As a Sydney paramedic he was used to certain standards, but here the medical equipment fell drastically short of what he was used to. For starters, there were hardly any oxygen bottles. Shmackers' words rang in his head. You couldn't dwell on the shortages or you would go crazy. You had to get over it. Improvise.

The Bravo part of the CASTA team came back that afternoon after having operated at Kesdam all day. They were satisfied with how everything had gone as they had actually been allowed to be useful. There had been some settling-in matters naturally, but progress had been made.

That evening the two SCAT paramedics, Adrian Humphrey and Jeff Gilchrist, together with Mike Flynn and three of the doctors—James Branley, Jeremy McAnulty and Paul Van Buynder—all attended a meeting at 5 p.m. in a building across and down the road from

Fakinah Hospital. It was at the International Organization for Migration (IOM) headquarters (the IOM was established in 1951 to resettle European displaced persons, refugees and migrants after World War II). The IOM premises were being used for the first few days by the United Nations Office for the Coordination of Humanitarian Affairs (OCHA), the United Nations (UN) itself and the United States Agency for International Development (USAID) until the latter two moved further down the road. The meeting was chaired by OCHA. The meeting was going to be a daily event. The building was well guarded and people needed permission to enter. Security was tight for various reasons, such as the safeguarding of aid supplies and the awareness of the conflict between the TNI and GAM. The main reason, though, was that there was a lot of important work to be done and organised, and interruptions would only stall everyone's efforts.

All the top representatives of the various aid agencies that had now arrived—about 23 already—turned up for this meeting. Charlie Higgins, the Bangladeshi head of OCHA—who reminded Jeremy of Sir Richard Branson with his British accent, beard and hairstyle—was in charge. Resources and supplies allocated to Aceh had to be organised and divvied up, so Aceh province was dissected into about six zones.

News that the military was accumulating thousands of bodies each day, which would soon become a public health hazard if they were not buried or burnt, was tabled. The aid workers who had scouted the area returned with reports of shortages of transport and difficulties in getting through on some roads due to the damage caused by the tsunami. All issues were pressing, all were urgent.

The pivotal problem reported by everyone at the meeting was the need to establish a reliable water supply. The water pipes had been damaged, limiting the water supply, and the water had also been contaminated. The Australian Army had a water purification plant which could supply 20 000 litres per hour. However, to purify that amount, you had to have an equal inflow of water. The piping was broken, and hard to locate and isolate, making the whole process tricky.

The next biggest problem was that although there was six months' supply of food available in Indonesia from Indonesian government and overseas aid sources, it had to be distributed to the needier areas and quickly. The whys and wherefores were all to be monitored by the various aid agencies who were spread around Aceh province.

The USS *Abraham Lincoln*, an aircraft carrier which was essentially a floating city of between 5000 to 6000 personnel was moored off the coast. It was commanded by Rear Admiral Doug Crowder, hosted seven different aircraft and had previously been sent to Somalia, the Gulf and Iraq. The *Lincoln* had just been to Hong Kong and was scheduled to head to Korea when it was diverted to Banda Aceh to provide assistance. The carrier had a hospital on board and the facilities to provide enough power to run the equivalent of 100 000 homes. It could process 400 gallons of seawater into fresh water each day. When Cyclone Tracy occurred, Australia's aircraft carrier at the time, HMAS *Melbourne*, plugged into the main electricity grid and powered the blacked-out city. These were the peacetime uses to which such ships could be put. The *Lincoln* was not required for electricity generation on this occasion, but it provided a vital platform to the fleet of helicopters for medevacs and for aid deliveries of food, fresh water and medical supplies.

Two thousand of its sailors volunteered to pack aid supplies, all day, each day, in the sun.

The local roads were initially impassable and most boats were too damaged to be used. It was rumoured that more than 150 bridges had been destroyed and the rebuilding of them would be a huge project. The American helicopters tirelessly searched the coast for injured people and each helicopter journey would return to Banda Aceh airfield with patients to be transported to one of the two functioning local hospitals.

By the following Monday, the Australian Navy would be contributing three more choppers to the operation, but the American contribution was incalculable. They had twenty helicopters fully laden, doing constant food and water drops along the kilometres of obliterated coastline. Had they not conducted these aid deliveries to many otherwise unreachable areas, thousands would have died of starvation.

With no warning the power went out. It was 7 p.m. and Annette was operating. The patient was a young woman who was very ill. Her wounds were extremely infected and she needed to have them debrided. This involved cutting away infected flesh and flushing away pus (the rationale being to not only halve infection but also to help healthy tissue grow again). Annette was operating with Sudhakar Rao. Ray Southon and Marj Raggett were the theatre nurses, Brian Pezzutti and Paul were anaesthetising. It was early days and everyone was still getting accustomed to all the shortcomings of the situation.

The instruments were not the right ones, there was a lack of sterile supplies such as dressings, the anaesthetic equipment for administering gases and drugs was non-existent, and there were no monitoring machines—the beeps and screens with wiggly lines were just not happening here in Banda Aceh. The list went on. Everything was being done manually, and it was laborious and slow. Now, a power failure. This they did not need. They all laughed when the lights went out. It was so beyond what was desirable, there was no other way of dealing with it. Humour was a mature coping mechanism; they had all learned that, in their medical studies and their journey of life. Suddenly, head-lamps and torches appeared from everywhere. Ken Harrison turned up wearing a headband with a light in it. He put one on Annette so she could see into the wound she and Sudhakar were working on. The fireys, Watto and Bruce, rigged up portable arc lights (Goliath lights) to enable the operation to continue in safety. By 8 p.m. the operation was completed and the lighting returned in the next half-hour.

As was becoming customary, there was a briefing from Mike Flynn that night in the dormitory. The members of the medical team traded information and updated each other. The team's mission was to establish a working surgical set-up which could be taken over by an incoming team. So far they were doing well. Jeff Gilchrist briefed them all on earthquake preparedness—they each had to have a pair of running shoes close at hand, and a bumbag or small backpack to grab in an emergency, containing their passports, underpants and a bottle of water. They were reminded that the fireys had hung a rope ladder over the balcony, in case of roof collapse or stairway blockage.

There was no respite from being on the alert.

The team crawled onto their stretchers at about 11 p.m., still cheery, still running on adrenaline. It was the end of their second day in Banda Aceh.

chapter seven

On the Ground in Banda Aceh

The team woke at 6.30 a.m., ate breakfast on the narrow balcony, then Alpha and Bravo would go to their posts at Fakinah and Kesdam hospitals respectively. Although the teams had combined into one team (CASTA), covering two hospitals had led to the original Alpha team working at Fakinah and some of Bravo going to Kesdam.

The balcony outside the team's dormitory sleeping area was about 1.5 metres wide and 12 metres long. It had become a thoroughfare, a cooking area, an eating area, a community area, and was even the lavatory, because the zip-up, plastic-walled tent toilet was down one end of it. It was not always pleasant eating next to a little tent that barely contained the noise and smell of human bodily functions, but there was nowhere else to sit.

Fakinah (sometimes referred as the 'police hospital' to distinguish it from Kesdam, the 'military hospital') had a courtyard in the middle. The balcony and their dormitories were on the top (second) floor along the whole rear length of the hospital, facing the courtyard. The theatres were on the ground floor and diagonally opposite, at the front of the hospital, next to the Emergency Department.

At the beginning or end of the day or during meal breaks, the team would return to the balcony and sit on grey-ridged plastic boxes, which their bony bottoms became accustomed to. Chairs felt so smooth in comparison. They brushed their teeth and spat onto the grass from that balcony, where there were no basins or mirrors. When someone needed to pass by, everyone had to draw their legs up to make room. When Scott Bevan from Channel Nine interviewed Annette on the balcony, there was literally no room anywhere for the poor bloke operating the boom mike, so he sat on the toilet. All 28 members of the team lived in this zoo for the deployment, and not a cross word passed between them. If you can imagine all the rooms of your house condensed into one smallish balcony, with 28 people milling around on it, during certain hours of the day—sometimes at the crack of dawn or last thing at night, when they were preparing for bed—then you would have imagined exactly what everyday life was like on that congested open-air balcony of Fakinah Hospital.

The nights were hot and humid. The team all slept on narrow Army stretchers with mozzie nets draped over them. Paul ended up sleeping in his underwear, flat on his back, trying to keep cool. With Dr Jeremy McAnulty, director of Communicable Diseases New South Wales Health, on one side and Dr David Scott, Lismore anaesthetist, on the other. Some of the luckier ones scored a spot under the windows. There was not a breath of moving air elsewhere.

Paul and the team who worked in Fakinah's theatre— Annette, Sudhakar, Ray and Marj, and some of the others—would usually sneak in late at night so as not to disturb the sleepers and climb into bed quietly in the dark.

They were quiet, but the room was not. It was like entering a cave of grizzly bears. Ray was a snorer, as was Sharwood. Paul contributed to the cacophony too, once he was heavily asleep. Soon Ray was banished, like a Big Brother eviction, to the small room Watto, Bruce and Paul had discovered during their expeditions. The tremors were frightening enough without nasal reverberations that reminded them of earthquakes.

Everyone periodically rifled through their bags, during breaks, looking for their stuff. There were no drawers or cupboards, nor a lot of room to move around either. Shmackers kept good-naturedly scratching his head and complaining he couldn't find his travel clock. He knew he had packed it. Everyone had something they either couldn't find, or that they would have packed if they had had a second chance.

The team were learning about each other. Picking up pretty quickly on who was a morning person, who was a night one. Larks and owls. Every morning at breakfast David Scott (Scotty) would breezily greet everyone, 'Good morning!' The less bright-and-bushy-tailed would grunt, stare back fuzzily or ignore him until they had woken up properly.

All were snaky about an alarm which went off every night, at about 2.30 a.m., waking them all for a bleary moment. It came from somewhere distant, muffled and not discernible, so nobody could turn the darn thing off. It sounded every night for the entire deployment, much to their bemused annoyance.

Sometimes the hauntingly beautiful strains of the Muslim call to prayer would filter through, between 4 and 5 a.m. Sudhakar would stir sleepily. He would be fully awake soon. He worked long hours, in that driven way

Above: A mass grave along the road to the coast. Identification processes were abandoned in favour of speedy burials for health reasons.

Below: Body bags lying in the heat by the roadside. Sadly, an all too common sight.

Above: A private moment for an Acehnese bus driver, as the enormity of the disaster sinks in.

Below: A tragedy that defies words.

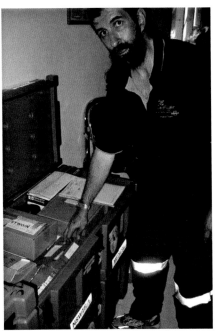

Above left: Ken Harrison, custodian of the cache. **Above right:** Nurses Lisa Dillon and Karyn Boxshall, complete with mask 'hats' and fireys' knee-pads. **Below:** The second relief team from Jakarta. Relations between this team and the Australians were excellent. Taken in Fakinah hospital courtyard, CASTA balcony is above right.

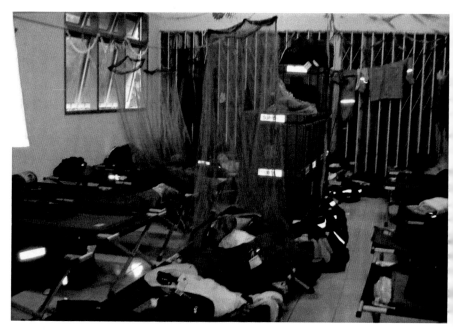

Above: The men's cosy sleeping quarters at Fakinah, complete with mozzie nets, grey space cases, clothing, bags—and the hidden alarm clock! **Below left:** Karyn, Peter, Scotty, Alan, Bruce and Jeremy on the balcony at Fakinah hospital. **Below right:** Watto and an Australian Army engineer working on the well at Fakinah.

some surgeons have. He was gratified to find that his anaesthetist Paul Dunkin was always ready to start early each morning, and understood without having to be asked that they were going to be working late.

Sometimes Sudhakar would open one eye and see that Mike Flynn's nearby stretcher was already empty. Their indefatigable leader was usually on the phone to the waking east coast of Australia—Canberra or Sydney, four hours ahead of Banda Aceh time—getting instructions or advice, providing feedback, giving details of requirements for this team or the incoming one. 'Send a fax outlining your requests,' Mike would often be told. Although he found this very amusing, he was too polite to laugh. Paper, fax machines and a reliable power source were not part of the team's Banda Aceh experience.

The team ate all their meals on the balcony and they were always ratpacks, the Army slang for ration packs. A typical evening meal might be the snootily named 'mushroom risotto', which was really just a fancy name for salty mushroom-flavoured rice. Chicken teriyaki was another. You added hot water directly to the food, or you could pop it on top of the urn to warm it up. Noodles featured more than any other dish, for the entire duration of the mission.

On about day three, some evening meals appeared with both French and English writing on the boxes. They were chicken and vegetables with *'poulet'* on the label. They were Canadian. Paul stuck with sausage and baked beans, at least they were identifiable. The fireys had loaded these meals before the team left Sydney, keeping them back until now for a change of flavour. The Canadian batch had a chemical heating mechanism whereby you put water into a sachet, then placed it next to the meal and left it for a few minutes to warm the food. The always inventive fireys had made contact with some of the sailors from the *Lincoln* and eventually the Australians were swapping meals with the Americans. Their meals were amazing—their meal bag for a single meal was the same size as the Australian allowance for a whole day. It even had chewing gum in it. Paul tried a New York Steak. It was manufactured meat, but was carefully coloured to look char-grilled. Paul told me it tasted heavenly and that it was great to finally chew on something. All the other food was soft and mushy like nursing home food.

They had a close call with the drinking water one day when the wrong type was put in the communal urn but nobody drank it, luckily, before they realised. The reliability of their help depended on them all remaining in good health and in good spirits.

A truck would arrive each day to take the Bravo part of the team to Kesdam, as per the deal struck at the airfield on day one. Bravo were very conscious that they could not go back and forth on a whim between the two hospitals as Kesdam was 5 kilometres away through militarily sensitive territory and there was no easy way for people to return, as there was no freely available transport, no shuttle bus. Resources such as fuel were precious. They needed local cash to buy anything, and they needed lots of it. If they forgot something, they had to make do, to their initial great consternation and eventual resignation.

Mike Flynn had bought some benzene (petrol) via a local called Marthoenis, a young nursing student helping at Fakinah. The Australians needed this fuel for the electricity generators which supplied the hospital with power and a couple of transportable backup generators the Australians had brought with them. The normal city power grid was out due to the earthquake and tsunami. The team had not been able to transport petrol on the aircraft due to its high flammability. Through Sudhakar Rao, who was happy to play interpreter, Mike asked Marthoenis whether he would accept a reward, over and above the cost of the fuel. Marthoenis was adamant that he would not take one cent for the labour involved, even though the Australians would have become involved in a major rigmarole if they had tried to obtain it themselves. 'I work for charity, for the Red Cross,' he said proudly. He set off on his scooter and returned with jerry cans of benzene. The Acehnese were showing themselves to be very likeable people, in myriad ways.

Mike was dealing with many issues. Everything from coordinating with aid agencies on the ground to liaising with Indonesian and Australian authorities there and elsewhere. The early meetings with UN representatives and aid agencies had resulted in the relief effort being divided into various categories. Health was one category, hospitals another. Health included public health concerns—everything from digging sufficient latrines at a camp to vaccinating against measles outbreaks. Hospitals was dealing with surgical matters, where people needed operations for wounds or fractures, or with very ill people who were suffering from inhaled saltwater pneumonia (aspiration pneumonitis), tetanus and other illnesses. The Emergency Department at Fakinah was treating the injured, some of whom were admitted if they needed longer or a higher level of care than could be given in Outpatients.

Mike had been put in charge of the hospitals category for the overall relief effort. There were field hospitals arriving from everywhere — Lithuania, Jordan, Germany, France, Norway, Qatar, to name just a few places. Most were tents, but a couple were what James Branley called 'blow-up hospitals', because they were inflatable.

One thing Mike was not having to deal with overly were personnel issues. Although the team comprised essentially a bunch of strangers who had come together under extraordinary circumstances and were having their professional and personal patience strained daily, they all got on remarkably well. They were all leaders in their own areas at home and, with such a bunch of mavericks, it could have gone either way. There were always some issues — they wouldn't have been human otherwise — but these were never major nor obstructive. There were some tense moments as a result of the pressure everyone was under, but they were always able to joke about them afterwards.

Paul was forever tinkering, trying to repair things. When they had arrived, there were two anaesthetic machines, neither of which functioned at all. He toyed with one broken one and got it to work. Desperate for another, so they would have a working machine in each of the two theatres, he tried to fix the second one. On one occasion, Brian Pezzutti and Paul were fiddling with the second machine and were carefully listening for escaping air as they tried to locate a leak in the oxygen tubing. Every time they got close, someone would cough, talk, move or rattle a door. Nurses and various team members kept walking in and out of the theatre. With each rattle of the door Brian was becoming more and more irate. He finally snapped at the miscreants, 'Either stay in or get out!'

Surgeon Annette and theatre nurse Ray Southon began tiptoeing around the theatre. Brian explained, 'It's important, it wastes precious oxygen. We have so little to start with and we don't want to leave a leaking hose for the next person and endanger a life!' He and Paul began afresh to listen for the leak when Ray's plastic apron inexplicably crackled. Brian exploded, 'Get OUT!!!!!'

Ray and Brian laughed about it together later. That bloody crackly apron!

Meanwhile at Kesdam, the surgeons René Zellweger and Peter Sharwood did hospital rounds and identified patients needing surgery. They were often accompanied by Wing Commander Greg Norman, who was working in the Emergency Department with about five hard-working ADF nurses and medics. The Australians did the day shift at Kesdam, the Indonesian medical teams did the evenings.

They would then head back to Fakinah and join the rest of the team, who worked late into the night. The Bravo Team were working on different cases over at Kesdam and under slightly different conditions too. It was a much larger hospital than Fakinah, and attracted more serious cases. At Kesdam, they were operating on two tables in one large theatre, prepared by the theatre sisters, Rosie Clifton and Rhonda Cowderoy, together with the paramedic Adrian Humphrey. The three of them were doing their best, but it was hard to achieve sanitary, let alone sterile, conditions. There were no shelves to put equipment on so they all had to work out of boxes. Surfaces were not sterile so things could not be put down. The hospital drapes were rinsed and re-used, literally after each operation. It stuck in your craw but there were no other options. There was no working steriliser, so they were using copious amounts of alcohol to sterilise the few surgical instruments that were available.

There was also a critical shortage of nurses for a 300-bed hospital. Where family members had survived, they looked after patients as best they could, cleaning and feeding them, interpreting for them, keeping them company and trying to make them comfortable. The team were deeply touched by what they saw.

Paul Luckin and David Scott were the anaesthetists for Kesdam. Shmackers was the only doctor available to do pre- and post-operative care of the patients. It was a formidable job. Pre-operative ranged from ensuring the patient was briefed, fasted and physically collected for surgery, to assisting with putting up drips for fluid and drugs. Post-operative responsibilities included ensuring the patient woke from the anaesthetic, was not haemorrhaging, and had responses such as pulse and blood pressure in the safe and healthy ranges. The patient would also have the opportunity to discuss any problems and future care requirements. Once the patient recovered, there was the handover to ward staff, the few that there were. Shmackers' role was a challenge—he was largely doing all the surgical patients pre- and post-op on his own, and the differing culture and language created their own hurdles. But Shmackers somehow managed. He was tender and caring too. It wasn't unusual for him to gently hold the hand of a patient or mop a clammy forehead, even in all the mayhem.

The team at Kesdam had a busy day on 2 January. Busy, and quite typical. There were a number of operations performed—at least four cases involved major wound debridements and there were another two patients each having a leg amputated. The leg amputations were the most demanding types of surgery as they required all the physical and mental resources which could be mustered, on the parts of all involved. They used more supplies than any other procedures done at Kesdam, and carried a high risk of infection, haemorrhage and death.

Adrian was the scout at Kesdam. The 'gopher'. The one who runs around doing things. He would open the dressings, pass the instruments. He enabled the nurses to remain as sterile as possible. As a SCAT paramedic, his work in theatre was completely different to his normal duties, but he rose to the occasion. Once he came back to Fakinah from Kesdam each afternoon, he would slip into theatre there to help out. Annette let him assist in wound debridements, to his great satisfaction. He was learning a lot and was gratified by her confidence in him.

Adrian had had much the same SCAT training as Jeff Gilchrist, and both were doing things on this deployment which were above and beyond their normal frame of reference. But they were used to rising to the occasion. Adrian had worked in the first-aid post at Denpasar airport, after the Bali bombings, treating anyone who was heading home. People mostly had burns from the intense heat and fractures from leaping out of windows and over fences to escape the fire. As well as injured Australians, there were Norwegians, Danish, English and other tourists.

He had also worked at the Thredbo disaster, which had become a matter of body retrieval rather than assisting survivors. Stuart Diver was the only one found alive of those caught in the massive mudslide, which brought thousands of tonnes of dirt and debris down a slope at around midnight one night in July 1997, crushing and suffocating those in its path. Eighteen people were killed. The large number of rescuers had been moving about on an unstable cliff-face in sub-zero wintry weather conditions, making the search a hazardous activity in itself, requiring the SCAT backup.

Adrian had done USAR (Urban Search and Rescue) training which was all about finding and caring for patients in urban disasters such as building collapses, as opposed to natural setting disasters such as bushfires. He knew some of the members of the CASTA team from exercises in the past. He had become a Queen's Scout in his youth, and at one stage had been in the merchant navy, training to be a captain. Adrian wore a beard, was fit and trim in physique and had a typically warm, friendly Aussie face, which went with his good nature — he was very much a 'people person'. Adrian was married to Kay and had three grown-up children, two sons and a daughter.

He was now here in case the team members themselves needed medical help, and he also was determined to help in any capacity possible. And he did — at both hospitals. He also was keeping a detailed log of the days in the disaster zone, so that lessons could be learned to improve future services and training. The team had been involved in moving heavy boxes, in heat they were unaccustomed to; the tremors were always a threat to their bodily safety and overall they were eating, working and sleeping in quite physically demanding circumstances.

The tally so far was within expectations. Nobody had pulled a muscle or popped a disc in the unloading process, but one or two had chafed their hands on the handles of the heavy tents and a couple of the men had keeled over from over-exertion; there had been the needlestick injury; one stye (infected eye); a few with swollen under-arm nodes and one had a swollen knee. But so far the team's health had been good. Adrian was conscious that not only was the work demanding for the members of the team, they were all working under intense media scrutiny also. One day as he was in the middle of something he looked up—straight into an ABC television camera. (Then he recognised his friend Gustav behind the lens, back from a war zone, and he relaxed.) Despite the challenges, the team's psychological health had been good too. Morale was high and people were functioning at par. He and Jeff Gilchrist were onto them all about keeping up their doxycycline and water intake, and also—most importantly— their mental wellbeing.

The fireys helped out here, opening their cache again on about day two or three (not too early), and bringing out coloured cordial and lollies of all descriptions. Spearmint leaves, chikkoes, minties, mentos, jelly babies. It was great timing. Such a contrast to what they were immersed in. Everyone got into them like excited children—there is nothing like deprivation to make you appreciate the small things in life. Little things become wonderful, when life isn't 'laid on' to excess. The secret to happiness surely lies in there somewhere.

The wounds of the tsunami victims were telling a similar story at both Fakinah and Kesdam. Rapidly moving, broken pieces of wood and sheets of raggedy-edged corrugated steel had gored and sliced people indiscriminately as they scrambled for their lives out of the swirling water. Now they had festering wounds, thick with hot pus and oozing black fluid (a mix of the noxious water, blood and denaturing pus). Pus is simply white blood cells and platelets; when freshly formed, it is a light, creamy-coloured fluid which rushes to the site of a wound. When it becomes infected—which can be quite a quick development, in a matter of hours—it begins to become offensive. Smelly, thick, greenish-yellow. As it ages, it becomes darker and even more offensive in odour, texture and colour. Its colour can become black, the colour of rot.

Some patients had been like this for days now. They were suffering greatly. A mere infected fingernail is distractingly painful. These poor people had red, inflamed, pus-ridden infections in many parts of their bodies. The Acehnese word for pain was *sakit* (pronounced 'suhkeet'). It was a word the team heard more often than they had hoped.

The team begrudged every day that they had not been there sooner. They did realise now how unstable conditions had been at Banda Aceh in the first days and how pointless it would have been to send in an ill-prepared, ill-stocked team. You never want to send liabilities into a disaster zone, or create more casualties. As it was, they had the bare minimum in stores and the aftershocks were still nerve-wrackingly sizeable and frequent. They couldn't have regrets; they just had to do whatever they could, with whomever was left.

There were no X-rays, but there were broken bones aplenty. The team were devising ways of detecting the nature and extent of injuries without any of the devices they relied upon back in Australia. Obvious breaks were easy. Especially if the skin had been broken and you could see a bit of snapped-off and bloody bone sticking out. Closed fractures were more difficult to detect. Sometimes the weird angle of a limb was a giveaway or bruising and swelling was another. Extreme pain when pressing the area or moving the limb signified something was not right.

The injuries were anywhere—on arms, legs, heads, trunks. Punctures, penetrations, perforations. Body cavities, such as stomachs and lungs, had been punctured; sharp wood and steel bits had penetrated muscles; bowels had been perforated. One little boy needed a colostomy bag.

One patient had her forehead and half her nose sliced off; she would need plastic surgery to have her face restored but, for now, radical measures were taken to prevent brain damage or death from infection.

Amputation decisions were being made, but never, ever lightly. The realisation that radical medicine was called for had dawned on the team quickly, as the infections were too deep in many cases. The victims from the tsunami had effectively self-triaged, creating a natural hierarchy of urgency. The worst cases had died already, and the very ill needed drastic responses to save their lives. It was gut-wrenching for the team as they knew that life without a limb for these patients meant hardship for life. There were no physiotherapists, no occupational therapists, no wheel-chairs, no crutches. The team had no knowledge of what welfare services would be available. They didn't want to speculate. But allowing the severely infected, ischaemi-cally gangrenous (lacking adequate blood supply) and sometimes pulverised limb to remain would kill the patient.

Some patients did not want to be less than whole. That made them imperfect and they were concerned this would deprive them of the chance to go to heaven. Paul remem-bered how a cat with no tail had fallen on him through the hospital roof. Since then, the team had seen many such cats and had asked about this phenomenon. Cats had their tails docked to keep heaven from being over-run. Some of the patients made the horrendously difficult decision to die staying intact, rather than have the life-saving amputation of a poisonous limb.

The medical care was the best it could be in the circum-stances. There were no medical records for the patients, no referral letter giving a background, no GPs to call. There were no pathology test results to shed light on conditions, no X-rays to examine, no ECGs. Any notes made, when paper was found, were useless to the Australians if written in a different language, and useless to the non-English speaking, if written in anything other than Acehnese or Bahasa.

Peter Sharwood and René Zellweger were operating at Kesdam with the barest of essentials. They were having to work with what was professionally unacceptable at home. No steriliser, precious few instruments, no blood supplies. They were flying blind, making educated guesses.

The fireys had given them protective goggles, because the sawing of the limbs caused blood to spray. Peter and René did not have a heavy-duty saw for amputating and so the job was harder. The two were using disposable scalpels for surgery and whatever else they could find. He and René had two gigli saws for the amputations, but only one set of handles. When both tables were doing amputations, they had to improvise with artery forceps as handles. A gigli saw is like a pipe-cleaner. It has a fine pebbly edge to it—it is like cutting through bone with very fine and spiky barbed wire. It became so hot from the sawing back and forth that it began to smoke and burn the bone. One of the team would dribble water onto the saw, to cool it. The surgeons worked themselves into a lather. A couple of times Peter had to ask for his mask to be cut off, as it had filled with sweat, and he could no longer breathe through the soup.

Peter did rustle up a proper amputation saw eventually. It looked like a carpenter's tenon saw, with a weight on it, so he didn't have to lean into it as he sawed. Doing a below-knee amputation was tricky as it involved cutting through two bones. In their situation you didn't want to cut more skin or have more blood loss than you could help. They were avoiding above-knee amputations because even though cutting through just one bone was easier, it was high-risk because of the blood loss when you cut through the large thigh muscles, which are richly supplied with arteries.

The team had no blood to give their patients and the tourniquets were woeful, just a bit of sucker tubing held tight with a clamp. In Australia, when a tourniquet was needed you had a pneumatic one which was pumped up to hold the limb tightly, cutting off the blood supply when you needed it stopped. They had no diathermy to cauterise the wounds. By burning the ends of cut tissue, it not only stops the bleeding but reduces the chance of infection. The surgeons had to make do with stitching up the stumps and leaving a bit open to allow them to drain.

It was difficult to take down a patient's history, yet it was never more important, because the treatments were extreme. Sometimes an Indonesian doctor who was bilin-gual was able to help. The patients, if they were in good enough condition to talk, generally could not speak more than a few words of English and the team could not speak Acehnese. Back at Fakinah, Paul was using a Bahasa word he had learned when he had travelled to Indonesia. *Bagus*, meaning 'good', became a word of common understanding. Communicating, even simply, was a way of connecting to the patients. Reach them. Ease fears. Confirm progress.

The international media drifted around the medical team, covering both hospitals, capturing the many challenges. Relaying what was unfolding, to a waiting world. A world in shock.

Out at the Sultan Iskandar Muda airfield at Banda Aceh, Bill Griggs had set up an Aero-Medical Evacuation (AME) system. Some USS *Lincoln* doctors had come ashore. American helicopters were bringing in badly injured survivors of the tsunami and they were being triaged by the USS *Lincoln* doctors at the airfield. The IOM had a triage tent set up which could treat some patients urgently if needed, as well as monitoring inbound patients due for Fakinah or Kesdam. This was also a holding place while the airlifting process got underway for the outbound patients coming from the two hospitals. The airfield was a hubbub of comings and goings, activity and aircraft noise. Despite the commotion, Bill had a system functioning.

Bill was well-placed to perform this pivotal AME role. He not only had experience professionally, he knew the various parties who were involved in making it work. He had arrived in Banda Aceh before anyone else and he knew what was where and who was who. He was liaising not only with IOM, but with the Americans, the Spanish and the ADF. He knew the members of the CASTA team who were working at the two hospitals. His work in the Gulf War, Bougainville, Bali, East Timor—and countless other missions—was going to serve him well now. He knew how to get people working and how to keep the goal uppermost in everyone's minds. Phone contact was very unreliable, especially in the early days, which added an extra layer of difficulty, and the tents had only torchlight after dusk. Language barriers made communication tedious, even when there was an interpreter available. Timing was everything with severely wounded people. The task needed a fast and good decision-maker. It needed Bill Griggs.

He met with the key people, including Mike Flynn and a doctor from the USS *Lincoln*, Lieutenant Lisa Peterson.

He needed their cooperation to coordinate the transfer of arriving patients to Fakinah and Kesdam for treatment. 'When we triage,' explained Griggs, 'we only do treatment we have to do. If the patients don't need treatment immediately now or if it's not simple stuff that's needed, we will send them on straight away.' He also negotiated via Lisa Peterson the acceptance of ADF casualties onboard the USS *Lincoln*, if it became necessary.

Some critically ill patients could not stay at Fakinah or Kesdam and needed to be transferred to Medan where they could be transfused with blood, X-rayed, tested, splinted, ventilated and monitored more closely. Medan had not been affected by the tsunami, as it was an inland city, and it had a number of comprehensive and fully-staffed hospitals complete with all necessary supplies and equipment. Patients earmarked in the two Banda Aceh hospitals as suitable for AME were sent to the airfield for airlifting to Medan, where Bill's friend and colleague Allan MacKillop was at the receiving end of the AME, co-ordinating the ambulances and hospitals to receive the patients.

Bill Griggs was everywhere. He stayed at Fakinah one night, where the team swapped mobile batteries with him and he re-charged his own battery by getting some food and rest. Sleeping out at the airfield was an exercise in futility. He went to Kesdam the next day, assisting anaesthetist Paul Luckin in theatre with a major above-knee amputation. He then stayed overnight on the USS *Lincoln*.

He had so much to do that eating and sleeping had become a low priority. His colleagues could see it in his face. Here was someone who needed a long rest. He was on the go constantly. Organising transport and aircraft, and ensuring patients are moved, fed and medically stable is a big job on its own when conditions are good and every service is orderly and reliable. In a disaster zone, it becomes a mammoth task. He had patients on stretchers being blown about by the strong, blustery updraft of dozens of helicopters, landing and taking off continually. The chaotic cacophony of rotors and engines of choppers, Hercs and assorted international aircraft only increased as the airfield became more and more congested by the hour.

In the middle of it all was this one tireless man, the Australian doctor Bill Griggs. To his credit, he was keeping it all together.

Back at Fakinah, the life-saving operations continued. There were no patient records. And no paper. Paul tore off box flaps and wrote down his patients' details in the operating list on them. Sudhakar had a paper towel list of his surgical patients on the wall.

The insect problem was constant. Paul found a bug zapper which looked like a squash racket and zapped flies and mosquitoes whenever he could. One night a mass of mozzies invaded the operating theatre through the air-conditioning vent. The room was thick with them. It was quite unpleasant—and risky. There were daily reminders about the dangers of vector-borne diseases. Some fogging (fine-mist spraying with pesticide) had taken place in the hospital grounds, in an attempt to get the numbers down.

Because patients were on the floor and the floor was putrid, the fireys gave the nurses kneepads, which were thick black-ridged rubber with a velcro fastening at the back. They also gave all of the medical team fluoro-plastic trousers to protect them from the squirting and splashing of blood from the debridements and amputations, and any other bodily fluids that came their way. This was not about neatness, but practicalities. They had few clothes, and a mere handful of disposable hospital gowns, and no washing machines available.

The weather was sticky and you could feel trussed up like a chook, but the options otherwise were worse. Ken had had smelly pus drip on him already and it occurred to him that you did not even want a tiny scratch in your skin where it could enter. His shoes were going to be left behind, no matter what. He would travel in others; some souvenirs you did not want—the dangerous kind.

The fireys also stuck down illuminated tape everywhere to make hospital areas safer. The hospital was dark and the tiled floor moist and slippery. Some of the access routes had low ceilings, which Paul and the taller ones, like Paul Luckin and Jeff Gilchrist, had already discovered with an abrupt smack to the middle of the forehead.

The stench was horrific, even through hospital masks. Death, decay, rot. Blood, sweat, pus. Ray and Marj put Vicks VapoRub inside their masks to make breathing bearable. They knew it was horrible for the patients to have their surrounds and own bodies reeking in this way, and the team's hearts went out to them.

Somehow they were all coping. And still smiling.

chapter eight

Improvising

The medical supplies were critically short but there was one thing the Australian team would not compromise on—pain relief. Especially during surgery. How it would be achieved in Banda Aceh was necessarily different to how it was achieved in Australia. In Australia, under normal hospital conditions, the way to have a person remain still, calm, unaware of being cut, and not in pain, is to give them something which will paralyse them and then, simultaneously, something to mask their pain. Make the brain unaware of the trauma of the incisions, the sawing, the removal of flesh, the flushing into the wound, the stitching.

If you don't get the mix right, the patient might be paralysed, feel everything yet be unable to scream. Or they might feel nothing but, if their muscles are not relaxed enough, they will move involuntarily, responding reflexively to touch. You don't want that either.

Ideally, patients metabolise the drugs during the appropriate period of time. You don't want them unconscious for weeks, just long enough for the surgery and a bit of recovery time. Then they can have post-op pain relief at a lesser level than anaesthesia.

Because they are usually in a deep stupor, if the drug dosage is sufficient, they need help to breathe. This is why you stick a tube down their throats—it's called intubating and has to be done early on, in case they vomit and block their own airway. Too early and the gag reflex and coughing make it difficult.

There's a lot that can go wrong, but trained people can carry out extensive repair work on a patient and rarely does anything go wrong. The drug to paralyse and the drug to take away awareness are mixed together. If the patients are elderly, or if they are very young, or if they have certain medications in their systems already, you have to work out how to get it all together in a safe and effective way. It is no good having one drug interact badly with another, or zonking someone out to the point where their heart stops beating. In a normal setting, in an Australian hospital, a range of anaesthetics can be used safely. There is the backup of staff, drugs and machines. This was not the case in the disaster zone of Banda Aceh. The anaesthetic best suited was Ketamine. This is a dissociative drug. It works by allowing the patient to enter a euphoric dream state. There were many pluses, including the fact that the recovery period was safer than other anaesthetic drugs, which required constant observation by recovery nursing staff due to the dangers of vomiting or blocked airways. Ketamine or 'Special K' as they were calling it, suited the medical team's limited facilities, as they did not have the luxury of post-op staff and there was a shortage of oxygen. Patients on ketamine could be left unattended in the wards quite safely.

It was a different experience for the surgeons. In Australia, their patients were paralysed and so didn't move. If they moved in Australia while you were cutting, you would stop immediately and alert the anaesthetist. Not so in Banda Aceh. Ketamine removed pain, but did not paralyse. These patients smiled and reached out to catch imaginary butterflies, sometimes they sang or prayed to Allah. Gasped at beautiful colours, smells and lights. Ketamine could produce a bad trip though, as it could cause flashbacks and nightmares. It was in the same class of drug as LSD. Pharmacologically, the brain was separated from the body, so during surgery the body might feel pain but the brain wouldn't register it.

The people in Banda Aceh had been through the worst of all nightmares. Despite the possibility of side-effects such as frightening hallucinations, ketamine couldn't bring the patients experiences any worse than those they had already undergone. Most times it brought respite from a cruel reality.

Paul worked mostly with Sudhakar and Marj in theatre, although he sometimes worked with Ray, with Annette and as a joint anaesthetist with Brian. They had no monitoring equipment so they were each other's eyes and ears. Under normal circumstances in Australia, they would be able to monitor with an ECG: pulse rate and rhythm and any irregular electrical activity such as arrhythmia or heart attack. They would have machines to monitor blood pressure, temperature, oxygen saturation of the blood (measured normally by a pulse oxymeter), and any anaesthetic gases being delivered.

None of these were present in Banda Aceh.

Paul finally had the two broken anaesthetic machines working satisfactorily, in his final days in Banda Aceh. He scrounged bits and pieces, made them fit. Even got some spare parts from a drawer full of scraps at Kesdam. An anaesthetic machine is a gas delivery system, which mixes and regulates the flow of volatile anaesthetic gases. It also absorbs carbon dioxide, and has a ventilator as well as a monitoring ability.

If anaesthetics could be compared to aeroplane flying, there is the 'take-off' phase of the anaesthetic (the knock-out), the 'cruising' phase (operating), and the 'final landing' (recovery). There is an outdated gas called halothane which, while not quite as ancient as chloroform or ether, is not normally used nowadays in Australia— although sometimes because of its sweet smell it is still used with children in the knock-out phase. Halothane was one of the few anaesthetic gases available in Banda Aceh and it was in short supply, so they used it for the more serious surgery cases. Ketamine was not the best anaesthetic for people with lung problems such as pneumonia, as it depressed breathing, so for those patients the team used halothane gas.

To understand what the medical team's working day in Banda Aceh was like, you must first understand what an operating theatre is like in a First World country, and one not in the throes of a catastrophic disaster. A typical theatre in Australia is well-lit, it is clean—the floors, walls, surfaces and machines are spotless. Everything—from the tubes and syringes to the masks and hats—are 'single-use', which means they are disposable. The people in theatre are an anaesthetist, surgeon, scrub sister and a nurse called a scout. They all wear a disposable or sterilised material gown, their shoes are covered in sterile, disposable covers.

Hair is covered with a theatre hat, the face is covered with a mask. Their hands and forearms are washed according to a protocol — three times with an anti-bacterial, disinfectant washing solution. Then gloves are put on. Germs are banished, summarily.

Supplies of dressings, sponges, clamps are opened and the sterile contents removed with sterile forceps and placed onto a sterile tray. The packets are discarded, their non-sterile covers not permitted to touch anything. A finely calibrated, computerised autoclave is used, which boils the instruments within an inch of their lives, using extremely high-pressured steam. For some instruments, powerful chemicals are also used, in a high-tech machine which does it all automatically.

A scrub sister guards against anyone going near the demilitarised zone of sterile instruments and equipment. If anyone even looks like sneezing in the vicinity, the sister is likely to scoop up the first set and will demand another, freshly sterilised set. If anyone moves his or her mask to be heard more clearly, or to scratch an itch, the sister will swoop like Cerberus, the mythical three-headed dog who guarded hell and missed nothing, and have the offender replace the mask. The usual background sound in theatre, apart from the beeping of anaesthetic and monitoring machines, is the shuffling of feet in covered shoes.

Before anything happens, the surgical site on the patient is shaved of any hair and cleaned. The surgeon will take a sterile sponge with a sterile pair of forceps, dip it into betadine, a powerful antiseptic, and paint the site he or she plans to cut. If this is done prior to going into theatre, it is covered with a sterile dressing which will sit there for hours, killing every microbe in its radius. The patient will be brought in by a hospital porter and moved onto crisp white, sterile sheets. If even a postage stamp of skin has been unpainted, the surgeon will not proceed with the operation. The painting procedure would have to be re-done.

The skin is the body's greatest protection; it is the immune system's strongest defence against outside bacteria and infection. Before making an incision, which could give germs a chance to invade, this invasion is prevented through 'triple-draping', where the patient is draped from head to toe. The first drape is plastic, the second is green sterile fabric, and the third is a drape with a window cut in it to expose the area, then a stretch-plastic 'skin', impregnated with iodine, is stuck over the whole area. The surgeon cuts into this with the scalpel, and the remaining area stays completely sealed. Protected. Germ-free.

The scrub sister counts out onto the patient five muslin sponges. They are thrown out afterwards. In some countries they are re-used after being washed in steam. The sponges contain a radio-opaque thread so that if a sponge is ever left inside a patient, the thread will show up on an X-ray. The surgeon is responsible for keeping count of these, but the nurse will advise if the count is correct or incorrect before he or she leaves the theatre and unscrubs. If the operation is very long, they may do a count half-way through. Everything is kept and counted. Needles, sutures, sponges. It is like the aircraft parts in a hangar, the maintainers must count everything. One unaccounted-for spanner clanking loosely around a flying aircraft engine could cause a catastrophe. If a sponge is discovered missing at the count, rather than immediately cutting open the patient again, the theatre staff will look everywhere in the theatre—on the floor, under the clothing layers of the staff—then they will X-ray the patient.

This is the regime in Australia. Those who cannot maintain this standard become identified as having poor sterile technique and are hounded out of a career in theatre.

In Banda Aceh, the operating team washed their hands in washing water then, if they were lucky, in drinking water, before squirting an alcohol liquid or a betadine concentrate on their hands. Marj or Ray might douse each other's hands, then they would put their own gloves on while their hands were still wet. They couldn't wipe them as there was nothing sterile to wipe them on.

Glove packaging was used for drapes. The sterile inside wrapping layers were used and even the packets themselves came in handy, placed sterile-side down. There were no surgical gowns, but they at least had some shoe covers and some hats. Paul wore the same one for the entire time he was there. He couldn't throw it out as there wasn't another one available.

They had an old-fashioned, boiling water steam steriliser on the floor outside the door. It was the equivalent of boiling water in a kettle. It got things clean, and the longer you boiled them, the cleaner they got. Obviously if there is a shortage of instruments you cannot let them boil forever, otherwise no operations would get done. You also had to leave some out for a while to cool, to prevent the surgeon's hand from being scalded.

There were not enough sponges to do the five-sponge routine. There was no X-ray to check if anything was left in a patient. The theatre was badly lit. There was a mat at the door for people to wipe their shoes on. As it became sodden and filthy, they abandoned using it — it dirtied their shoes.

As a scrub sister, Marj worked very hard in Banda Aceh. The conditions were totally different to what she was used to. She normally worked in the operating suite of Westmead

Hospital in Sydney. This was her first deployment and she had been asked to go by her Assistant Director of Nursing. While she naturally had some trepidation about what she faced, she thought she could help the local people of an affected region, which was why she agreed to go.

Marj liked how the team all mucked in and did what was necessary. There was no demarcation according to rank, station in life, or job description. If the task needed doing and you were the closest and available, you did it. A surgeon might grab a mop to clean the floor after finishing on one patient and before the next one arrived in theatre. She felt privileged to be with such people. She noticed the media moving noiselessly around, performing their work of reporting, and thought how fortunate it was for the viewers back home that it was television, and not *smell*a-vision. She sometimes had to breathe through her mouth, the air was so foetid.

Paul offered to help her sometimes. At the end of a long day the theatre had to be cleaned thoroughly, and then set up for work the next day. He noticed how late it had become and how tired she was. Marj thanked him, but her look said it all — the sooner you leave, the sooner I can get on with it. He left.

Although she never uttered a word, Paul knew that Marj had her patience tested one morning when she came in and found the theatre dirty and in disarray after she had stayed on late the night before, as usual expending her last vestiges of energy swabbing it down and arranging the instrument and dressing set-up. The Indonesian doctors occasionally used the theatres overnight and vacated them before the Australian team came in. She rationalised that they would have been strapped for time and would have struggled to leave it in any better state.

There were simply no spare personnel for all the tasks at hand. Clean-up and repeat preparation was hard work, pretty thankless, and you had to be your own motivational coach at times like that. What Marj liked most of all was the appreciation of the Acehnese patients. They had lost so much, yet always smiled and showed wholehearted gratitude for their care. Marj found it warming—and quite humbling.

Marj used to come back to the women's dormitory tired and drawn and flop gratefully into bed. She had previously noticed Karyn always had her mozzie net very neat and taut and had asked her for her secret. A limp net would sometimes sag and cover your face, and you would wake suddenly, startled and gasping for breath. After following Karyn's instructions, Marj's bed and net looked pretty good too. But one night, when they all leapt up because of a large aftershock, Marj hurtled straight into her tight mozzie net. It trampolined her straight back into her stretcher, to everyone's vast amusement. It was a great way to break the tension created by the alarming tremors. The tremors threatened to pull the rug out from under the team, both literally and figuratively. Their morale and determination to overcome hurdles were repeatedly pitted against these seriously undermining, unnerving and recurring forces of nature. They had seen first-hand the harm that nature could cause. It was not encouraging.

The particular one, experienced overnight on 2/3 January, was the third aftershock they had experienced since the dangerously large one on New Year's Day, which had registered 6.7 on the Richter scale. This had followed one the previous night (New Year's Eve) at 5.8, which had sent them fleeing out of their dormitory.

During their time in Banda Aceh there were approximately 25 earthquakes which registered over 5.0, over the course of nine days.

The quakes would creep up on them. Paul and the others would hear a rumble like a peal of thunder. It would grow louder and louder until it was too loud for them to talk normally—they could no longer hear each other. The building would start shaking violently; sometimes they would hear a snap as a building seam wrenched apart. In theatre, the drips shook and things fell over. Their feet would shift from under them and they would lurch and grab frantically at whatever was near which seemed sturdy. They gasped out whatever invocations came to mind. It was horrible. Nobody enjoys being terrified.

Jeff Gilchrist had the most bizarre response to them. He seemed to see things happen in slow motion when he was in near-death situations. It had happened to him a few times previously in his life. Once, he had been in his car turning a corner when he realised he was heading into an inevitable smash with another vehicle. Everything had slowed down in his mind, enabling him to bolt out of his car (a Mazda RX3), run a distance and stand and watch it happen. He had even turned the ignition off and taken the key out. Witnesses were incredulous afterwards—they couldn't comprehend how he had had time to react, because to them the speedy approach and loud impact had happened in a split second.

Now here he was in Banda Aceh, seeing these aftershocks in slow motion. He lay resting in his stretcher one time and saw the tiles on the floor compress and crack, as though a film was being shown, frame-by-frame. Microscopic shards of white glazed ceramic floated up in a cloud, the particles all moving in slow motion. Jeff leapt up and dashed to the nearest door-frame. He figured that, although the building might come down, the door-frame could hold up. You had to believe it. It was too frightening otherwise.

The tremors brought them out in a cold sweat. You were helpless. You were not in control. For people who were normally in control, this was disconcerting in a big way. Although no one died or was injured by these aftershocks, there was always the fear lurking that a really big one would come along or that the cumulative effect of these smaller tremors on already weakened structures might have some unexpectedly fatal results.

They were surrounded by death. Everywhere they looked were reminders of their own mortality. They had known that coming here would be risky, but they still expected to return home alive to their waiting families and friends.

At Kesdam, Adrian Humphrey was finding that he could not put anything down without someone moving it. He could never discover who did this or how to get the stuff back. Drip stands, instruments, even the rubbish bin to put the amputated stumps in, would be moved. There were many people at Kesdam in addition to the medical team — patients, relatives and milling world media. With the language barriers, it was not always easy to discern people's roles and responsibilities. Predictably, the only thing that failed to move quickly was the rubbish from the operating theatres, all the swabs, dressings, paper towels and cloth rags. They were all put in a plastic bag, which would sit for up to twelve hours outside the theatre. As there were no cleaners — they were either dead or looking for missing relatives — the medical team did most of their own cleaning up.

One afternoon Adrian stopped and stared blankly at the thirty or so body bags lying at the rear of the Kesdam Hospital building in the car park. They contained patients who had died. It was a sight he had never seen before. It was a shocking sight. But as others in the team were also finding in response to appalling scenes and happenings, his brain adjusted and eventually such things seemed normal—even acceptable.

chapter nine

Building Bridges

There were some cultural differences which confronted the team early. They had to resolve them; they had a job to do.

Nobody wants to be awake when a knife goes into your skin. You don't want to feel the needle stitching you back up, either. This is one of the biggest fears of people about to have surgery. They put such trust in the anaesthetist—if you have to be awake, you don't want to feel a thing.

So when Sudhakar came into theatre one day in tears saying, 'You have to do something, Paul,' Paul leapt into action. Sudhakar had just seen a child aged about nine, having a wound stitched up by the Indonesian doctors, without anaesthetic. Something had splintered inside the normally mild-mannered Sudhakar and he had roared at the nearest person in authority to 'Stop it!' Then he realised it was an Indonesian policeman wearing a side-arm. 'Stop it, PLEASE.' Hot with angry tears, he ran out of Emergency to find Paul.

Sudhakar had been burnt as a child. He knew what pain was about. He was also, by nature, kind and empathetic.

Paul could hear the child screaming in agony as he approached the Emergency Department. It was the little boy, valiantly fighting off six people who were all trying to restrain him. Paul quickly approached and said, 'Whoa, whoa, let's just hold on a tick. Give me two minutes. Please give me two minutes.' He had to be polite, but he was determined to sort this out. Doing a quick calculation in his head, using his knowledge of drugs and dosages (and making his assessment of the child's weight by comparing his body size to that of his own son, Liam's), he injected into the boy's arm a syringe of what seemed to be the appropriate amount of ketamine.

At Paul's behest Sudhakar had gone to get the oxyviva (a self-inflating bag that sucks in room air instead of bottled gas, then the doctor deflates it by squeezing it to aerate the patient's lungs), and a mask from theatre, in case the child stopped breathing. Paul had never before given ketamine into the muscle, only into veins. It works more slowly in the muscle, but you can jab it in quicker, and if the patient is thrashing about you will never manage to get a cannula (tube) into a vein.

Gradually, the child calmed right down and entered a dreamy, relaxed state. His eyes began to wander until he had a thousand-mile stare as he entered the 'space travel' that ketamine is renowned for. His parents, who were present and worked up into a terrible state, visibly relaxed and burst into tears with relief. The mother touched Paul's arm and looked at him, murmuring her thanks. He said to her again and again, 'It is okay, it is okay.'

The Indonesian doctors went back to their task. Paul left soon after, privately horrified that they were sewing up a wound which should have been irrigated, dressed and left to dry out and heal. Sewing it up would potentially trap pus and create a hotbed of bacteria, encouraging infection to spread into the flesh and then into the bones; it was a recipe for gangrene. He felt complicit in the exercise of bad medicine, because the child's quietened state meant the doctors could now close the festering wound.

The incident with the little boy was not the first, nor the only, occasion when the Australians would hear agonising screams coming from the Emergency Department. These Indonesian doctors acted in a way which initially led the Australians to believe that they thought pain was not unbearable or life-threatening, and therefore should be borne.

There were many reasons for the Indonesians' different approach to emergency health care. It could not simply be dismissed as cruelty. Not at all. One of the Indonesian doctors at one stage took Paul aside and politely explained, 'We are a lot stronger than you are. Indonesians are strong.' Paul knew the man was right to an extent. The patients he was seeing were incredibly resilient. The antibiotics worked so well because most had rarely, if ever, been exposed to them. Up until now the Acehnese immune systems had fought every bug on their own.

Because it was still early in the developing relationships between the Australian and Indonesian doctors Paul, despite strong mixed emotions, felt compelled to keep the peace and the communications open. It was all very tricky. Paul usually had a vibrant nature, but he kept a quieter, more laid-back profile in Banda Aceh. There was a lot going on, and he was happy to let others verbalise, to let others say the words that needed to be said, make the complaints that needed to be made, bond with the patients who needed it, cry the tears that needed to be shed. He kept his mind on what he thought had to be done by him. His mantra was to keep a cool head and work very hard.

There was tension everywhere. Everyone was working in a war zone, they were outsiders and there was danger from a number of quarters. The team was constantly in the company of armed personnel. Some people were affected by the death which surrounded them and reacted in sometimes strange ways. Paul had already been briefed that there was a heavily armed colonel over at Kesdam who had gone completely mad. Paul learned very early that you couldn't assume that people and situations would be normal or that reactions would be as they were at home.

Paul sensed a lot of emotion around him. It was enveloping, but he didn't want to be engulfed by it. He mostly closed his ears to the sounds which came from the Emergency Department and tried not to think about it too deeply. He didn't want to be judgemental. Everyone in the team adopted his or her own personal strategy for psychological survival. At the same time, everyone looked out for each other. If you looked like the situation was getting to you, there was always someone who noticed and shared the load. The team was very strong on support, kindness and loyalty.

Infection sometimes compromises the effectiveness of local anaesthetics, and drugs were in short supply. The Indonesian doctors were not trained anaesthetists. But the Australian team included highly trained anaesthetists and specialist emergency physicians. They had had years of cutting-edge learning, with access to the latest knowledge, from the world's best in these disciplines. If you did not have such specialist training and you administered anaesthetic drugs or certain kinds of pain relief, there were real dangers to the patient. If the anaesthetic or heavy pain relief compromised the patient's breathing, then there was a risk of death.

The Australians recognised that tempers could become rather raw when fatigue set in. They had to be careful. Build a bridge, they reminded themselves. They had always known that they would have to get used to other methods and differing cultural approaches; likewise, the Indonesians knew they had to work with the Australians. Both sides knew there was work to be done and they had to work side-by-side because they needed each other. They had been trained differently and viewed suffering differently. One side believed it had to be avoided at all cost; the other saw it as an inevitable part of life in a developing country, where expectations could not be elevated unrealistically. Neither perspective was completely right, neither was completely wrong.

In one view, not using anaesthesia as you hacked into a patient was barbaric; in the other view, a doctor with incredibly limited time and resources was attempting to save a life at a time when there had been massive loss of life. Each life saved was investment in the future of this community, which had been ravaged and would need years to restore itself.

Mike Flynn knew what was going on. He had made a leadership decision to let the team work it out for themselves. Micro-management was not his method, and throwing his weight around had never been his way. It could have poured petrol on a volatile situation in any event. He reasoned that it was far better to have smart people deal with it in their own ways. He saved his advice for the regular evening briefings, which were being held at about 10 p.m. each night in the dormitory.

Mike had worked in different cultural situations many times. He had served on Australian naval ships that had gone to Indonesian ports and cities such as Surabaya and Denpasar, and he'd gone to Sabah, Sarawak, Malaysia and Borneo. He had spent time on Indonesian ships in the 1990s. He had served in East Timor with Interfet as a Naval medical physician and public health consultant in 2000. He spoke pidgin from his time in Papua New Guinea. He had a heightened awareness of the varying mores and idiosyncrasies of societies. Every nation had them, including Australia. He had been involved in the Bali effort behind-the-scenes when New South Wales doctors were sent at short notice after the bombing; and he had also been involved in medical supplies going to Baghdad. Mike was the man of the moment; it somehow just worked out that way. That was why he had been chosen to head up this team, which was working in the epicentre of the tsunami devastation.

Mike had even been in China when the Tiananmen Square massacre occurred in July 1989. He just happened to be the Naval medical officer at the Australian embassy in Beijing at the time, and ended up helping with the casualties. The sensitivities had been incredible. Thousands of students demonstrating against the communist government regime. Armed tanks were sent into the square, and many students killed. The stakes had been high, but he felt he understood why it had ended up so tragically—issues had been forced and 'face' had become paramount, even at the cost of death. It had been a complex and highly charged event, which gave him a lot to think about later.

There were ways and there were ways. While Mike did not advocate peace at any price, or capitulation, he didn't plan to sail with a fixed rudder at ramming speed over the top of obstacles either. He steered things gently from the stern, tacking and jibing as required.

Differences surfaced from time to time, causing challenges for the team. They were very conscious of being there with permission. It was a privately owned hospital and it was not their country. They did not want to overstep their welcome.

By 2 January, the team were a couple of days into operating, and were bemoaning the lack of surgical instruments. It was becoming very frustrating. Annette was using a gynaecological ring curette to scrape away rotting flesh from wounds. 'If only the instrument cabinet wasn't locked,' said Marj. 'If only we could get into it.' There was a glass cabinet between the theatres, but it was locked. It had glass shelves and instruments on display, taunting them.

Paul observed, 'There was a key in it earlier.'

'Really?'exclaimed Annette. 'Let's get what we need!'

A young Indonesian doctor was working with them at the time, he said nothing.

The team trooped out to look at the cabinet.

'The key is gone!' said Paul, puzzled.

The young Indonesian doctor quickly disappeared and was seen talking to his superior. He returned with a key. Marj took out as many instruments as she could and put them in the steriliser. Things were looking up.

What the Australians did not appreciate at the time was that they had effectively confronted the Indonesian doctor about the key, and the obvious lack of sharing of vital instruments. It had become a matter of face. The refreshingly direct and typically Australian approach had somehow backfired here. They got the surgical instruments, but it had built up tension. They were soon to discover by how much.

Shortly after the key discovery, Annette was virtually thrown out of the operating theatre. A young Indonesian surgeon called Dr Panini[1] seemed to regard her as a foreign woman who was insolently masquerading as a surgeon. Naturally, Annette was distraught and incredulous. Furthermore, she was being prevented from doing indispensable work for what seemed like an insulting and ludicrous reason.

There was a natural attractiveness to Annette. Womanly rather than girly, she stopped short of being blokey. She had a short boyish cut to her ash-blonde hair, pale skin and pink cheeks; she was of medium build and average height. Not elfin, but rather, someone substantial and to be reckoned with. She had an openness, an inclusive manner which was very appealing. Annette had been wearing a pink fluffy stole at Richmond when Paul met up with her. It was more a token of her confident freedom and sense of humour than of any extreme femininity or tizziness. She wore pearls in theatre in Banda Aceh.

Annette was the only orthopaedic surgeon the team at Fakinah had; the other orthopaedic surgeon, Peter Sharwood, was over at Kesdam. Orthopaedics was about mending broken bones. The tsunami had broken many bones in many Acehnese bodies and these stoic people, broken in body but not in spirit, were waiting to be fixed.

The Indonesian surgeon would not accept a woman working in the capacity of surgeon. Unless perhaps enough deference towards the men was shown. Humility. If she could be slightly apologetic, *then* she might be allowed to help — a little bit, but there were no guarantees.

Annette had started this particular day ('knife to skin', as it is called) at 8 a.m., as was her usual practice. The anaesthetist had met and prepared the patient earlier. This

[1] Name has been changed.

patient, a man in his fifties, had a tibial fracture that needed setting in plaster. The Indonesian surgeon appeared and said to Annette in English, 'I am in charge of theatres and you should not be in here operating.'

Startled, she replied, 'We agreed yesterday on the ward round that I could operate on this patient.' Annette then quickly thought she should offer solutions. 'Perhaps we could use the other theatre?' she said.

'My friend is using the other theatre,' the surgeon replied stiffly.

'Well, maybe after him?' she suggested.

'No,' he answered firmly.

Annette, realising she was not making any headway and beginning to feel hurt, said indignantly, 'Well, I guess we will pack up our stuff and leave, if that suits better.'

'No, we need your supplies and your nurses,' he said very quickly.

Further discussion did not resolve the impasse. Annette was by now shedding tears of frustration. She left, heading for the women's sleeping area upstairs at the back of the hospital. As she walked off, she was stopped by the son of the patient.

'Aren't you going to operate on my father?' he asked, concerned.

'It *was* going to be me,' Annette answered flatly.

'I would like it to be you.' He went into theatre as Annette continued on her way, hearing him berate those inside. The son had seen another, less invalided woman patient with a small foot wound walk unaided into theatre and take precedence over his father in the surgery list.

As fate would have it, a new team of Indonesian doctors and nurses had arrived that day and were overlapping with the original team. The new team observed this encounter and its aftermath, and went to great efforts to be conciliatory. The working relationship with this second team would prove very successful.

Annette was unusual, and not only in Indonesian society. When she graduated as an orthopaedic surgeon in 1989, she and Linda Ferris (in South Australia) were the only women specialist surgeons graduating in this field in Australia. Annette now worked as a specialist in trauma surgery at the Major Trauma Centre of the Alfred Hospital in Melbourne.

A mother of three children, Annette was quite a remarkable person. What she had achieved in life was no accident. She was no shrinking violet, but a natural leader and a high achiever. She didn't know how to be retiring or obsequious; it wasn't part of her psyche. She took charge and made decisions. The team admired her style. In the situation of urgency that confronted them in Aceh, she did ward rounds and worked in theatre making major decisions swiftly and accurately. She was matter-of-fact and friendly. Each procedure she undertook was life-saving—this was not elective surgery, and it was far from cosmetic.

Annette also had something which made her immeasurably valuable to the team.

She had worked in a tidal wave disaster before. It was in Vanimo, Papua New Guinea, after the Aitape tsunami in July 1998 killed over 2000 people and destroyed the homes of almost 10 000. She not only had specific post-tsunami surgery experience, she had seen what happened if you left wounds unattended—people died.

Annette sat upstairs with a cup of coffee, writing up her notes and telling herself to get over it. But in the scheme of all that had happened in the tsunami, it seemed nothing short of an iniquity. It was a waste of a life-saving skill for what seemed petty, antiquated and ultimately debasing views about the status of women. If a woman had brains and certain gifts, wasn't it wrong not to use these gifts to help others?

Peter Sharwood had warned them all to tread carefully. In the aftermath of the Bali disaster, Australians had scooped up burns victims and bundled them out of Indonesia, post-haste. Time was critical. In retrospect, they might have tried to make those remaining feel less deserted, been more sensitive. Everyone was learning, but life was often about resolving differences and learning how to treat each other with respect, which was a two-way street. You would never get it if you never gave it.

The Australian team had a couple of male nurses (Terry Jongen and Ray Southon) and a female orthopaedic surgeon (Annette). In one view, these professionals were a celebration of overcoming pre-conceptions about what is normal. Right now, she could easily have been with her family—enjoying her Christmas holidays, perhaps sipping piña coladas beside the pool at Jupiter's Casino. If she had been the type to go there. But she had chosen instead to do something that was meaningful, and now her gesture appeared futile. And the many needy patients had not had a say in it. She wondered how the admonishment by the patient's son had been received.

On a more personal level, Annette missed her children, Lachlan, Caitlin and Alys, and her partner for life, Simon. The SMS messages from her family made her eyes prickle and her throat constrict. 'We miss you Mum, we love you.' She had kept that one in the message inbox of her mobile, and looked at it now as she slowly bit her lip.

Sudhakar and Brian Pezzutti hit upon a plan.

Brian was not just your average rural hospital anaesthetist. He was a brigadier in the Army Reserve and had been everywhere. He was in the surgical team that went into East Timor to serve the 11 000 Interfet troops, where he was photographed with a smiling patient who was none other than José Ramos-Horta, the Nobel Peace prize-winning leader of the East Timorese Independence movement. In fact, Brian had served in East Timor on six separate occasions, in Bougainville twice and once in Rwanda. For fifteen years Brian had also been a member of the New South Wales Upper House. He had always kept his professional qualifications and skills up to date so politics would not be the be-all and end-all. This had kept him grounded. He had grown up in Lismore, New South Wales, studied medicine at Sydney University and was an anaesthetic specialist in private practice by the time he had turned 29. He was the father of four young adult children and was married to a doctor, his supportive wife Chris. Part of Brian's role was about helping the team push into new frontiers. In the matter of Annette's difficult situation, Sudhakar knew what would work culturally and Brian's political nous now came in handy.

A case came into theatre a little later that day. It was complicated. An Acehnese patient in his mid-thirties had a hand injury, which looked like it had been caused by a deep rope burn, and he had broken some fingers and his thumb. He stood to lose the use of his hand. Sudhakar became concerned as he watched Dr Panini try to re-attach the man's hand. The case was difficult and it required an advanced skill level. He and Brian said they could offer the services of a hand surgeon—a professor in the field, in fact.

Sudhakar rang Annette. He described the case and his concerns. Could she help? 'I have told the Indonesian surgeon that you are a professor of hand surgery,' he said.

Annette, shaking her head and smiling, assured Sudhakar that she would come to help. It was well within her abilities. She left immediately for the theatre, the heavy weight across her chest lifting as she walked.

Unbeknown to Annette, Liz Cloughessy had headed to theatre and put it as straight as she could in her best head nurse style: 'Annette is here to operate. No Professor Annette, no nurses.' The surgeon saw her point, and indicated he would cooperate; nurses were in desperately short supply.

Brian Pezzutti, Ray Southon and Marj Raggett were there, working alongside the Indonesian surgeon when Annette re-appeared. Paul and Sudhakar were also assisting. Watching. Helping. They were all being careful, not wanting to 'push in'. It was all being handled gently, carefully.

Annette walked into theatre. Hesitant, but determined. Brian addressed her as 'Professor'. The others took his cue. Annette watched carefully, courteously asking questions as Dr Panini showed her the problem. His eyes were downcast as he agreed to her scrubbing up. Eventually he handed the case over to her. Assisted *her*.

Brian had given the patient a brachial plexus block, an injection of local anaesthetic in the bunch of nerves which go from the neck to the arm. The patient was conscious and could speak some English. Brian said he could stay quiet if he wanted, he didn't have to make conversation. 'I must pray to Allah,' he told Brian. And he prayed out loud in Acehnese throughout the operation.

The rope had cut the skin and muscles. It was like a loop had been cut into his hand, from the ring finger down and around the thumb and back up to the ring finger. He'd broken three metacarpals, the long bones in the hand that have the fingers attached to them. The most important is the one that has the thumb attached to it.

Annette wanted to drill a hole in each end of the broken metacarpals and suture the bone ends together to oppose them and allow healing. If they met up, they would knit neatly. She tried to make a hole in the wrist side of the bone with a heavy needle, but the bone was too hard. She needed a proper surgical drill. Unfortunately, there was no drill. This was not the time to dither or lament the inadequacies of supplies. They simply could not send this poor man away. It was, once again, time to improvise. Paul got on the radio: 'We need a useful man in blue down here.'

Jeff Gilchrist appeared moments later, in his paramedics' uniform, handing Marj his stainless steel Leatherman pocketknife. Marj opened it up and threw it in the steam steriliser. Among the collection of gizmos and widgets in it, there was one called an awl, which could be used to make holes. Normally used for wood or leather, Jeff had yet to try it on bone. Annette found it worked perfectly. Jeff always carried his pocketknife. It was a very useful tool to have with you. He had used the pliers in it to extract teeth, when he had worked in a tribal village in Papua New Guinea, some years ago. The team's rich backgrounds, skills and habits were proving useful.

While Jeff was in theatre he couldn't help noticing how Paul had adjusted his theatre hat so he was wearing it French beret style, and had adopted some accompanying jaunty mannerisms, making the others laugh. It broke the tension. Even Dr Panini joined in.

Panini questioned Annette as they worked, asking about when she had graduated, and when she had finished her orthopaedic training. He appeared satisfied that she could well have gone on to be a professor. He appeared contrite and they were able to work together quite congenially and productively. She also let him know that she worked at a major trauma centre in Australia. It was a long-ish operation. As they worked together, mutual respect grew. Dr Panini was young and very junior in experience, but he was having a go. Annette's brain was ticking over, considering the whole scenario, but she shelved it for later. He had obviously had to put his own feelings aside too.

It was gratifying for Annette in the days that followed to have some of the Indonesian staff come and apologise for the earlier upset. What she was able to deduce was that it wasn't her, and it also wasn't necessarily an Indonesian problem. It was the actions of an individual, and you get them everywhere on the planet. Annette figured this surgeon might become more secure as he matured. He departed on the Monday, and the team began working until late at night, tip-toeing softly through darkened corridors and along verandahs, taking patients to surgery. The second Indonesian team clicked with them from the beginning, so there were no longer any issues about usage of the theatres.

Annette was concerned that her own professor would get wind of her spruiking that she was a professor. As soon as she could, she sent word through Louise, the trauma program manager at the Alfred Hospital in Melbourne, to tell him about it before he heard it on the news. Louise must have relayed the message well because the amused response was along the lines of 'whatever it takes'. The goal of saving lives and limbs was paramount; delicacies were not. Annette had called Louise before, when she was banished from theatre. These mobile calls to the outside world and the SMS messages were invaluable for morale. Louise supported her through that difficult patch, when Annette thought all was lost and her going to Banda Aceh was pointless. They chatted. Louise told her she had found some new weighing scales, well priced in the Harris Scarfe sale. Comfort talk. Hearing Louise talk about shopping in Melbourne reminded Annette that what she was involved in was temporary, and to keep it in perspective.

The patient was later reviewed by the surgeon Peter Sharwood, who actually did have considerable experience in hand surgery, and the results were judged promising at that stage.

These issues of contrary medical practice and equality of gender, which could have made things unworkable in Banda Aceh, were coped with and worked through. The team members knew they simply had to build a bridge and get over it. The theatre incident and Annette's impressively deft use of the pocketknife in surgery was the topic of discussion that night. A good surgeon could operate with a knife and fork, they jested.

What the team would also discern is that some things are human nature and nothing to do with race or culture. You might find an intolerant or rude person in the most enlightened of environments. Conversely, presentation was not the definitive gauge of a person's character. Polished charm was no guarantee of goodness. A brusque exterior often hid a genuine heart. There were also good people to be found everywhere across the globe.

Brian Pezzutti was coming into his own, and there were going to be many occasions in this deployment where his political skills would come in handy. He was bringing people together, helping break down barriers, and taking the younger practitioners under his wing. He was helping them acclimatise to work in a disaster zone, with all its shortcomings and stresses.

'Have you thought of this?' he would ask. 'This was tried in East Timor and it seemed to work.' Always ready with a laugh, always willing to listen and offer an idea if the moment seemed right. Sudhakar Rao and Paul Dunkin found his approach invaluable. After surgery, needing to wind down, the three would often talk about life—or anything other than what they were immersed in—on the balcony, in the dark of the Aceh night.

chapter ten

The Bridge of Death:
a Bridge of Hope

Paul Dunkin was told he would be visiting town on
3 January. Mike Flynn thought it was important that
they all take a break, to have a change of scene and also
get some understanding of what they were in the middle
of. It was easy to become cocooned in theatre. If you
didn't have respite you might either get cabin fever and
go crazy or, worse, start to become over-reliant on the
safety of your little sheltered world and become under-
confident about ever leaving it. It was healthy to get out
and about.

Mike also wanted members of the team to understand
the patients they were treating. You had to know where
they came from, what they were talking about, what they
had been exposed to. Patient histories and doctor recom-
mendations were going to make more sense if you had a
realistic impression of their lives. Even telling them to get a
prescription filled, get bed rest, take medication an hour
before food, change sterile dressings daily, take vitamins
and see the physio—all of which might be perfectly normal

doctor advice in Australia—would be meaningless right here, right now.

Paul started the day at 4 a.m. He stole quietly out of the dark room full of sleeping bodies. Steve Liebman was on the line. It was a live cross for the Channel Nine *Today* show. Steve started asking questions. Paul was bone-weary and felt drugged. He had just woken up and it was the first time he had really thought about anything he was doing in Banda Aceh. He explained to Steve you just do it. He hoped nobody noticed the catch in his voice. He just wanted to be strong and give a lot of detail for those at home who wanted to know what was happening.

Later that day, Paul was driven into town with some of the Fakinah theatre team by Jackie, an Indonesian medical student who had tried to outrun the tsunami and ended up climbing onto a roof to avoid its onslaught. Brian Pezzutti, Sudhakar Rao, Marj Raggett, Annette Holian and Ray Southon accompanied Paul and Jackie. The Ward and Emergency Department groups had already been out on an earlier day, and the fireys had gone even earlier.

Firey Bruce Cameron had taken photographs of sights which were very disturbing. The worst scenes in anyone's lifetime, and something he could never forget. It was not normal. Not even for a disaster. A vast wetland filled with thousands upon thousands of splayed olivey-purple bodies, beaten to a pulp, bloated, their clothes shredded from them. The others who went later were spared some of this blatant horror. The bodies remaining were more hidden, discolouration disguising them in the rubble. It was confronting nonetheless. Up close, individual patients' injuries were easier to deal with, at least you could help. Mass death and destruction were another thing altogether.

The sights shocked Paul, even though a lot had obviously been done in the last seven days to clean things up. There was ruination wherever you looked. On the coast, where the water had entered the land beyond the normal tide mark, the trees and buildings had been mown down. It was a plain of acres and acres of nothingness. It looked as though someone had taken a giant whipper-snipper and cleared the land, leaving everything flattened. Now and again a lone tree still stood, its branches shorn off for the first few metres from the ground up. In an expanse of wasteland a solitary small building was still standing—one home, the only perpendicular structure. It was as though the all-powerful wave had decided to spare it, for some inexplicable reason.

The coastal area was particularly glary. The absence of trees caused a lack of shade. There was none of the variegated light you normally take for granted.

Paul wandered as near to the shoreline as he could safely get. There was a road, but they did not drive closer as there was a lot of mud and swampland; it was not a safe area. He found a little brass bell on a piece of twine in the churned-up earth. Someone had worn it and cherished it— you could tell by the careful double knot in the yellow cord. It was just long enough to be worn around the neck. It seemed there had been a kindergarten here, judging from some broken concrete playground equipment and patches of what appeared to be painted children's games in hopscotch-style patterns. But it had vanished.

It was eerily quiet on the deserted coast. No birds. No children playing. The sounds of life were gone.

Jackie drove the group into town, where, in loud contrast, noisy bulldozers were moving wreckage. There were no delicate rescue operations for trapped survivors, as there were none. There were just decomposing bodies and mounds of wet, rotting rubble needing to be moved. The mounds were all becoming the same dull prison-like shade of grey and brown. Now and then lakes of water could be seen next to buildings and roads, strange sights in the cityscape. Beside the roads were piles of spiky pieces of wood and metal, smashed chunks of concrete, broken-off wooden posts, fencing, roofing, walls. Bravo team had been to see the devastation a day or two earlier. They had been given a tour by the doctor who was the bizarre army officer in charge of Kesdam Hospital. He had pointed out the gaol where all the prisoners, locked in their cells, had drowned. Paul thought about this chilling account as he looked across the devastation. The wave had been 15 metres high in places and had swept through the land for some 7 kilometres. Paul pondered on these facts, putting them into a home perspective as it occurred to him that if a comparable earthquake had taken place a similar distance off the coast of any of Australia's coastal cities, an equivalent wall of water with the same force would have demolished those densely populated cities and their beach suburbs. He shivered involuntarily.

They had now arrived at the Baiturrahman Grand Mosque, a mosque in the centre of town, which appeared mostly untouched. Its forecourt had been cleared, but there were signs it had recently been full of flotsam. The mosque was a huge, solid building, very beautiful, with impressive pillars and domes. It stood reassuringly substantial and blindingly white in the sun, a tribute to the faith of its creators. It seemed to be a symbol of strength in these troubled and tragic times. Paul thought that, for the sake of the local community, it was a divine mercy that it had been preserved. Faith was so important in times when a two-dimensional perception of life held no answers, and gave no fortitude.

The sombre tour continued. Paul noticed a very large, heavy book which was full of writing in a foreign language. It looked as though it was some sort of sacred text. It appeared to have been saturated, thrown about, and was mulched in parts. It was now mouldy, greying and dried-out. The pages were ruined.

Everywhere else was still wet and stinking. Humid wafts of mould and decay enveloped the group as they viewed the scene. To minimise the stench, they all breathed through their mouths sporadically and Brian smoked. They saw many upturned cars, partly or wholly crushed, dinged and dented beyond repair. People had been gored and ground down by the deadly swirling sludge of sharp metal, glass and broken wood. The wave of water had quickly become thick with refuse it had collected as it mowed down everything in its path and moved it all along with the inexorable force of a mighty ocean current. Now some of the bodies were still trapped beneath the debris.

Property of every description had been smashed and crushed against other bits and pieces; it looked like it had all been picked up and mulched into a series of garbage tips. A rubbish dump sat incongruously in front of the graphic-designer-decorated 'Perdana Tour' shopfront. A gaily patterned blue awning, now ripped and tattered, hung limply out the front of the damaged building. One of many such buildings. Too many. Two giant fishing boats sat inappropriately in front of the Suzuki car dealership. Huge, uprooted trees with full branches sat festively next to them. It was a world gone mad.

Paul wanted to restore order, to put it all back where it was supposed to be. His head had started throbbing early in the tour. After working and concentrating for days in a dark theatre, he was like some nocturnal animal blinking against the bright sunlight and frowning with the effort of deflecting any emotional feelings.

Paul and the group reached the bridge in the middle of the city.

A river wends its way through the heart of Banda Aceh. Spanning it is one of the city's main bridges, made of concrete, which had clearly provided a buttress against the force of the tsunami. The river's great cargo of moving wreckage had smashed to a grinding halt at this point. Large fishing boats were concertinaed against the bridge, together with bodies, planks of wood, walls of homes, pieces of glass, cars and refuse of every description.

The boats had had their main trusses and supports ripped from their anchoring hull planks. But the hulls now provided a dramatically vivid visual juxtaposition of bright, primary colours against the otherwise drab and sorrowful scene. Reds and blues were splashed about randomly in a brownish-grey palette. Paul saw a dove strutting about on the ground near the bridge, eerily clean and white, in stark contrast to the dirty disarray behind it.

Signs of the lives once lived there, but now gone, were everywhere. Mattresses, clothing. All interspersed with strips of bent metal, bits of roof, fence palings, boxes, sprung bed bases. The heavy concrete pillars of the bridge were cracked and the railings were broken.

Some people, obviously locals, wore face masks and picked their way in the steaming heat through the danger-ously unstable piles around the bridge and along the banks of the canal. They appeared to be looking for something. Maybe for a relative, a friend, a neighbour, a workmate, a child. Perhaps hoping to find some precious belongings. It seemed a mind-numbingly hopeless task. There were thousands upon thousands of bodies in these piles of dredged-up refuse, and it was difficult to distinguish the bodies. The heat had accelerated the decomposition, and the bruising and wounds had made the skin of the dead appear unnaturally dark.

Paul saw photographs sticky-taped to doors and street poles and fences. Notes on them asked for any details of missing loved ones. There were rumours that one in every two people here had been killed, that half of Banda Aceh had died.

Every now and then on this grisly tour, Paul spotted something which his mind quickly catalogued as innocuous before it could create psychological pain, before it made him dissolve inside—a child's tricycle, bent and rusting now, a mangled toy, occasionally something intimately personal, like a shirt or a family photo album.

A couple of trucks were being steadily uncovered in one of the streets. One of the streams of rubbish had reached the obstacle created by these trucks and had quickly formed massive piles around it. It was now a deadly, putrid, papier-mâché fortress. A few odd shoes sculled around on top, signalling that life had once existed here, where now there were only death mounds.

There were few animals around, apart from a few cats with no tails, the occasional gecko and the odd cow roaming through rubbish near the hospital. Paul noticed a starving dog. Its owner gone, the dog was foraging for itself. It joined a couple of other dogs feeding greedily on something in the rubble. Paul knew what the dogs were doing. They had found a corpse. This was too gruesome to acknowledge, let alone watch.

Paul returned to the bridge, the scene of greatest destruction in Banda Aceh. It was being called the Bridge of Death. He noticed something nearby which made him catch his breath. In a pile of heavy beams, branches, strips of galvanised iron, his eye picked out a hand. It was reaching out, its fingers ever so slightly upturned. He was shocked. His brain knew instantly its owner was beyond rescue. The hand was unmistakably decaying, it was attached to an arm that was greyish-yellow and purple with injury in places. He turned away, but changed his mind, deciding to capture its image with his camera. When the Emergency Department group had returned from their earlier tour of Banda Aceh, James Branley had tried to explain the inexplicable with the phrase 'such a mass of crushed humanity', which had stuck in Paul's memory. It was what this disembodied hand now represented for him. It seemed as though its supplicant gesture acknowledged the help he had come all this way to give. To Paul, the hand was a symbol of hope. He would not have been there to photograph it if he and others had not come to Banda Aceh to help. Australia and other countries, upon whom the future of this place would rely for rebuilding, would never know the extent of the damage and what was needed unless images were captured and relayed to the outside world.

He was here, as were the others, to help build a bridge.

After taking the photograph, Paul went back to Jackie, their waiting driver. He and the others piled back into the car. Paul asked Jackie to pull over so he could buy them all some soft drinks at a roadside shop. Thin Indonesian cans of Coke and Sprite, slightly warm but a welcome change from urn coffee and bottled water. The sugar and caffeine seemed to help cure his pounding headache.

They were all quiet as they returned to Fakinah Hospital. Paul felt the weight of it too. Sadness.

The scenes in theatre seemed so safe and familiar now, even as dire and gory as they were. He was accustomed to them. They were not as troubling as the scenes in Banda Aceh.

chapter eleven

Support at Home

I put baby Pierce down, raced into the back room, took the videotape out of the machine and pushed a blank one in. Toddler Francis immediately started protesting, crying for 'Doo doo'. He wanted Thomas the Tank Engine back on. I SMSed this rather amusing fact (under the circumstances) to Paul. I had warned young Francis that we needed to tape Daddy on TV. It fell on deaf ears. Francis cried throughout the broadcast. I kept turning up the volume louder and louder so I could hear Paul. I hung on his every word. I didn't know what I would do if he didn't make it back. I stopped myself mid-thought; I could never let myself think that far.

Paul was technically in a war zone and, although hostilities between the GAM and TNI had officially been halted, a few gunshot deaths had been reported in Aceh province. The medical team was very conscious of the dangers and sensitivities. The police who ran Fakinah and milled around the team as they worked were heavily armed. There were earthquakes every day. Disease was now considered the biggest threat to life. The team was too busy to focus on all this, they were just getting on with the job.

The death toll across all the tsunami-affected countries was now 130 000, with twelve Australians confirmed dead. Many bodies had been washed out to sea and the final figures would never be known. From what I could gather from news reports and Paul's phone calls, the team were surrounded by more death than they would see in their whole lifetime, and a succession of patients with the most hideous injuries they had ever seen. There was sometimes pain which even their efforts could not remove. Dead brothers and sisters, children, mothers and fathers. The team was saturated in the sadness, but they could not allow themselves to give in to it. I thought Paul must be feeling pretty overwhelmed, deep down, and I wished I could physically put my arms around him, to hold him and comfort him.

Steve Liebman asked Paul whether anything could have prepared him for this. The interview was a live voiceover, but the footage shown was pre-recorded—people lying in hospital corridors, children with amputated limbs, hungry people reaching out their hands as they were thrown boxes of food from American helicopters. A 360-degree view of flattened homes. Rubble, body bags. Paul replied with an almost imperceptible quaver in his voice, 'Nothing could, Steve . . . and nothing should. We just get in and do our job. We're taking each step as it comes, each new patient who arrives. You can't stop. You can't think. When we get home we'll do that.'

I wondered whether any of the viewers would be able to tell that his voice was thick with emotion. Maybe it was just me because I knew him so well.

In this interview, Paul provided a great deal of information. He was asked about many things, including the children.

I knew from a conversation with him that many children had not survived, that the elderly had fared badly too. The children did not make up the biggest group of patients and there was a reason for that. Most had died when the wave swept through. The little ones had had no chance.

Those who had survived and were at the hospital were asking: Why? They told Paul they had been in a war and now this. Why? It was a good question. One to break your heart.

There had been just over twenty primary schools in Banda Aceh prior to the tsunami. Paul later found out that the surviving children only filled one school.

One of my brothers SMSed. He had seen the interview and was very proud Paul was there. My brother had been a fighter pilot and he had been on many deployments in his own military service. He understood what separation from family was like and the effect unfamiliar circumstances and unusual threats could have on your emotional state—how you had to hold it together, compartmentalise. My brother was a brave man, and he knew how much the love and support you had behind you mattered. It cheered me up to have him make contact. My mobile beeped again. It was my friend Julie and her son, Jai. Another SMS message, and another, then the email inbox started to fill, all day. Paul's best man, Paul Ryan, emailed me from the United Kingdom. 'Pat and I are honoured to know him. No doubt the events will have had some effect on him, but he is made of pretty stern stuff. He is very lucky to be able to come back to a stable and loving family. The boys will be just the tonic he needs.'

My friend Lisa Hill also reassured me with: 'Hope that you are not too worried about Paul. As you know, he is extremely capable and sensible. He is the perfect person for the task at hand, if there can be such a person. Please let me know if I can do anything for you.' She then outlined plans to take two of my sons, Liam and Darcy, to the zoo.

The phone began to ring. My friend Kate made contact with me every day Paul was away. People came to help. Within an hour of the interview being shown, my brother-in-law, Ross, was on the doorstep to take the two older boys to play and have a sleep-over with their cousins. Nanna collected Francis for the day. The Disaster Control Centre rang. They would return Paul's car for him from Richmond and did I need anything?

I put together an electronic email address list and called it my 'Paul Update Group', and began typing. I kept the television in the lounge room on all day and all night, muted, I did not want to miss one report. Anything that looked like a tsunami report caused me to drop everything and put a videotape in. I didn't have time to watch—the activities and needs of our four active little boys ruled that out—but I hoped I might get a chance one day to watch the tapes, perhaps after Paul returned home.

The children were no longer thrilled when Daddy was on TV. The promotions for the news programs often showed snippets of the Australian medical team at work and Paul was shown many times. Francis didn't seem to make the connection and Darcy started kicking the wall. Children, even if they can talk, cannot always verbalise their concerns, so they manifest them in other ways. Liam sometimes couldn't sleep and would come and sit with me. We would sip hot green tea together and chat as I cleaned up or gave Pierce his night breastfeed.

Liam said to me one evening, 'If my dad dies, he will be a saint, as he will have given up his life for others.'

Dismayed, I realised Liam had been carrying a lot of worry around with him and had been too thoughtful to dump it on me. I hugged him and reassured him that his dad was safe. I hoped he was, I couldn't think otherwise. This was my private prayer that played non-stop in my head.

Paul called home one time and Liam answered the phone. After a while, Liam asked, 'Did you get me a souvenir, Dad?' It was revealing that, even with the television footage of demolished Banda Aceh, he thought there were souvenir shops still standing, doing a roaring trade. Children are resilient, sometimes simply because they do not grasp the depth of the horror.

The news that night reported that a charity cricket match was being planned. Shane Warne was promoting it in various ad breaks and Steve Waugh was being asked to play. In his typically self-deprecating manner, the former captain indicated to the media that he thought that nobody wanted a 'has been' wheeled out. 'Oh yes, they do,' I thought. Like many Australians, I am a bit of a longstanding Steve Waugh fan. There was talk of a rock concert to raise money.

My friend Stu Lloyd emailed. He was involved with a charity fundraising event at West Pymble Bowling Club, planned for 16 January. The news was full of similar events taking place all over Australia, in every club, in every pub—picnics, dances, barbecues, door-knocks, raffles. Every pharmacy, newsagent, bakery, general store and gift shop had a tub on the counter with a little 'For the Tsunami Victims' notice. Church plates were filling. Famous figures were pledging sums. Australian entrepreneur Dick Smith and his wife gave $1 million. World Champion Formula One racing car driver Michael Shumacher reportedly gave $US10 million. Someone else gave a small fortune too. And people who did not have very much were giving what they could. One story told was that one of the men's prisons passed a hat around.

The mind-numbingly huge extent of this tragedy was triggering just as momentous compassionate action. It was a wave of its own, and it was sweeping through everywhere.

chapter twelve

Reaching Out—Sigli

Sometimes, the moment you think you cannot do more than you are doing, you are asked to do just that. The medical team had become very close. Those who went to Kesdam returned each day to Fakinah, where they shared stories and dramas, ate and slept alongside each other. They were like a tight-knit family. They cried sometimes, when the death and the stench and the revolting injuries became too much. The stories of the patients were affecting them. The team always hugged each other and affirmed that each person was doing a good job. They had to keep going.

A strange thing happens to time when you are working in a disaster zone. It is compressed, at the same time as it is elongated. A day becomes a lifetime. You experience a range of emotions, and work at a rate that is far more intense than at home. All your senses are heightened and time seems like a hyper-reality. This physical response is not sustainable in the long-term, of course, or you would simply burn out. It is especially concentrated if you are present in the more acute stages of the disaster. 'Get in early and get out early' was the advice of those with experience of working during times of intense crisis.

It was 4 January and the team felt as though they had been in Banda Aceh for months and as though they knew each other deeply. Even though they were doing a succession of patient cases back-to-back, they all felt that they should be doing more—that what they were doing was somehow not enough. It was strange, but their reactions were perfectly normal. It is a phenomenon experienced by many who have worked in mammoth tragedies. And this tsunami was the most monstrous of them all.

Paul and the others were talking one day as they worked about how they were hearing from home that some people in Australia were even re-evaluating what they did for a living since the tsunami. This was how strongly they supported what was being done in Banda Aceh and elsewhere. It made the team feel better, knowing that what they were doing was considered so worthwhile that people would question their own life occupations. Sometimes the team thought what they were doing was a drop in the ocean—there was just so much work to be done, such a relentless stream of sick and injured people, and there were always more. The flow never abated. What they did not know was the impact the media images of their work effort was having in Australia and in the rest of the world. This by itself would prove vindication of their presence there.

Médecins Sans Frontières (MSF) asked the team if someone could be spared to go to Sigli General District Hospital, as the surgical ward was overflowing with cases. The local surgeons were missing, all believed to be with their stricken families.

The team did not necessarily want anyone to go anywhere. There were hundreds of needy people presenting at Fakinah and Kesdam every day, but Brian Pezzutti thought the team members could extend themselves. The head of MSF worldwide was a young Australian plastic surgeon, Rowan Gillies, who had been a registrar at Lismore Hospital where Brian was an anaesthetist. They had worked together and, feeling that he didn't want to let anyone down, Brian spoke to Mike Flynn. Brian's attitude was, 'No worries, can do. Let's find a way.' He was always upbeat, positive and never shied away from the next challenge.

MSF had been set up in 1971 by some French doctors who had worked with famine victims. The doctors had worked for the Red Cross during the Biafra war in Africa and were frustrated by the bureaucracy they encountered, and outraged by the degree of government interference in the delivery of aid and relief services. They decided to form a lean and independent group, which would be unhampered by red tape and all the administration which sometimes accompanied the bloated organisations. They often did not accept funding from governments (depending upon the crisis) — only private donors, to keep themselves free from political influence. In 1999 they had received the Nobel Peace Prize for their ability to work so effectively, and without politics. They were now helping out in Banda Aceh at the northern tip of Sumatra, at Sigli on the east coast, and Lamno and Meulaboh on the west coast. MSF were waiting on a surgical team to arrive from Belgium. Their nurses were already helping out in the wards, but they needed a fill-in surgeon and anaesthetist in the meantime.

Mike Flynn was conscious that the safety of the team was in his hands. He couldn't guarantee anyone's safety anywhere, and going to Sigli would put them at risk. It was about 200 kilometres away from Banda Aceh. Some of the roads had been opened along the coast but were still not in the best condition and were putting pressure on the inland roads. Many bridges had collapsed also. Adding to the impact of the physical devastation was the ongoing political turmoil. Aceh province had been in a state of emergency since mid-1993, with nobody allowed in or out without permission. There was presently an unofficial ceasefire between the TNI and GAM but there were still pockets of fighting, resulting in deaths since the tsunami. Mike did not want any international issues or incidents, his mission was to be a constructive one. Danger was to be given a wide berth. There would be no avoidable deaths in the team. Nobody would be shot at—he couldn't live with that.

Once again, the team was enriched by the resources within its ranks. Paul Van Buynder had links to MSF, partly because he had been born in Belgium and spoke French, and partly because he had been dealing with them already since arriving in Banda Aceh. He had been going to the 5 p.m. meetings across the road from Fakinah at the UN/USAID headquarters with a couple of the other CASTA physicians—Jeremy McAnulty and James Branley. These had quickly become regular meetings with non-government organisations (NGOs) in the area. There were two dozen agencies represented in these early days but there was little feuding about who was going to do what, probably because there was so much work to be done. The agencies included Oxfam, CARE, Red Cross and Red Crescent, Médecins Sans Frontières, UNICEF, Save The Children, the Jesuit Refugee Service, Caritas, Catholic Relief Services and many, many more.

Paul Van Buynder used to talk to MSF about what was happening at these gatherings because they were too engaged to go themselves. OCHA needed to know what MSF's plans were for surveillance for disease outbreaks and other activities which might have an impact on aid work, or their plans for first-line malaria treatment and Paul would feed MSF's plans back to these meetings. There were a few diseases around which needed to be pounced on, before they became a major problem.

MSF wanted the option of using the Australian team as a personnel safety net. If their staff became ill they wanted to be able to ask the team to fill in for them. They thought Fakinah Hospital could be a useful fall-back receiving station for evacuations of patients they couldn't deal with 'out bush'. The CASTA team also had invaluable supplies, which MSF could take out to their remote clinics in Aceh province where there was no protection against certain diseases. For example, the team had tetanus toxoid and tetanus immunoglobulin for warding off tetanus.

Paul Van Buynder was the priceless intermediary between CASTA and MSF. When Mike Flynn finally agreed that three of the team could spend some time at Sigli, Paul Van Buynder stepped into the breach and started working in theatre at Fakinah. Paul was the principal medical consultant in the Office of Chief Medical Adviser, Western Australia. He was the head of the emergency response section of public health in that state. Despite his position, he was very down to earth. With his sparkly eyes, cheeky moustache, reddish-tinged unruly short hair, he had a face you instantly liked and felt comfortable with. A genuine Aussie man—roguish, intelligent. Married to Jan. He was a fearless Carlton supporter and, no matter where he lived, would fly to Melbourne for key games. He was yet *another* Paul on the team. (Out of 21 men, four were called Paul. Brian Pezzutti said it was easy in the early days when the team members were still getting to know each other—whenever he was in doubt about a name, he just called the bloke 'Paul'.) Paul Van Buynder was kind-hearted and mindful of the team's good health. He brought them eggs, bananas and mandarins. Paul Dunkin put his hard-boiled egg in with his noodles, making them taste like real food. Fantastic.

Paul Van Buynder's years of research and experience working with under-resourced Aboriginal communities in the remote Australian outback were going to serve him well in Banda Aceh. He had worked in clinics in outstations and Aboriginal settlements in Western Australia, Northern Territory and Queensland, including the Torres Straits. He had given anaesthetics and done every type of operation— from caesarean deliveries to vasectomies. You became an expert in everything, by necessity, when you worked in isolated communities. He was also an officer in the Army Reserve. In his public health role he had reviewed issues for the government such as the health response to the World Trade Center bombing, and the anthrax release in the USA. His varied background and wealth of experiences equipped him with skills which were very helpful in the Banda Aceh setting.

As he was fluent in French but normally spoke with a broad Aussie accent, he entertained Sudhakar and the surgical people in the team hugely with his French impersonations. '*Pardon*,' he would say throatily, as he moved elegantly past someone in theatre. He might have been officially a public health doctor, but he really rose to the occasion in theatre. Once again, the team members showed that there was no demarcation—you did what you could, you learned fast and got on with it.

Although one of the main public health officers of the biggest state in Australia, who had been admonishing the team about the risks of sunstrokes, malaria, drinking water and so forth, Paul Van Buynder decided at one point that it was a good idea to rescue a rabid cat out of a water well.

There were only two major health emergencies for the team during the deployment. Brian's needlestick injury was one and the attack of a feral and possibly rabid cat was another.

Paul Van Buynder was woken one night—again—by the mamp-mamp-mamp sound of a faint alarm clock. Exhausted but unable to go back to sleep because of the communal snoring, and aware that the nearby mosque's call-to-prayer would start in an hour or two, he fuzzily contemplated the respective merits of finding the clock's owner and maiming him; or doing something constructive, like writing up a public health report on Banda Aceh. He chose the latter.

He left the dormitory. As he sat typing on his laptop in the team's office, he heard a strange noise nearby. He investigated and saw a cat drowning in a water well. These were the square-tiled tubs out of which the team used to scoop water with a dipper to wash themselves. He reached in and put his arm under the cat. The frightened cat, clearly blaming Paul Van Buynder for its whole predicament, scrambled to safety by ferociously scratching its way up the flesh of his arm, and promptly made itself scarce.

Paul Van Buynder worked mostly with Jeremy McAnulty and Mike Flynn. Jeremy didn't know many people in the team before going to Banda Aceh. He had met James Branley when working on an outbreak of parrot fever (psittacosis) in the Blue Mountains in 2002. Jeremy was the director of the Communicable Diseases

Branch of New South Wales Public Health. Tall, dark and handsome—think actor Tom Hanks, with a stronger jaw line—Jeremy was in his early forties, quietly brilliant and genteel almost to a fault. Married to Paula, he had three boys, William (fifteen), Henry (twelve) and Alex (nine). His work in public health had seen him involved in everything from cryptosporidium in the New South Wales water supply to outbreaks of disease on pleasure cruise liners, responses to bio-terrorism and respiratory outbreaks such as SARS. Jeremy was finding that the Acehnese were very sensible about disease control—they exercised proper personal hygiene and knew the risks about food contamination. Unfortunately, however, the tsunami had fouled many of the water wells in Aceh province, and homelessness and camp living had led to bathing and washing taking place in higher water reservoirs, which otherwise might have been useful for drinking.

Jeremy had experienced his own sombre moments at Banda Aceh. One day he was travelling to a camp with Mike Flynn, and as they approached a river near Kesdam Hospital they saw the local people slowly rowing out to floating bodies, tying ropes around them and gently hauling them, hand over hand, back to the riverbank. They saw a pair of bodies which looked like a couple embracing—they appeared to have died clinging to each other. It was too sad. All the team members had moments which touched them, and would never leave them.

After some quick negotiations with MSF, Annette Holian, Brian Pezzutti and Ray Southon set off for Sigli. They sneaked out of their quarters at first light to join the waiting MSF cattle truck—or what looked like a cattle

155

truck loaded with supplies—and a four-wheel-drive car. There were three MSF people sitting in the car. 'There is no room for your bags!' they called out in cheery French accents. Annette and Ray pulled out all the boxes and bags that were already in the car, re-packed the lot and discovered there was plenty of room for their bags after that.

They set off with Udi the driver, an MSF member François, his wife Gabriele, Afe the translator, Eunice a nurse, and the three Australians in the back. Annette asked light-heartedly, 'Where's the champagne?!' They were, after all, French. 'It is in the back, in the portable refrigerator,' Gabriele assured her seriously, in her French accent. Some things you did not compromise on.

The trip was uneventful. The roads were inland so had not been directly affected by the tsunami, but it was unclear how far the earthquake had been felt. At one stage they passed what appeared to be yards and yards of coloured cloth, being washed and dried in the sun. Life still went on. Clothes still had to be made. Many fabrics and furnishings had been ruined beyond salvage in places on the coast, if not by the immediate wave and wreckage then by the seeping rot and mould afterwards.

What struck Annette most as they travelled was that they occasionally passed heavily secured TNI vehicles, that looked like tanks on wheels. It was a two-and-a-half hour drive to Sigli and they had originally planned to go by twenty-minute helicopter ride, but MSF cancelled this plan due to the risk of being shot at by those involved in the fighting. MSF had also given them zip-up sleeveless vests to wear, which identified them as medical personnel.

The city of Sigli was about 8 kilometres inland and had not been directly affected by the tsunami. Thousands of refugees were arriving daily because the fishing villages on the coast had been ravaged. They drove in the driveway of a hospital, which was not unlike Fakinah Hospital to look at. A white single-storey building with verandahs and grassy courtyards. When they arrived they were met by the middle-aged director of the hospital, who was very friendly and took their passports. Their arrival had to be recorded with the police.

The director told them that 50 per cent of his staff was missing from duty, either killed by the tsunami or with their families, dealing with the trauma of losses and damage. He knew a great deal about the new arrivals, clearly having done his research. 'The internet,' he explained, smiling. He even knew that Brian's birthday was 6 January.

The hospital was desperate for an orthopaedic surgeon. Hospital staff looked at the group and, after a quick query, singled out Annette. 'Come this way please,' they said, setting out on a ward round. The others followed.

They were taken to look at the theatres. One was blue-tiled, dark and dingy. It looked very well-used. Down the end of a corridor was another theatre, which was a beautiful, white-tiled room with bright sunlight pouring in through large glass windows. Natural light! Annette thought. How different to Fakinah. She had assumed they would be going downmarket when they left Fakinah, expecting to rough it further and get even more out of their comfort zones, professionally and personally. Sigli was a complete surprise.

More was to be revealed. A veritable feast! Surgical instruments. Suction units, anaesthetic machines, diathermy machines. Annette wondered how she would operate with all of this paraphernalia, as she had grown used to making do without it. Brian was in his element. He was so thrilled to find an anaesthetic machine that he could barely contain himself. He was photographed as he examined it, beaming. He couldn't find an oxygen hose.

'Where is it?' he asked the staff.

'We were given it as a gift,' he was told, 'it has never had a hose.'

'When were you given it?' Brian persisted, searching in cupboards. He hoped to find the hose stored nearby, or something that would do the job.

'Twelve months ago.'

Brian couldn't use it. He was fuming inside—such a disappointment. But then it was the usual matter of getting over it. Again. He just laughed, which was always the best response.

Ray had set up the theatre with instruments, dressings and other supplies. Annette gave MSF a list of her surgical requirements, and when they didn't blink, she kept adding to it. This was luxury. They had supplies such as surgical drapes, gowns, instruments. She almost felt guilty about her colleagues slumming it back at Fakinah.

They identified a number of patients needing immediate surgery. Annette looked at one of them having his dressing changed. He was biting down hard on a dirty, rolled-up towel. He was in agony. Shocked, she looked around. There were other patients doing the same thing, as their dressings were being changed. The gauze dressings were stuck to jagged-edged wounds, where the sharp debris in the tsunami had sheared off skin and roughly cut away flesh as it whipped past. She thought of how much a Band-aid could hurt as it was ripped off. These were tearing and snagging at the large, infected, deep gashes. She shuddered and her eyes prickled in sympathy.

The differing pain philosophy was again evident. What to do? Order immediate, appropriate pain cover for all the patients? She knew from her work in other countries that there was a fear that pain relief suppressed breathing. It was all about adequacy of education, training. She couldn't change the world in one day. She knew there was no intention to be cruel. She would do what she had come to do. You cannot take over and throw your weight around. You do what you have come to do.

Annette, Brian and Ray commenced operating. The power gave out almost straightaway. The theatre quickly became like a greenhouse with steam rising from their hot bodies and the sun streaming attractively but relentlessly through the large windows. The three put on bandages as makeshift sweatbands around their foreheads, laughing at how with every challenge you had to dream up a way of turning it into fun, otherwise it could all become too annoying for words. Power was restored shortly and, wonder of wonders, MSF was also able to put in running water for them. Ray did not have to run the 20 metres up the hall to the other theatre every time he needed to wash something or scrub up. Brian was impressed with how Ray managed to team-build with the local nurses. He was very organised, smiled often and although he couldn't speak their language, managed to have a good working relationship with them as they helped each other.

They knew it was a day-to-day proposition whether they were going to be able to return to Sigli but for now the three would just do their best to alleviate some of the patient workload.

Ray was very moved to be asked to go with them. He was a nurse at Westmead Hospital in Sydney, working in general surgery. He worked as a scrub nurse and occasionally the scout (the former remains sterile, the latter obtains what is needed for the surgery). The general surgery he was involved in covered anything from varicose vein removal and bowel repair to burns and fractures. Ray's background particularly suited him for this mercy mission. He had been a minister of religion in the Seventh Day Adventist Church for 28 years. Fifteen of those years had been in a chaplain's counselling role. He had been exposed to many of the crises of life which people suffer and had had to help people find a way out of their pain.

He had never been in the military but he had been trained in outdoor activities such as abseiling and boy scout-style camping.

Ray was married to Margaret, who was also a nurse and was from a family of nurses. Together they were the parents of two grown-up daughters and a son. His vocation was nursing but, when his time was his own, Ray made homes structurally safe and beautiful. He was the ultimate handyman.

He had been on duty in the Royal Melbourne Hospital the day the West Gate Bridge collapsed in 1970. He had worked in East Melbourne and Adelaide on the community disaster response for the Ash Wednesday Bushfires of February 1983. He was experienced in dire situations, where injuries were horrific. He regarded the request for him to help in Indonesia as an honour for his hospital, his community and his country.

Annette, Brian and Ray found the Indonesian hospital staff at Sigli very friendly and highly receptive to outside assistance. So much so that the trio volunteered to stay on the next day, and were rewarded with a magical meal that night of ducks' eggs and banana leaves.

That night the remainder of the CASTA team back at Fakinah experienced the biggest earth tremor since their arrival. It hit at 10.30 p.m. and registered 6.5 on the

Richter scale. It shook them to the core, but they all had adopted a fatalistic approach—if they were meant to survive they would, but if your number was up then it was up. There was not much you could do about it.

chapter thirteen

Helping and Coping

The US Secretary of State, Colin Powell, and Florida's Governor, Jeb Bush, visited Banda Aceh on 5 January. Both men had been sent by President Bush to assess the situation and report back on what role the United States could play in the recovery, and to raise the profile of the area in need. The world press swarmed to capture this amazing visit.

After they landed at Sultan Iskandar Muda airfield, they boarded a Seahawk helicopter to get an aerial appreciation of how badly the region was affected.

Powell sounded staggered on his return. 'I've been in war and I've been through a number of hurricanes, tornadoes and other relief operations, but I've never seen anything like this,' he told reporters, in an aghast voice. 'Flying over Banda Aceh and seeing how the wave came ashore, pushing everything in its path. Cars, ships, freighters overturned all the way up to the foothills. I cannot begin to imagine the horror that went through the families and all of the people who heard this wave coming and had their lives snuffed out by this wave.'

Powell then visited the IOM tent in the middle of the day.

Bill Griggs had a number of patients at the airfield. He had had a tough couple of days trying desperately to airlift patients to Medan. Earmarked for departure were a number of cases from both Fakinah and Kesdam. He and Sudhakar had done a ward round the previous day, Tuesday, 4 January, and identified those patients who needed to go to a fully equipped, fully staffed hospital for treatment. These were mostly surgical patients that Paul had anaesthetised and either Sudhakar or Annette had operated on. These patients had to be stable enough to travel but they required further and better hospital care than could be provided locally. They were mainly patients who required ongoing surgery and rehabilitation. There was also a fifteen-year-old aspiration pneumonia patient called Zahara who had been added to the list as a special request from James Branley, on behalf of a local Indonesian doctor. These patients were moved onto the verandah at Fakinah to make way for incoming admissions, while they waited for transport to the airfield. They were unable to depart on the Tuesday, as a plane coming in to land had hit a water buffalo on the runway, causing chaos and shutting down the airfield. The incident relayed by Griggs to Fakinah by phone, to complete disbelief at the other end: 'A plane hit a cow. A *cow*. Yes, a cow.' It was not the most comfortable of arrangements for the patients as they waited, lying on body bags in the outside humidity, and the plan was for it to be strictly temporary. The patients were uncomplaining and cooperative at every step.

Another group of evacuees from Kesdam had been treated and stabilised and were now waiting with their relatives at the airfield. Griggs had rejected some prospective patients as they were too ill to travel and unlikely to survive, wherever they were. It was hot. The usual noise and chaos of aircraft activity was not present. The pre-arranged flight was cancelled. All aircraft movements had suddenly been halted due to Powell's visit.

Griggs got on with his job and continued to do what he could to keep his patients in a comfortable state until the flight embargo was lifted. He had a tarpaulin placed over the patients to shield them from the hot sun. No sooner had he secured the shade for them than a Seahawk suddenly flew over at low altitude, blowing the tarpaulin away, its updraft pulling out drip-lines from the patients. It was carrying Powell.

Hydrating and feeding the patients was difficult, let alone keeping them cool, comfortable, toileted and medically stable. The security arrangements accompanying Powell's visit were such that if he had to leave at a moment's notice, then everything was on standby for this to happen. Security on the airfield was tight as there was the potential for a terrorist attack. The whole world was watching. People were pre-occupied and vulnerable. With such considerations in mind, the security needs of this prominent world figure were paramount.

Colin Powell found Griggs and spoke to him. 'If there's anything I can do to help, anything at all?' he offered.

Griggs responded politely, 'My patients need to go to Medan for hospital treatment, Sir.'

'In that case, my leaving might help,' said Powell.

'Yes, Sir,' replied Griggs. Powell understood immediately. He had been in the military himself. He was not afraid of straight talk. He had served his purpose by coming, in drawing the world's attention to Banda Aceh. The world was already responding. Money needed to help these desperate people was starting to pour in.

Powell left. But the impact of him being there was enormous.

The team members' backgrounds often gave clues to how they had ended up in the disaster zone. Their particular personalities were also a factor. These two aspects combined seemed to be what helped them perform well under pressure. Unless you were okay yourself, you couldn't help others. Expectations had to be realistic, and endurance was crucial. Experience and character. You needed both.

Paul had been unwittingly preparing for this important role in Banda Aceh throughout his whole life. He had watched the television program *MASH* as a fascinated teenager, with family and friends telling him he reminded them of Hawkeye. He spent years in Venturers, the teen version of scouts, and he was also a Queen's Scout. He had gone camping, caving, abseiling, rock-climbing, canoeing — combining loads of activity with the joys of improvising and roughing it. Their food would usually be creations that smelt great but looked awful, cooked on a campfire which had been painstakingly made, sometimes with rain-soaked wood in icy winds. There were many situations of danger, when the tenacity of the team meant that the person trapped in the too-narrow cave did not panic, and the person dangling at the end of the abseiling rope was confident of being rescued. Rick, their calm and confident leader, had let them make mistakes and learn. Paul had kept the tin plates he had eaten off, as souvenirs of many happy and character-building experiences.

Paul was an ordinary Australian boy who grew up in the Sydney suburb of Ryde. His mother was a mathematician who also taught English as a second language to migrant adults, and his father was a professor of teacher education. When Paul joined the Navy in the 1980s, he was required to do survival at sea training. He went to sea on various ships, where he lived in crowded messdecks and learned to tolerate lack of basic creature comforts such as long showers, comfortable beds and privacy, all of which are sacrificed as part of shipboard life.

Paul completed flight-surgeon training in Pensacola, Florida, in 1995. He and his group of 40 fellow doctors were put out in the bush and left without food or water for days. Four US Army Rangers had died of hypothermia in survival training there, in an exercise a month prior to his arrival.

It had been bitterly cold and his group had become hungry. Paul caught a turtle, cooked it and ate its eggs, even as his classmates watched and turned slightly bilious. They couldn't touch it, or anything else for that matter. He felt he had to be able to stomach living off the wild—he had to know what he was really made of. He ended up the only one out of that class of 40 to successfully fly a military jet solo. Mike Flynn had been another Australian who did that course, back in the 70s.

Paul specialised in anaesthetics and transferred to the Naval Reserve. He also became a cardiac anaesthetist, and joined the heart–lung transplant team at St Vincent's Hospital. Cardiac anaesthetics was the most complex of anaesthetics. The patients were the most sick, they were usually on a cocktail of drugs which made interactions tricky to calculate, and operations such as heart and lung transplants were lengthy and high risk. But Paul thrived on challenges.

Paul always said it helped that he married someone who understood him, was used to coping with separation (because I came from a naval family), and who backed him in his aspirations.

In his time at sea he had certainly had moments when things were hairy. Boat transfers at 2 a.m. in pitch darkness across heaving seas to another vessel to treat a patient (the much-loved son of a Thai admiral) were not for the faint-hearted.

There were other dicey episodes from time to time. A young pilot fell from a helicopter in a winching exercise on the New South Wales South Coast and Paul had to reach him using the same set of equipment which had just failed. He would never know which felt worse — being unable to save the young man's life, because his body had been completely broken on rocks — or returning to tell the bride of a few months that she was a widow.

There was always the element of your own 'human-ness' which had an impact upon your ability to function and achieve goals. Paul had packed for Banda Aceh on the 'keep it simple' philosophy. He was now regretting ditching my packing choices. When he rang me one day, and actually got through, he asked 'Do you know the first thing I had to borrow? Fungal powder!' We laughed heartily. It was hot and he was, manfully, not as hairless as some. Constant sweat over your entire body meant rashes and discomfort. The 'shower-in-a-can' as he called his anti-perspirant, did not quite do the trick.

At 11 p.m. on the night before he left Sydney, he had disdainfully thrown aside the vital provisions I had heaped on the kitchen nook table, after a frenzied rummage through cupboards. I had been mad about creating survival kits as a child. I knew exactly what he needed:

candles, wind-up torch, fungal powder, waterproof matches, sunblock, Rid insect repellant, Pine-O-Cleen antibacterial wipes. He had taken only the Rid and the wipes from my proffered pile. 'They think I'm a legend because of the wipes, Soph!' he later teased. They did once end up operating by torchlight, he also had to confess.

The food was something Paul had to 'get over'. The RAAF ration pack they had been given for the flight out of Richmond Air Base had been pretty lame—a bit of devon or something, a lonely piece of unbuttered bread, an Anzac biscuit and a granny smith apple. These days Paul remembered it longingly. He hadn't known it then, but it was to be the best food he would have on the whole deployment. It had had a fresh apple in it—and he didn't even eat it! He would have done anything to have it here. The ratpacks they had now contained no fresh food.

Paul had heard about Al Stafford when he was learning to fly in Pensacola. Al was an American who was shot down in the Vietnam War. On his first day in captivity he had been given a revolting fish-head soup, which he couldn't touch, let alone consume. Al later said he wished he had known it would be the best meal he was offered for the next six years. He'd been given it because some feast day fell on the same day he was shot down. It was a gift horse.

Paul thought about how he was starting to appreciate the things he was now deprived of. Here in Banda Aceh, you ate because you had to, to keep your strength up. Although he had a strong stomach, some nights Paul felt he couldn't eat, even though he knew he had to. He would sometimes just grab a cup of coffee and head back to theatre to do more cases with Sudhakar and Marj, with Adrian often helping. Sometimes the disgusting smell of infected and sick bodies, which clung to every inch of you, combined with the revolting sights of the day—rotting, pus-encased open flesh—would saturate your senses. It just overwhelmed you.

More and more, Paul would walk along the balcony to get to theatre, rather than going through the ward. He found that this routine—not seeing the people lying there with wounds, not seeing the little babies or the children, not breathing the pungent air—enabled him to come to theatre emotionally strong and ready to perform professionally.

The nurses—Karyn Boxshall, Lisa Dillon and Liz Cloughessy—and the physician James Branley were working on the ward, and doing it very well. As an anaesthetist, Paul didn't have to do this. He could just get on and do his job and that suited him fine. Removing people's pain while they were being operated on was how Paul knew he could best help them. During his working day at Fakinah he saw case after case, until well after nightfall. It was enough.

Paul did do ward rounds with the others on the team. He remembers vividly an incident involving a man in his late fifties, who had a severe head injury which had become fly-blown—flies had laid eggs and maggots had started living in the wound—and it needed to be debrided. The maggots were not the problem. Maggots had been used in World War I to clean wounds of rotten tissue and deadly bacteria. It was a painful injury, but this patient was a very stoic man. At one stage there was a drip-stand in the theatre—one of those horrid, unsteady three-legged ones. Suddenly there were earth tremors and people lurched about, causing the stand to rock and fall, smashing the man full in the face. The cracking sound of the impact on his skull was horrific. Paul was beside himself when he saw it happen, but the man just took Paul's hand and squeezed it reassuringly, saying brightly, despite all he had gone through, 'It is okay, it is okay!'

Increasingly, the team was getting an impression of the Acehnese as strong and kind people, who saw the humour in situations, no matter how dire.

Watto, Bruce and Ken Harrison spent most of their days sorting out everything which would enable the hospital to function. Repairs and supplies. One of the ongoing challenges was the water supply for the hospital. The tsunami had put water, water everywhere, but not a drop to drink. The team had bottled water and the hospital had a tank, for all purposes including showering and the washing of hospital cloths. Prior to the tsunami, the water from the tank would be pumped electrically through the hospital system. But the pipes leading from the town had been broken in the massive earthquake which triggered the tsunami.

The hospital water now had to be trucked in and the tank had to be filled from the truck. Australian Army personnel provided 20 000 litres of purified water from the water purifying plant they had set up in the grounds of the Catholic Church, close to the centre of Banda Aceh. It was opposite the rubble of a huge shopping centre which had collapsed in the initial quake. An Australian flag fluttered over the plant, signalling the presence of the service which steadily provided 480 000 litres of water, every 24 hours, for the people of the city of Banda Aceh.

The 20 000 litres for Fakinah Hospital were meant to last the whole of the hospital for a few days, but Watto and the others were discovering that the tank would be drained by morning. The first morning it happened, they thought the tank or the pipes throughout the hospital might be cracked and water possibly leaking out, so they decided to isolate the pipes to the hospital. That evening, they shut off the electric pump which sent the water into the pipes. In the morning, the tank was drained dry. The tank must be leaking, they thought. It cannot be the pipes after all. To check there wasn't another, less dramatic explanation— such as extravagant water usage overnight for clothes laundering or long showers—they cut the plug off the power cord which ran the electric pump. Again, in the morning, the tank was empty. It had been re-wired overnight and plugged in again, with an Indonesian plug. Watto asked the Army to refill the tank again, which caused some concern about the rate at which the hospital consumed the water. Clean water was gold. The Army wanted to continue to be able to meet the demand. They had their own pressures. The water purification relied upon a steady flow of water in order to purify it, and the city's pipe maze had been damaged. There was also a time factor involved in the purification process, and a queue of patient but thirsty people. A queue which stretched forever.

Watto, aware that the supply was precious, cut the power cord so short it could not reach the power socket. He made himself a power cord which went from the cut length to the socket and kept it hidden away.

If people wanted water overnight he reasoned, they could fill a bottle and take it to their rooms. The Indonesian police objected, saying that they did not carry water, it was beneath their station. Watto and Bruce offered to carry their water for them to their rooms. Shamed into accepting that the tsunami had created different conditions for everyone, the police capitulated. Although Watto and

Bruce never quite solved the mystery of the disappearing water, from that moment on, the wastage stopped.

The police had a good relationship with Watto and Bruce. One time they had locked themselves out of their room and one of them called on the firemen for help. 'You are like thief!' he said admiringly to the bemused fireys. This particular policeman had watched as Watto and Bruce deftly broke into rooms on security rounds. Bruce had been keen to find some oxygen supplies, as they were so desperately needed. The firey was overjoyed when he shone his torch into the room on rounds one night and saw a number of oxygen cylinders. They appeared to have fallen this way and that during that first earthquake, firmly blocking the door. Bruce had a little boy and his Indonesian family help by slipping the boy through a small gap in a train-ticket-type window. The boy moved the cylinders and Bruce was able to get the door open and distribute the cylinders to the grateful doctors and nurses. Whilst supplies of everything mattered, oxygen ranked as particularly important. Pain relief, given in the levels required for serious discomfort, could cause depressed breathing. Weakened patients, or patients labouring to breathe due to pneumonitis, often would have plummeting oxygen levels. Lack of oxygen could lead to brain damage, or even death. Bruce's find was a godsend. He gave the little boy a torch for his help. He was thrilled.

Supplies were a constant challenge. Ken Harrison was the team's puppetmaster in that area. When it came to logistics, nothing got past him. He was in his early forties with a long dark ponytail and beard. Married to Jill and father of pre-teens Luke and Rachel, he was running the CareFlight Cache (supplies) at Westmead Hospital when he heard about the tsunami. He promptly contacted David

Cooper, who headed up the disaster response section in New South Wales Health. Ken was a qualified anaesthetist, but the role disaster response wanted him for was to use his calculating logistical ability. He was a medical equipment expert and was fast accumulating disaster response expertise. He had assisted with the Sydney to Hobart yacht race tragedy in 1998. He had helped at the Waterfall train crash in January 2003, at bushfires too numerous to mention, and, in contrast due to its nature, the Olympics in Sydney in 2000. But he had never been to anything on the scale of this tsunami. Nobody had.

As well as manning the supply situation, Ken also had responsibility for team building, and he did it well. He got the whip out in the early days to get the job done so the work could start. He knew that morale would stay healthy if the work could get started—there was nothing worse than being somewhere, all revved up and then not being able to do what you had travelled there for. The earthquakes were what unnerved Ken, he would never forget them. The bad ones were those you could hear before you actually felt them; you were in their power and there was nowhere to run. They were not only disquieting, they made you feel shivers of terror in your bones.

He had had experiences in Banda Aceh which would probably never leave him. Battlefield protocol or disaster triaging is so different to normal working procedures. You saved those people who were most likely to survive, so that they could rejoin the community and help their remaining family members. A theatre could not be tied up all day by one case—particularly if the patient would probably not make it anyway—when ten people with better prospects could have been treated in that time. The only option for very ill patients was making them comfortable.

On one occasion Ken had had to let a young boy die. The boy was about twelve, his own son's age. It was a tough call, one of the toughest of his life, and it seared him to the core. The brutal reality was that the resources had to be used elsewhere, as many more people would only be able to live if the team conserved the medical supplies and didn't use them irresponsibly. There were only four surgeons and the boxes of supplies were finite and dwindling fast. There were hundreds of people lining up at Emergency, all needing help. Hundreds and hundreds per day in fact.

Hard as it was to do, Ken did his job.

Sudhakar shed tears some days. It was completely understandable. Paul felt Sudhakar cried on his behalf, as Paul had battened down his own hatches emotionally. He had to, to make it through.

Sudhakar worked extremely hard. He drove himself. He also knew the language, and therefore had no buffer from what was being said around him. He was in a different position from the rest of the team in that respect. Although it was an advantage, it brought with it a certain rawness of experience.

There was a lovely little child to whom Sudhakar became particularly attached. Zulfahmi was about nine and could have been a playmate of Luke, the oldest of Sudhakar's three boys. He came to the hospital on 4 January. The Americans had picked him up in one of their helicopter trips along the ravaged Aceh coastline, and he had been triaged at Banda Aceh airfield. He was alone and suspicious of all these strangers around him. He was admitted to Fakinah Hospital because he needed surgery on his festering arm and foot. Zulfahmi was an unusual patient because so many children had died in the tsunami. He was silent and looked warily at them through lowered brows. His eyes were dark and dull, not how a young child's should be at all. Paul anaesthetised him and Sudhakar operated on him.

As the ketamine coursed through the boy's veins, working its marvel and separating his mind from the pain, a magical transformation occurred. Zulfahmi began to smile, and make contact with them. They realised he had some English and they started chatting to him. He began counting animatedly and singing the *Sesame Street* version of 'ABC'. He called out spiritedly '1,2,3,4,5,6,7,9,10!'

Paul teased him. 'What about eight? You left out eight!' Zulfahmi laughed and concentrated harder: 'Oh! Eight! Eight! Okay! 1,2,3,4,5,6,7,9,10!', leaving it out again. And so it went on. Paul blew up a glove balloon for him. It was so wonderful to see that little face uplifted. Paul playfully called Sudhakar 'doctorrr', rolling his r's. There was a simple joy in hearing Zulfahmi chuckle merrily at his pronunciation. Zulfahmi laughed with them and they bantered happily as they helped fix him up. Now and then he broke into a stream of Acehnese and would then burst into tears. Sudhakar, listening, suddenly had tears streaming down his own face.

He interpreted for Marj and Paul that Zulfahmi had just said, 'I will never see my mother again! I will never see my father again! Everyone in my family is dead!' Marj gasped and folded her arms around the little boy. Paul stroked his hair. 'Yes, you will. You will see them again,' he murmured, choking back his own tears. This child gutted them all.

Sudhakar learned that Zulfahmi had been running out of his home, away from the tsunami with his father, mother, sister, brother and a young baby sibling when the mother told them to go ahead as she could not keep up. She had been through a hard pregnancy and had only recently given birth.

Zulfahmi did not see any of his family again. He had also become separated from his only surviving relative, his grandmother, when the helicopter they were on became too heavy to take off safely. Some of the passengers had been obliged to alight, to alleviate the overloading problem. His grandmother was one of them.

chapter fourteen

Kesdam

Kesdam Hospital was nothing special to look at. From the front, this white, one-storey building was rather plain and a bit grotty, but out the back it was quite lovely with grassy courtyards and covered walkways.

Inside were rows of serious patients with hollow expressions lying on beds. Dazed relatives milled around them, doing what nursing staff normally would do—giving them water and food, offering medicine, assisting with toileting and liaising with the doctors on their behalves.

The Kesdam experience was different to Fakinah. The Bravo team who went there worked in a cramped theatre with two operating tables, with next to no suitable instruments, no proper steriliser, and battled with the overwhelming heat and flies. The hospital was large and there was only a handful of medical staff, including some who had come from Malaysia. Most amputations were done at Kesdam rather than Fakinah, which was fortunately not as bad on the surgical trauma scale. But surgery performed at both hospitals was what some surgeons would call 'Tiger country'. It was dangerous, frightening, and challenging.

The officer in charge of Kesdam was Dr Arasanda, a colonel in the TNI. He had been severely affected by the tsunami and appeared to be suffering from some sort of post-traumatic stress disorder. He had apparently lost people close to him. He was armed and waved his weapon around. Later on he invited Mike Flynn to enjoy some Elvis Presley karaoke with him. The team was warned by the Indonesians to be careful of him.

Paul Luckin had initially gone to Kesdam on 1 January for an early 'recce' with Bruce Cameron, Adrian Humphrey, Ken Harrison and Mike Flynn in Greg Norman's Army truck. They looked at the two theatres there and Luckin met with a young Indonesian surgeon, Dr Panini, and an Indonesian anaesthetist. Dr Panini was in his thirties and was young and determined; it was he who clashed with Annette Holian at Fakinah. He spoke English and said pointedly to Luckin, 'We do not need your assistance, we do not need your help. We want your equipment.' He was almost aggressive in his demeanour.

Luckin was a gentleman—he had exquisite manners. He was Bond, James Bond. Except he was here to do life-saving anaesthetics, rather than car-chases, seductions or elegant shoot-outs. 'I will go to speak to our team leader,' he said diplomatically, deliberately not taking offence. 'Please do write down a list of your requirements. I would be happy to meet with you again, say in one hour?'

'We don't need you,' repeated the young surgeon.

People who go to other countries do not go as themselves alone. They stand for the country who sent them. It is a fact of life. And the reception you get from an individual you feel is the reception that country gives you. Unless you can limit it to the individual because you know what is behind it. Luckin knew this. He had lived in a number of different countries and he had served in many too. He had been to Bougainville in 1998–99, East Timor in 2001, the Solomons in 2003 and was in the military medical team that went to Bali, arriving 30 hours after the bombing which had taken place late at night on 12 October 2002.

There were any number of reasons for why this man had such a suspicious attitude. It might have been something other than a simple personality problem or a personal wariness of strangers, it may have been a culturally based 'face' issue. Some things cause loss of face. Some people do not like to be at the receiving end of assistance. There were also all the other sensitivities that had been outlined by Mike Flynn—religion, history, the TNI/GAM relationship. Luckin suspected that the man's attitude could be related to past events where Indonesia and Australia had medically interacted after a disaster.

Luckin had attended the last bi-annual 'Controversies in Civilian and Military Trauma Conference' in Brisbane, where a couple of senior Indonesian doctors had spoken about how they felt after the Bali experience. The conference had been about improving approaches. Issues were on the table for discussion, brainstorming, learning for the future. The atmosphere was one of trust, where people could open up and be frank.

When Luckin had arrived in Bali as part of the military medical team to assist after the bombing in 2002, there were dozens of patients waiting to be returned to Australia. They were already at Denpasar airport when he arrived. Pain relief was the most important thing as all the survivors were burnt. Most had burns to 70 per cent of their bodies. Their pain was indescribable. Many had inhalational burns from the intense heat, flames and dense smoke. Some people had ruptured ear drums, some had blast-lung, where the explosion had caused tears in the alveoli of the lung. For some the blast sent shockwaves through the delicate tissues of the brain, liver, kidney and spleen. Luckin had looked after these people the whole way back to Australia.

The Indonesian doctor who spoke up at the Brisbane conference was blunt. The Australians had rescued their own during the aftermath of the Bali bombing and, in doing so, had left the Indonesians without help. This had caused unhappiness for his people. Understandably, Australia had been caught up in its own national grief and shock. Yes, time was critical with burn injuries. Sterile surrounds were needed. Top-level medical care. Balinese facilities couldn't cope with the numbers. And yes, Australia had since poured money into refurbishing the Intensive Care unit at Kuta Hospital. All that aside, the Indonesians had needed them at the same time. Bali had been host to Australian holidaymakers for years. They were 'family'.

Luckin knew all this. He and the Australian team were here to make amends. If the Australian team could be given the chance, they would do their utmost to help. That was why they were here.

As brusque as this man was, Luckin was not going to take offence at anything. Now was the time to start afresh. It had to start somewhere, sometime. There was no point in harbouring grudges or labouring your own case. It was time to close the chasm, to build a bridge. That initial meeting at Kesdam had a satisfactory outcome. The Australians could help.

Paul Luckin had had a holiday booked to go to Tasmania with his wife Geena and pre-teen daughter Melissa when he received Peter Sharwood's very early morning phone call on Monday, 27 December. After telling Peter dutifully that he could be counted on to go if needed, he had rolled over in bed and groaned. It was the first time in seven years he had had a break over the Christmas and New Year holiday period. 'It is not really convenient,' he thought aloud to his wife Geena, who stirred beside him. 'It is rather more inconvenient for the people of Indonesia,' she said quietly, snapping him into reality.

Now here he was in Banda Aceh. Not that you would know it from looking at him. Luckin always looked like he was at a country gymkhana, in the members' tent. Pressed shirt and trousers. Every day. Even in a disaster zone. He never had a hair out of place and was always clean-shaven. About six foot four, wide-shouldered and perfectly groomed. Shaken not stirred, that was Luckin. Unflappable, he would have ablutions anywhere, in the most disgusting of places, but return as though he had been to a men's salon. He sat with a ram-rod back in theatre, and you fully expected to see a Rolex peeping out of his theatre gown sleeve. When others were stuffing dirty clothes in with clean into their backpacks, blueys and duffel bags, he had two bags, one with clean, one with dirty. He was organised. Scrupulous. He even had coat-hangers. But while clothes mightn't make the man — manners might, and he was always courteous.

Luckin lived his life to help people and he couldn't stop now. He had been born in Johannesburg, South Africa, moved to Rhodesia at age five (now Zimbabwe) and decided to do medicine at age eight after being a frequent visitor himself to doctors, as a result of falling off bikes and having scrapes, and generally having an adventurous spirit. He moved to Tasmania at age nine, and grew up there.

His parents were teachers. By age eleven, he was an ambulance cadet and by sixteen an ambulance volunteer (with a motorbike licence); finally, as a young adult, he worked his way up to being a paramedic. His introduction to death and disaster was earlier than most. In his first year of medicine, Luckin had studied in Papua New Guinea, where his parents had moved some years earlier. He later returned to South Africa to study the remainder of his medical degree at the University of the Witwatersrand in Johannesburg. His undergraduate training was at the Barragwanath Hospital, Soweto (reputedly the largest hospital in the world, with 2000 beds and 110 per cent occupancy). Soweto was renowned for violence in the 70s and 80s. Luckin became accustomed to seeing machete and gunshot wounds. A common one was the classic stabbed chest. One night he did his PB—30 chest drains in one evening.

In Australia, handling a pneumothorax puncture would be the work of a specialist emergency physician. In South Africa, if you weren't doing it confidently by your fourth year of varsity (uni), there was something wrong. He qualified in anaesthetics in Durban at the King Edward VIII. Here he dealt with something else in addition to the gunshot or other wound—disembowelments by assegai, a long Zulu blade. The action was in fact a traditional courtesy to allow the dying spirit to escape.

He was becoming conscious of concepts which to normal practitioners would be strange, unethical and confronting. Pain relief, for example, was an essential in a highly developed country, but it was considered a low priority elsewhere. Luckin learned to work even where you were constantly being reminded of a certain lack of humanity towards one's fellow man, although he never quite got used to people sometimes walking straight past an obviously stricken person on the footpath.

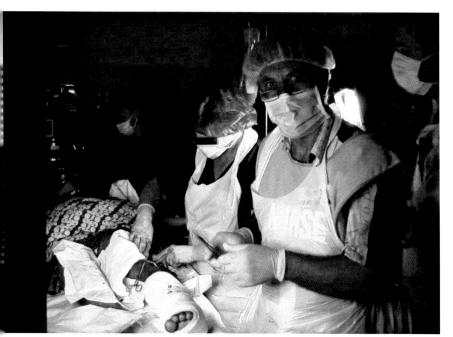

Above: Power failure! Annette Holian, Ray Southon and the team operate by torch-light at Fakinah.

Below: A normal day at Kesdam—amputations are in progress on two tables in the same operating theatre.

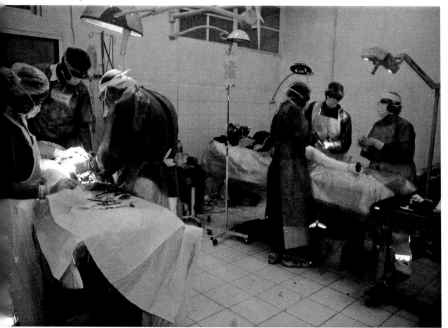

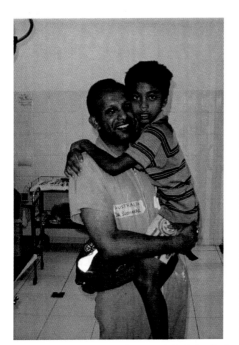

Above left: Sudhakar Rao and Zulfahmi, the little boy who stole everyone's hearts. **Above right:** Paul Van Buynder taking care of the team's health ... with a welcome bunch of fresh bananas. **Below:** Improvising—Paul Dunkin in the operating theatre. Behind him is one of the anaesthetic machines he cobbled together.

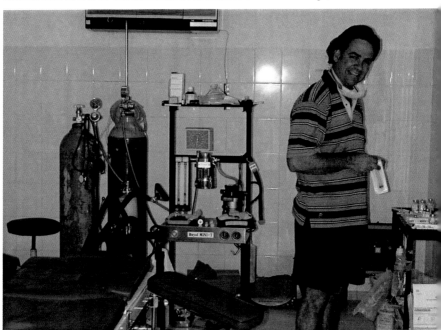

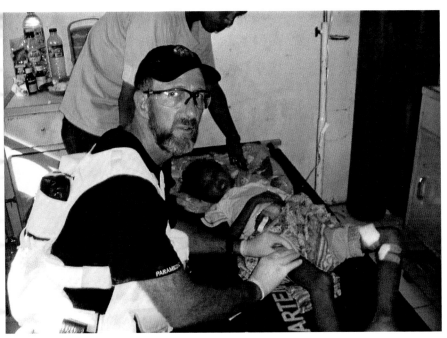

Above: Adrian Humphrey giving a tetanus shot. Caring for injured children was always a moving experience for the team.

Below: At Kesdam. L to R: Terry, Adrian, Rhonda, Shmackers, Rosie, Peter, Colonel Arasanda in camouflage gear. Luckin and Scotty at the back, René in front.

Above left: The future of Banda Aceh's society: resilient, cheery children in the IDP camp. **Above right:** An IDP camp, visited by Jeremy McAnulty. **Below:** Local Acehnese queue patiently for water purified by the Australian Army.

Fortunately, you could also find in any society good people who cared. It kept your faith in human beings.

Luckin was clever. He had trained in cardiac anaesthetics, as well as general.

His overseas experiences before Banda Aceh meant that he knew that cultural sensitivities would always be present, and that there was always more than one way to do things. If you wanted something to happen, you had to make it happen. You just had to work out a smart way of achieving it.

On their first day at Kesdam, Bravo Team and the Indonesian doctors did a ward round together to identify patients who would need surgery. Luckin was tactful, and sought the opinions of the Indonesian doctors, listening carefully to what they had to say. The Indonesian surgeons led the ward round. The anaesthetists, Luckin and Scott, followed the entourage and noticed that occasionally they skipped a patient, saying, 'It is okay', 'No no, no need.' Luckin was not sure why this happened but he hadn't come this far to overlook anybody who needed care. He hung back and started to make his own observations.

He noticed one young lady who appeared to be very ill indeed. We will call her Jamirah.[1] She was burning with fever and Luckin could tell she was dying, even without examining her. When he was studying medicine in his youth, he had scoffed at lecturers who said things like this, but now he knew what they meant: he could see the pallor of her skin, detect the laboured breathing, see the colour of her lips, her fingernails; he noticed the pulse rate in her neck. He was sure her lungs were full of phlegm and fouled seawater. She clearly had pneumonitis. Luckin lifted up a dressing and her injured leg literally burst open with offensive pus. If he

[1] Name has been changed.

had been a weak-stomached type, he would have been retching at that point but he simply said in his refined way to his Indonesian colleagues, 'She needs urgent surgery. Don't you agree?' They demurred, but he insisted. With due savoir faire. His years in the Soweto hospital as the young medical student had made him no longer shy—it was sink or swim.

They took Jamirah to theatre. Peter Sharwood operated on her, cutting away all the dead and rotting flesh in the leg wound. If he could save her leg, he would. But saving her life came first. None of the team held much hope for her but all did their best.

The next day, when Luckin called into the ward, Jamirah was in a much better condition. 'Thank you,' she said to him, clutching his hand, and smiling up at him. He was touched, even a little overwhelmed. He never expected that.

Before Luckin and the team departed from Banda Aceh, Jamirah was discharged from the hospital. She left on her own two legs, because nobody had had to cut either of them off. She was so happy and relieved, she didn't just *walk* out of the hospital—she *skipped*!

Kesdam had shocked theatre nurse Rosie Clifton to the core on day one. 'Where are all the supplies we should have had?' she ranted angrily when they got back to Fakinah that night for their regular briefing. 'Do you realise how busy we are, how desperate the situation is? We are overloaded, it is dangerous, people will die because of our understaffing! Where is the rest of our team? We don't even have half of Bravo out there with us!' And so she went on, not caring about etiquette. She had seen more gore in that one day than most theatre nurses see in a month, and was exhausted, and like the rest of the team, she was being stretched professionally. She had worked before in trying conditions, but these were the worst.

Liz Cloughessy took Rosie aside afterwards: 'You need to watch the way you speak,' she admonished.

'On the contrary,' said Rosie. 'It had to be said.' Nurses catch and kill their own. Rosie's bravery paid off—Terry Jongen and Adrian Humphrey were sent out to Kesdam the next day to help, for the duration of the deployment. They were hardly surplus at the understaffed Fakinah, but it was a gesture of support. The team forgave her her outspokenness. They were family now, and the reality was that they were all straining under similar pressure. Their experiences were bonding them, and airing your grievances was not going to be held against you.

Rosie was an attractive brunette, whose age was never discernible. She was petite, had her hair pulled back and held her head high. Before becoming a theatre nurse, she had been a ballerina and had danced all over Australia, New Zealand, Europe and South America. She had had four husbands. 'I told them to shape up and if they didn't, I showed them the door,' she explained to Paul cheerily. Rosie's figure never showed that she had had four children. Her face didn't give away that her eldest child was almost 30, either.

Rosie had done rigorous live-in training with the Red Cross, where faux terrorists would burst in on the trainees, without warning, during the course. She had done a mission with MSF for three months in 2004 in the former Soviet republics of Abkhazia and Georgia. Abkhazia had been involved in sporadic fighting for independence for some years. She had gone there principally to assess the operating theatres, but she had also assisted in the surgery. The operations included everything from the standard appendectomies and hernias to amputations of limbs shattered by landmine blasts.

Her philosophy was that, rather than throw a person a fish and have them fed for a day, you taught them how to fish and they fed themselves for a lifetime. To Rosie it was galling that the team would be in Banda Aceh for such a short time, offering medical services which might never be able to be replicated after they left. That was life though, and she got on with it. She was a professional. They rarely stopped for lunch, and if they ever did, it was for a quick bite from the ratpacks. They were swimming in blood and pus from morning until night. They did about fifteen major limb amputations in about five days, in amongst the wound debridements and other procedures.

Rhonda Cowderoy, Rosie's colleague for the deployment, had long given up on trying to keep the flies out of her sterile field in theatre at Kesdam. The smell of the blood on the floor and operating tables brought them in and they crawled all over everything and everyone. They swarmed on the pile of lopped-off limbs. She had also become accustomed to the 'What does this woman want now?' look which the Indonesian medical staff humoured her with as she asked for this and that, with gesticulations behind her mask and without touching anything. Nurses are generally considered 'servants' in the medical hierarchy in Indonesia and it was up-ending the usual order to have her taking charge. However, by the time she finished her deployment, the Indonesians were in tune with her routine and happily helping her, even anticipating what was needed.

Rhonda had short blonde hair, with fair skin and a radiant face, and had been married to Bruce for 33 years. They had had a son Rob and daughter Sarah. Rob had worked as an electrician with a telecommunications company. Almost two years ago, Rhonda was told Rob had been in 'an accident' and she rushed to the Royal Prince Alfred to be with him. She never thought the worst—her husband was an electrical engineer, she was a nurse. Sadly, Rob had been electrocuted at his worksite and died. Rob's death had had a huge impact on Rhonda and her family. Coming to Banda Aceh had been a blessing in disguise. In this disaster zone, she worked on people who were suffering greatly, people who *all* had experienced loss. It changed her outlook. For the first time, she was not thinking constantly of what she had lost. It didn't diminish her loss, but it did make her look at life with new eyes. Although not overtly religious, she believed in her Creator and had a private spiritual dimension. When the violent aftershocks in Banda Aceh threatened to bring the roof down one night, she asked Rob, from her heart, to bring her home safely to Bruce and Sarah.

Rhonda and Rosie worked solidly on case after case. Their work was going to save someone's life. There are times when you do not need to be told to put your best effort in.

Most afternoons the team at Kesdam finished by 3 or 4 p.m. and usually hitched a ride back to Fakinah. Sometimes Shmackers or René would stand by the roadside and flag down a car or truck. Almost invariably someone would stop and give them a lift, often for nothing in return. The goodwill towards the Australians was overwhelming.

The idea of a stump where your leg should be sends a cold shiver down most spines. The pain before, and afterwards. Then the phantom pain, or the itch in the ankle you no longer have. The changed life. The altered expectations.

Luckily, most people in modern times never have to experience losing a limb. And when they do, they have no say in it, it just happens, by terrible accident. Say in a car accident.

At Kesdam Hospital, many of the patients were in parlous states. Their conditions were serious and they needed radical care. Amputations were taking place daily. René Zellweger, the trauma surgeon on Bravo team, performed amputations at Kesdam, alongside his colleague Peter Sharwood, at the two operating tables. One surgeon at each. The theatre soon became a disgusting mire of spattered blood and infected fluids. Despite his many years of surgical work, René never quite got used to seeing human limbs, with a large bone sticking out of the middle, being dropped into the bin. It just wasn't how it was meant to be. Not in modern times. You rarely saw people with missing limbs in Australia and you certainly didn't saw off a number of them, one after another, in any one day. It would sicken you if you thought about it for too long, but you had to remember that the limbs you had examined were fast becoming fatally toxic to the rest of the body — and there were no other remedies at this late stage.

René felt thwarted on one occasion. He had advised a lady patient that her leg would have to be cut off and she had said 'No'. Surgeons like to solve things. She would not be getting a second chance — if it didn't come off, she would be dead in days. Whatever had broken her leg bones had left deep gashes, which had now become so infected that her leg was dead. The sultry climate didn't help: the heat had made it fester worse than ever and suppurating wounds become deadly. What an ironical situation — to survive the tsunami and then to die because you refused medical treatment. He could understand it. You learned to understand all manner of bizarre things. Life as a cripple could be cruel if you had no support. No crutches, no prosthetic limbs, no homecare, physio or occupational therapy. Who knew what her personal circumstances were? You couldn't judge anyone, not after this event. René tried to persuade her, firmly, gently. It was life or death, and there was no time to waste. He had such feeling for her and her suffering. She was being offered a below-knee amputation, but she refused. A few days later she died.

René had seen extreme suffering before. He performed trauma surgery at the Royal Perth Hospital in Western Australia, and was also an Associate Professor in Traumatology at the University Hospital in Zurich.

René was fair, athletic and of slim build. He had David Wenham-style looks and physique. René was at the peak of his professional experience and had worked in other disaster situations before, including war zones. In 1995, he had been an emergency doctor at an earthquake in Kobe, Japan, and in 2000, he was a surgeon for the International Red Cross during a civil war in the Sudan.

A world-class surgeon, who could have been living the high life with fast cars and mansions in the best parts of exclusive suburbs, René wanted to make his life worth living in a different way. A selfless, out-reaching way. Without fanfare and aware that some might be cynical—or think it unusual to the point of being eccentric—he did not mention his life's work to anyone, not even to those in the team. His altruism was a joint effort—his wife Katrin, a beautiful blonde physiotherapist, supported and fully shared his idealism.

In 2002 and 2003, he had worked in South Africa, in Cape Town and Johannesburg hospitals. He had operated on injuries sent in by the truckload from the strife in the townships. Ballistics, knife-wounds, axe and machete slashings. He had repaired the injuries of war and lived among human misery, coping with dramatically less than ideal situations. These were desperate situations, in violent times. The memories of those injuries would be with him for life.

René enjoyed working with this highly motivated team in Banda Aceh, where everybody pulled their weight. He knew he would be sad to leave, partly because he wanted to continue helping the tsunami victims and partly because he knew that he would rarely see these team members again, people that he had come to regard as friends. They enriched each other's lives with every passing moment and he would always treasure that. Everybody helped each other and nobody exploited any weaknesses they might have noticed. Quite the opposite. They bolstered each other, which was how they could continue to work under such demanding circumstances.

If you live cheek-by-jowl with a small team, and share harrowing experiences together over a relatively short space of time, you either bond or you strain apart. René had been in the military in Switzerland years ago in the crack mountain forces, where one slip in the dark, in the blizzards or on the ice, could mean death. His measure of a person's worth was whether he would have trusted that person with his life in those conditions. He felt there were people in the Australian team he would definitely have chosen to have alongside him on the mountainside.

The poverty of the Acehnese and the hope in the eyes of the patients also kept him going. These people had so much to complain about, but they didn't. They were good-natured and thankful for every bit of help. Always. It grabbed René's heart.

He sensed that the Acehnese wanted to be treated by the Australian medical staff in preference to any other. Although this was affirming of the team's skills and expertise, he tried to ignore it as he was conscious of the feelings of the Indonesian doctors, who were offering tremendous assistance and with whom he got on well. The Indonesians had shown that they were willing to be taught and some of them had discerned the limits of their own training.

He found their enthusiasm to learn very humbling and wondered whether he and his colleagues would have had the same humility were they in the same position.

On 3 January, René was interviewed by Daniela Lager from SFDRS, the main Swiss television channel. It was one in a series of interviews he gave to SFDRS.

René's Swiss background gave him fluency in German. He was able to talk about the destroyed infrastructure, the high number of casualties, and the major surgery being performed under the most extraordinary of circumstances.

These news reports about the tsunami relief work were broadcast across Germany and Austria. René's media coverage, which highlighted the work being done by the team, assisted in galvanising European generosity. He and the team were written up by Jane Perlez, a reporter from *The New York Times* and the story also appeared in the European edition of the *International Herald Tribune*. The activities of an Australian team in a remote Indonesian 'village' might not ordinarily have captured European attention but the tsunami itself caught their initial interest, and the medical work being done in its aftermath was brought into their consciousness via René.

The German contribution to the relief effort was to be among the world's most generous—they donated over $600 million.

The team members at Kesdam were always conscious of the sensitive relations with their hosts. One day, mid-afternoon, Shmackers came into theatre white-faced and tight-lipped. 'Let's go, pack up,' he said. One look at him and the team complied. He had been ordered to leave at once by an unknown, high-ranking, armed Indonesian. That was all Shmackers needed. There were no recriminations or arguments. The team returned the next day apprehensively, but the man was gone and all seemed well. No explanation was ever given and, in these unusual times, none was really expected.

There were heavy times at Kesdam but there were moments of levity as well. Shmackers one day turned a corner and came face-to-face with a local who had been given one of the Australian Army ratpacks. He had anointed his many cuts and scratches on his arms and legs with Vegemite out of the pack. 'It is good! Very good!' he told Shmackers earnestly. Shmackers, his suppressed desire to laugh almost causing him pain, acknowledged him politely with a nod and smile and quickly moved on.

Terry Jongen, emergency nurse, spread himself around. He had been hard-won for Kesdam by Rosie's understandable ranting in a briefing in those early days and he wasn't going to lounge about. Some days he helped in theatre, sometimes in the ward and often in the Emergency Department, with Greg Norman and some army medics.

Terry was a clinical nurse specialist in charge of the nurses in the Emergency Department at Royal Perth Hospital. He was single, in his late thirties, dark-bearded and into motorbike-racing. He had been at the receiving end for the burn victims of the Bali bombing, when he had had at his disposal the full resources of the Royal Perth. But Banda Aceh was different.

One day he and Shmackers had a patient who had severe and septic leg wounds. During the operation it became apparent that her infection had spread further than they had realised. The amputation was a difficult one, and it became clear after the operation that she was dying. She was tiny, in her forties, and was a very sweet and stoic lady. Her family was around her, and her English-speaking niece was the translator for the nurse and doctor. The woman died soon after the operation and her family wanted her body for a speedy burial for religious reasons.

Terry and Shmackers put the body into a body bag and the niece hugged Terry. 'Thank you,' she said, trembling. The family then asked if they could have the woman's severed leg as well. Terry thought it over. The leg had been wrapped and discarded already. It was not going to be a pleasant task. He decided he would go that extra mile for this lovely family. Donning a pair of gloves, he rummaged in the heat and thick swarms of flies through the putrid rubbish in the back alley until he found the leg. He was surprised at its heaviness. He carried it inside and placed it carefully in the body bag under the family's watchful and appreciative gaze. They wanted her as intact as possible.

Shmackers found Terry after the family had left. 'Thanks,' he said. Nothing more was needed.

Peter Sharwood, the other surgeon at Kesdam, was a complete saint. He didn't wear a halo and he didn't have saintly charm. You just had to see how he spent his life. He had obviously decided at some stage that he would dedicate his life to serving others who were needy in the worst kind of way. Being catastrophically injured in a developing country might qualify for his help. And he wasn't afraid of being uncomfortable, in danger, or without any of the items which could make his job easier. Although a prestigious surgeon in his 'normal' life, he didn't shirk from any job. The higher your professional status, the more you have to overcome to do what is demanding and sometimes lowly. Peter carried boxes with the best of them. He would mop the floors when not operating. The operating team had no suction machinery, so blood dripped and occasionally flooded over the edges of the tables. It stank. Sometimes it was a quarter-of-an-inch deep on the floor, becoming dangerously slippery. Peter's tradition of swabbing the floors had started when he was in Rwanda. The others wouldn't let him help put equipment away, as he put it in the wrong place. So while that went on, he mopped the theatre. When the *Bulletin* magazine in Australia did a write-up on him and some of the team at Kesdam, they photographed him mopping the floors.

Peter had done 41 years in the Army Reserve by the time he went to Banda Aceh, and was now a colonel. The others in the team all talked about 'When we', as in 'When we were in Rwanda we did such and such', and 'When we were in Somalia' and traded stories about the disasters they had been to and what they had dealt with. Peter had a few stories. He was entitled to be a When we.

He had heard about the tsunami on the 5 a.m. news on 27 December and had immediately called in his contacts in Queensland and Lismore. A surgical team was not being put together yet, but he was told to stay packed and ready. The next thing he knew he was farewelling Monica, his wife, and his four daughters and was in the government jet, the one Queensland Premier Peter Beattie used, flying to Richmond with three anaesthetists and a physician — Brian Pezzutti, David Scott, Paul Luckin and Paul Shumack.

The first day Peter had come to Kesdam, he had been begged by an American doctor called Scott to stay and help. The two Indonesians, Dr Arasanda and Dr Edison, had talked in their own language in front of him about how they didn't need any outsiders to help. The American understood what they were saying and chastised them animatedly for being so unrealistic and ungrateful; Scott was very helpful to the team that first day, but they never saw him again. In that discussion Peter let Dr Arasanda know that he was a senior officer in Australia's military reserve. Dr Arasanda visibly relaxed, sensing that Peter was responsible and understood chains of command. He allowed the team to stay.

Within one week, Sharwood and the others had turned the initially resistant opinion around. When they were leaving, Dr Arasanda gave the nurses double-cheek kisses, calling them 'his friends from Australia' and videotaping them. They were mutually sad to say goodbye to each other by that stage.

David Scott was asked one day via an interpreter by an Acehnese man, 'Where are you from?' David replied 'Australia'.

The man was amazed and asked, 'Why are you helping us and asking for nothing in return?' David replied simply, 'Because you are our neighbours.'

Both teams were now winding down operations. They had been briefed since 4 January that they were due to return home the weekend coming up. They began the gradual process of farewelling patients and mentally preparing themselves for their eventual return home to normal life, work, comforts, and loved ones.

chapter fifteen

Australia Responds

I woke bleary-eyed on Thursday, 6 January 2005, to images of Prime Minister John Howard on morning television and breaking news of some description. Too tired to get myself back to bed, I had flopped during the night onto the couch—the nearest horizontal surface—after breastfeeding Pierce for the third time. There had been no catch-up naps for days. I was half out of my mind with fatigue.

The strip of information running across the bottom of the screen began to sink in. The slight nausea I always felt upon waking too early after one too many nights of broken sleep, began to give way to excitement as I realised I was not having a self-satisfied dream about the prime minister doing my bidding in an important matter—this was real.

Howard was busy hugging someone in front of the international media. Even then, in my under-the-weather state, this struck me as not only quite moving, but a spectacularly insightful thing to do. What nation's leader could resile from an agreement that had been sealed with a sincere embrace and beamed all around the world? John Howard was hugging Indonesian President Susilo Bambang Yudhoyono. They were hugging each other. You could never have imagined it. Never. They were at some kind of regional summit and the prime minister was being interviewed: 'This is a human tragedy on a scale that none of us in our lifetime has seen and it does require a response above the ordinary,' he intoned. 'This is a terrible tragedy for mankind. On humanitarian grounds alone, a lot of help is needed. But what we are saying to the people in Indonesia in particular is that we are here as your friends. There is an old saying in the English language. "Charity begins at home." Our home is this region. And we are saying to the people of our nearest neighbour that we are here to help you in your hour of need.'

The Indonesian president was also filmed speaking at the summit: 'We are overwhelmed by the Australians' generosity and we will never forget it,' he said. 'Your presence here means so much to us in Indonesia. It means that you care,' he stopped, and then went on. 'And you care *deeply*.'

The toll from the tsunami was being reported as at least 145 000 people dead in eleven countries, with almost as many missing. Eighteen Australians were believed to have died. Faced with these appalling statistics, politicians had found their hearts.

My phone began to ring. Funnily enough, none of the callers knew about the letter I had sent to John Howard. They just knew me well enough to know that I would be thrilled by the latest outcome. They knew Paul was there and that my level of involvement in the crisis was personal. The first call was Jen Lloyd, Stu's mother and a long-standing friend of my mother's. Jen was enraptured by the prime minister's decision and slightly incredulous. We chatted for a while about the tsunami, the horrific losses of life, Paul being there, his television appearances and those of the team, the appropriate responses of a nation to such an event, and how Australia continued to amaze us both.

Then my brother-in-law Graham Swan, who was a project manager for his own residential building company, rang to say he was willing to throw his hat in the ring and contribute his skills gratis. He was drafting a proposal as he spoke. Paul's groomsman Guy Sullivan rang. He was a plumber. He'd seen Paul on the news on Channel Ten. The two of us discussed the huge plumbing and re-building issues thrown up by the devastated city of Banda Aceh. Paul's sister Linda rang in disbelief and excitement. Linda had lived in Jakarta for a few years and knew of the poverty in the kampongs.

When Paul and I had visited Linda while she lived in Jakarta, we had been struck by the abject poverty juxtaposed with the incredible wealth. You could dine at the opulent Dharmawangsa hotel having passed people who had no running water in their homes on your way there. You could not live in Indonesia, working and travelling through it, without becoming uncomfortably aware of the great divide between rich and poor, and the many culturally and territorially sensitive issues, such as East Timor and Aceh province.

The poverty seemed so depressing, because you felt that you could never do anything to change these wretched lives, and their government would not permit our own rich nation to interfere in an effort to improve their lives. Our motives would be judged, perhaps undeservedly, as suspect. To change this perception, it needed something of unprecedented magnitude. Such as a tsunami.

Animated out of my round-the-clock lactation stupor, I suddenly saw the prime minister transformed into someone who could perform miracles. I emailed a summary of the *Sydney Morning Herald*'s lead news article to all the people on my 'Paul Update list'. Interestingly, the print version of the *Herald* had the headline 'Australia takes charge in Indonesia', while the online version proclaimed 'Howard promises $1 billion in aid', a far less inflammatory and more diplomatically helpful headline. Nobody wants to be bossed about, and that was never the intention.

I felt euphoric. An Alan Moir cartoon appeared in the *Sydney Morning Herald* showing a staunch ALP voter despondently admitting to flashes of admiration for Howard. This particular decision was not going to be a mistake. He was Australia's Prime Minister, not simply the leader of a political party, and today he had made a wise decision, which he cannily guessed most Australians would back to the hilt. He showed he was aware of how aghast normal Australians felt about the tsunami and how keen they were to help. He did not underestimate Australians' generosity. This gift from the Australian people to the people of Indonesia was going to be administered by Australians, with the Indonesians assisting. Indonesian President Susilo Bambang Yudhoyono agreed wholeheartedly and it was sealed with a hug with our prime minister.

I picked up more details on the internet. The aid package Howard had announced on behalf of Australia included $500 million in direct aid and $500 million in concessional loans. Indonesia would receive $1.8 billion over the next five years, which included existing aid from Australia. Kofi Annan had already made the point that the disaster was of unprecedented proportions and would require an unprecedented response.

Australia had first sent over doctors and nurses, plus logistical support, but the next step was to send Australian tradespeople and town planners. It was a golden opportunity to help put proper sanitation, roads and safe infrastructure into place in the rebuilding process. What would be re-created in these impoverished, desperate regions would hopefully be a testament to both a regional neighbour's generosity and the wisdom of the Indonesian president — help was being diplomatically given, and diplomatically received. The gesture was generous and constructive, and the effects would undoubtedly be long-lasting.

I was so excited that I couldn't eat, couldn't think. Whenever I had travelled, especially in parts of Africa and Asia, my heart had been weighed down by the intractable poverty I witnessed. In the late nineties while visiting Indonesia, I had dreamily looked out of an upper window in Jakarta to suddenly observe a whole family below washing with what appeared to be a soup ladle, scooping water from a square tub. The heat, the smells, the ugly dankness and the incongruity of my own comfortable setting gave me a feeling of hopelessness and frustration beyond description.

I had experienced this before, in Africa one winter when I had seen families packed into small, smoke-filled and smelly farm sheds. I gave some clothes and colourful little books to the people I met, for their children. I will never forget the looks of disbelief on their faces. It made me feel sad and overall rather useless, in that it was a one-off gift which would probably have very little impact upon their lives in total.

I was also conscious that material things, of themselves, are not the answer in any event. Feeling that you are worthwhile is the key. Loved and respected. Although true self-worth can never be achieved through possessions — because it is something deep within you — under these extreme conditions, where the surroundings are not even basic and are a constant reminder that you are low in the human pecking order, how could you rise above this and experience self-worth? My two sisters, Ingrid and Libby, had done charity work in the Philippines. Despite the grinding poverty they had witnessed, they had reported that the people were very cheery and outreaching. It was one of the ironies of life that those with no material things, and no fretting about worldly advancement, were carefree and happy. It seemed the clue was in the real love they had for each other, because the greatest sadness they experienced was when they lost the people they loved. Life expectancies were often low in poor regions, due to some of the negatives which came with crushing poverty, such as disease, malnutrition, poor health services and harsh living conditions. Sometimes these were compounded by conflict and extreme regimes. International poverty is the true ongoing challenge for the nations of the world.

These thoughts and feelings about the suffering of people in the world had been gnawing at me for years. And then the opportunity to do something tangible had come up. Paul went to Banda Aceh, and I wrote a letter. Now here was the Australian prime minister responding, it seemed, almost in person! Who knows if he ever saw it? There may have been 6000 similar letters faxed that same day. It didn't matter. My far-fetched wish had been granted, before my dazed eyes. Nelson Mandela said, 'It sometimes falls upon a generation to be great.' My nation and generation were taking up the gauntlet.

I drafted a reply to the prime minister, thanking him.

In Jakarta, the Australian embassy staff broke into a cheer. They had every television set on and had just heard the good news. The prime minister of Australia had just made his announcement. Brigadier Ken Brownrigg, one of the top Australian Defence personnel seconded to the embassy, slapped Bernard on the back: 'I have never in my life been as proud to be Australian as I am today, Bernard,' he said.

Bernard grinned. He felt the same way.

The next day I checked my emails. There was a steady flow coming in. There was one from my tutor back in my early readership days at the Bar, Sandy Street SC. In his usual upbeat and supportive way he had written, 'Good on the Saint! Happy New Year and keep up the sterling effort!' It was a longstanding joke between us. He used to tease me that Paul should be canonised, for his father and husband skills. Now Paul was in a disaster zone.

My sister Ingrid emailed from Frankfurt. Ingrid was an in-house counsel for Deutschebank there. She had just read in the European edition of the *International Herald Tribune* an article about the Australian civilian volunteer medical team in Banda Aceh operating at Kesdam on a patient named Zaini, who had had half his leg amputated. Dr Paul Luckin was quoted as saying sadly that the chances of survival were still pretty grim. Ingrid went on to say that she was picking up on the very positive press that Australia was receiving. In all the mass of news in Europe, a small Australian team in a remote corner of Indonesia were getting detailed coverage in Europe.

Australia was being portrayed internationally as a highly professional, humanitarian country. The prime minister's donation of aid had been covered separately and had also been very well-received. For days, CNN and the BBC ran a league table of donor countries and Australia consistently topped the list.

Germany was coming a close second on the donation table, followed by Britain. Japan, the Netherlands, Canada and Norway were close behind. Ingrid felt the Germans really admired the generous move by Australia. A few colleagues had asked Ingrid if it made her even more proud to be Australian, as her countrymen were so generous. She proudly mentioned that her brother and brother-in-law were in the thick of it, and her colleagues marvelled that someone they knew of was there. They were only six degrees of separation away from the desperate tsunami need, and the practical, real-life response.

People in the world felt the need and were responding to the call in every way they could. In all the bombardment of bad news, to hear of Australia's generosity was very welcome.

chapter sixteen

Emergency Care

If a few hundred car crash victims, some with pneumonia, presented to an Australian Emergency Department in one day, it would make headlines. If some had tetanus too, a police cordon might be formed around the hospital. Yet this, with a few exceptions, is what Norm Gray and Lisa Dillon were effectively faced with every day in Banda Aceh.

In the Emergency Department at Fakinah Hospital, patients were presenting at a rate of at least 300 per day. Norm Gray was running the department in conjunction with an Indonesian urologist. Nurses Karyn Boxshall and Lisa Dillon and SCAT paramedic Jeff Gilchrist were working between the Emergency Department and the ward and there was a mere handful of Indonesian doctors and nurses. It was ridiculously busy, but, as Mother Teresa once said, 'Never worry about numbers. Help one person at a time, and always start with the person nearest you.'

Lisa was an emergency nurse from Westmead. She was married to Chris, a fellow nurse. She was pretty, with golden hair and a big smile. She was in her mid-thirties and always ready with a laugh and a quip. When she had been telephoned by her Senior Nurse Manager late one night and asked to go on a trip, she had initially thought it was an invitation to go on a shopping jolly. This could not have been further from reality but, once the request had been clarified, she was more than happy to go. Lisa had undergone disaster training in the past and had also been to Korea with the Australian paralympic team. Her sense of humour was helping her in Banda Aceh, and it was a boon for the suffering patients, and for her team-mates. She and Norm bounced ideas off each other and kept morale high. They shared the desire to keep patients pain-free and cared for in a way which most resembled what they could offer back at home.

Norm Gray and the urologist initially did not think much of each other's skills. Their techniques and approaches to patient care were different. Everything— how they diagnosed, triaged and treated—was different. It was training, it was culture, and it was influenced by resources and expectations. 'Oh, no—this is bloody hopeless,' thought Norm on day one. His heart sank. He had a huge job ahead of him but this doctor, in whom he had no confidence as far as professional trust was concerned and whose methods seemed so unorthodox, was his stable-mate. In Australia, where two doctors are working side by side, they share observations, advice, and often assist each other. If there is time, they may quickly run a treatment plan past the other to see if they agree, or have a professional comment to make. They would make sure that the patient was being assisted to the maximum degree. In Fakinah, the other doctor was keeping information to himself, even though this might compromise the care being provided. It was frantically busy, but the frost was palpable. Any advice sought or offered by Norm was rebuffed. No clinical opinion on a case was ever proffered. But Norm persevered. Polite, inclusive, and clinically very competent, he wore the other man down. After the first few days, the urologist began to say good morning to Norm when he arrived, and the forbidding scowl was eventually replaced with a smile. The ice was beginning to melt.

Many of the cases they saw had multiple dirty wounds, with infection creeping into the muscle layers, fat and tissue. One day the urologist asked Norm to give some sedation to a patient. The wound was so ingrained with dirt that cleaning was not going to help. It would become a vat of bubbling pus if they didn't do something. Norm gave the patient ketamine while the urologist scrubbed the wound with a hard brush dipped in iodine. It was one of a myriad similar cases, but now at least they were working together.

Norm adopted the technique of cutting away dead flesh with a scalpel or a pair of scissors, whilst he had the patient prone on a white plastic body bag, on a bench. Sometimes there was an abscess which needed to be pierced and drained. He would open it to let the brownish 'sewer water' out. Sometimes gas would escape and, more often than not, greenish-brown pus. He always anaesthetised first.

One day he had watched speechlessly as an unknown Asian doctor walked up to a sitting, fully conscious patient and started cutting her mangled foot with a blade. She shrieked, as one might expect. It was spine-tingling and it made Norm ill. Reacting instinctively, from the core of everything he stood for, he grasped the doctor by the front of his shirt. 'I'll take it from here,' he said firmly, while the patient sobbed gratefully. The seeming savagery was what shocked Norm. He was a tough Aussie bloke, renowned for his calm, quiet nature, but he was knocked about by

Tagged patients at Fakinah awaiting medevac to Medan. Their departure was delayed after a plane hit a water buffalo. Every space was used, including verandahs.

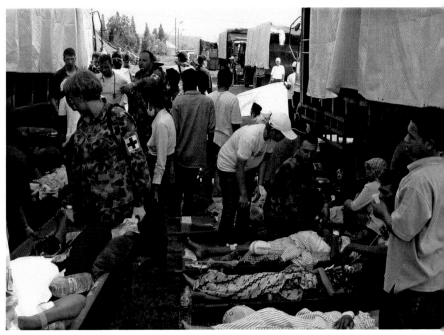

Above: What Colin Powell saw first-hand: Griggsy directing patient traffic at Banda Aceh airfield.

Below: Can there be a harder decision than to remove a child's leg? What makes it bearable is when a young life is saved, as here.

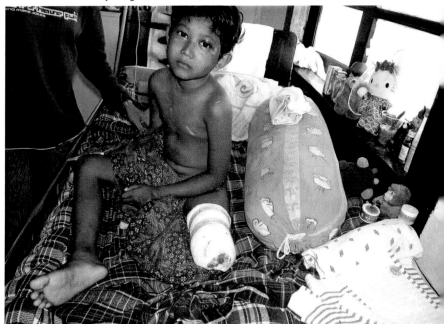

Above left: CASTA leader Mike Flynn briefs the team. **Above right:** Wing Commander Bill Griggs in the Kesdam transport truck, focusing on the day's work ahead.

Below left: Lieutenant Commander Bernard York RAN, always ready to help. **Below right:** Annette Holian at SIM airfield, with signature fluffy pink stole and pearls.

Above: New South Wales' tsunami relief volunteers receiving Meritorious Service Awards at Government House from Governor Marie Bashir, then Premier Bob Carr, and then Health Minister Morris Iemma.

Below: L to R: James and Valeria Branley, Governor Bashir, Paul Dunkin, his wife Sophie and baby Pierce Dunkin.

this seemingly primitive outlook towards a fellow human being. He heard many screams from elsewhere in the department, but he couldn't be everywhere at once.

He was aware that the theatres were always in demand and so, whatever procedures could be performed in the Emergency Department, to quell the flow to theatre, were being done. If the debridements were serious, or if amputation was required, he sent the patient to the ward for inclusion in the surgery list. But you had to be careful that the patient didn't die of septic shock in the meantime. Pustulent wounds and lung infections could be a fatal combination.

Sometimes a patient presented with suspected tetanus. This horrific disease causes paralysis as the muscles throughout the entire body gradually stiffen. One young man admitted to the ward became so stiff he could no longer open his mouth to drink. They gave him fluids (Hartmann's fluid or saline) intravenously and pain relief. Eventually, his chest wall hardened and breathing was no longer possible. They put a tongue depressor in his mouth to prevent him grinding and eventually crushing his own teeth together. He foamed at the mouth and died with what was known as a 'devil's grin' or 'sardonicus', a contorted grimace caused by the muscles of the face being pulled back into an unnatural grin. It was the visible irony of the disease that the patients grinned in this manner, while they suffered greatly and died a ghastly and drawn-out death.

Tetanus usually took two to twelve days to manifest itself, if the spores were in the body. These came from the soil and manure in the community's farms, which the tsunami had washed everywhere. When patients presented in the Emergency Department, Norm was usually told by the accompanying family member that the person was suspected of having tetanus. The team tried to make them as comfortable as possible—hydrated and pain-free—but they could not cure them as they simply did not have the resources. Such patients eventually became hyper-sensitive, at the slightest sound or movement, even a hand clap or when brushed by someone walking past.

Tetanus was almost never seen in Australia. There had been one case reported in New South Wales in 2003, none in 2002 and none in 2001. Most Australian cases tended to be older women who were never immunised. They were too old to have been given it as a regular childhood innocula-tion, and became exposed when tending their gardens in their retirement. It was a cruel disease and it relied upon a decent vaccination program to keep it at bay in a population such as the one in Aceh province. It was not something you might have looked for immediately, but Norm had seen cases when he had worked in Rwanda and recognised it.

There was one thing which didn't faze Norm at Banda Aceh—earth tremors. Coming from New Zealand he was used to them. Norm was a major in the Australian Army Reserve. He had studied at Otago University in Dunedin and ended up in Perth, where he was a specialist emergency physician at Fremantle Hospital. He was now an Australian, except for the All-Black barracking bit! Fortunately, citizen-ship didn't depend on denouncing this. He had seen a bit in life from his time serving in East Timor and Rwanda.

His dad had died when he was in Rwanda. That was hard. Norm was a father himself with two boys, Connor aged twelve and Rory aged nine. And unless his sons happened to play one day for the Wallabies, he would keep his secret rugby loyalty and never switch. The boys' Scottish mother had left her husband, Norm, three years ago. The boys loved their dad, but the Army was never going to be their choice of career, they assured him. Why go out bush and get dirty and tired, when you could be having fun on a ship or in a jet, they asked him. His boys made him laugh.

By the end of his time at Banda Aceh, Norm and the urologist had developed a genuine admiration for each other. They had each learned a great deal from each other. Norm found his colleague tireless—on duty from early morning and there all day, never taking breaks and never seeming to leave at night. The patients they were seeing and the work they were dealing with was beyond what normal doctors in everyday life ever have to deal with, yet they were managing, they were developing a strong professional relationship and even eventually sharing the odd macabre joke to alleviate the tension.

Karyn Boxshall divided her time between Norm's Emergency Department and the ward at Fakinah Hospital. An emergency nurse from the Royal Perth Hospital in Western Australia, she had always wanted to work in a disaster situation, where her emergency skills would be used to their utmost. For her, Banda Aceh was the ultimate. It was all she had ever trained for.

Every day they would do a ward round. Sometimes they would be accompanied by some of the Indonesian nurses and doctors. The strangest aspect for Karyn, in this climate of very unusual happenings and experiences, was the total absence of paperwork. Paper administration dominated her practice in Australia. Here, radical life-saving care was the paramount concern and the luxury of documentation came second. Pens, paper and clipboards were simply unavailable.

Each day, as they changed dressings on wounds, they wrote on the dressing what date they changed it and when it had to be next changed.

Initially rather sceptical about what type of people she would be tending in Banda Aceh, Karyn soon realised that the Acehnese were unusual people. Given their injuries and personal tragedies, it would have been completely under-standable if they had been irritable and incessantly complained. Instead, each day the patients on the ward greeted her with happy smiles and warm appreciation. Their situation had not crushed their spirits at all. She couldn't quite believe it, but it was very rewarding for the nurses.

Karyn, Lisa and Adrian went through the ward, inoculating dozens of patients against tetanus. The babies cried but the team persisted—they would thank her one day, she thought, if they could understand.

After days of no real showering, no shampooing, no blow-drying, Karyn's hair stank and was becoming slimy. Normally her long blonde hair was glossy and swung freely, shining as she walked. The sweat build-up, com-bined with insect repellant, sunblock and particles which landed in the humidity on her blonde mane had made it thick and dull. Her hair had become so rancid that she wanted to retch one night when she rolled over on it and breathed in the smell. She had one of the other nurses braid it back away from her face. She had also developed painful cysts under her arms from blocked sweat glands from anti-perspirant build-up, and possibly from the doxy-cycline she was taking for malaria protection. There was one small plastic, low-walled camp shower in the court-yard which the fireys had set up with a bag of water at the top which sat warming in the sun. The bag hung low due to the weight of the water, so you had to crouch to get under it. Smelly water trickled out of it and you ended up hot and sweaty just trying to get washed.

On 6 January, the day before the team left, it rained heavily. The monsoonal rains were starting, making life even more difficult for the many homeless Acehnese. They were sheltering under bridges and in damaged buildings, attempting to cook food outdoors and stay in good health in remote areas along the West Sumatran coast, far from support. The last thing they needed were chest infections, fungal problems and diseases, which thrived in moist, muddy conditions where sewers over-ran and drinking water became contaminated. Puddles were a perfect haven for malaria-carrying mozzies to breed in.

For some the deluge was welcome for one reason—you could have a long-awaited shower in it. Terry Jongen offered Karyn his shampoo and conditioner, sweet-smelling liquid gold. Karyn was concerned about going in the rain in her swimming costume, not wishing to offend her devout Muslim patients. But James Branley (in his best infectious diseases physician capacity) urged her, as an important health measure, to take advantage of the opportunity to have a thorough wash-down. Tentatively, she walked out of the door of the hospital, self-conscious in her swimming costume top and board shorts. The patients all burst out laughing at seeing her becoming drenched. But it was utter bliss.

chapter seventeen

Last Days at Fakinah

Dr James Branley was making headway on the ward at Fakinah. One of the first patients he had seen after arriving was Morita, a young woman of about 27 years of age. She was septic with pneumonia, after inhaling seawater in the maelstrom of the tsunami, and was near death. Her lungs were heavily congested and she was coughing up thick, brown 'gutter water', while gasping for breath. The water had been contaminated with everything imaginable—sewage, fuel, soil, bits of wood and metal. It was salt water, so it burnt her lungs too. Then, as so often happened, the fluid in her lungs became infected, killing off some of the lung tissue, which is normally clear, pink, vibrant and spongy. If you could have seen these lungs, they would have looked brown, partly necrotised, slimy and flaccid. Morita was very dehydrated and had not eaten for days. Her husband, who had survived, encouraged her to live.

James' work overlapped with that of Norm Gray in the Emergency Department, and with the surgeons, Sudhakar and Annette. He was also helped greatly by a doctor who had come from Switzerland, Dr Rolf Streuli.

Some of the patients James cared for were medical, meaning that they had illnesses caused by the tsunami. Many had pneumonitis (inflammation of the lungs), or aspiration pneumonia, infected eyes and eardrums. At one stage he, Lisa and Karyn went through the ward with the Indonesian staff and put drops in every patient's eyes and ears. The filthy tsunami water had seeped into these sockets and pockets in their bodies.

Some of James' patients had injuries which required an operation, and were classified as surgical patients. The truly unlucky had both illness and injury, which had a big impact on how well and how quickly they would recover. A lung disease, which makes you weak and struggle to breathe, is hard enough to bear without having a painful, infected leg wound as well.

Fitri was a young girl and a surgical patient in the care of Sudhakar and Paul. She had bled so much that her haemoglobin level had dropped to 3.5 (normal is 13). There was no blood to give her. She also appeared to have had some sort of malnutrition prior to the tsunami and, by the time the team saw her, she had not eaten for days. She had deep, penetrating injuries from tsunami flotsam. Pockets of gas had started to form in the poor girl's legs, which were becoming like popping bubble-wrap (this is called 'crepitus' and can be a sign of gangrene). She had to have her wounds attended to surgically.

James would never forget Fitri because, as she recovered, she would beam at James and the other team members. Despite her suffering, she would always give them her best smile. The TV journalists wanted to film her as a poster-girl for the tsunami. James, always conscious of people's feelings, said to them, 'Perhaps you should ask her first?' Startled, they did. She was still a patient with the right of privacy. 'No,' she said. So they didn't.

Meulwati was eighteen, but looked even younger. She had pneumonia and had become hypoxic (her brain had become oxygen-starved) in the water which had engulfed her. She was constantly hallucinating, re-living the tsunami, every day. James felt intense compassion for her. He used the oxygen saturation meter on her, and guarded it carefully—it was the only one, and it was vital equipment.

James and Karyn would do ward rounds together, where Karyn would note what happened and where possible get it put into patient records by one of the Indonesian staff. The charts were kept in the office, rather than at the end of each bed—since the beds were stretchers on the floor, there was no place for normal hospital apparatus.

Zahara was a twelve-year-old girl, in hospital because she had aspiration pneumonia from inhaling tsunami water. Her uncle was with her. He was the only surviving adult in her life. James needed to get patients like Zahara to move the dense build-up of fluid in their lungs.

Annette had given him a great idea she had seen used in Vanimo, Papua New Guinea. James made a bubble 'machine' out of a bottle of water and a straw, with a tiny dash of green (or sometimes red) cordial added to colour the water. The patient would blow through the straw and try to get bubbles happening. To do this they had to take big deep breaths and blow hard, which in turn exercised their lungs. It was a very simple, ingenious way of getting sedentary patients to assist their own recovery. Some of them were depressed, having lost their families, their homes and so when they finally got a hospital bed, they often lay there stagnating, which was dangerous because phlegm would settle in their lungs and fester.

This was another example of the team's improvisation skills. Their resourcefulness was evident everywhere. The SCAT paramedics, Jeff Gilchrist and Adrian Humphrey, had solved the problem of few drip-stands by stringing up ropes like ceiling streamers, then successfully hanging the patients' drips from them. Terry Jongen had even managed to create traction for a lady's broken leg, using a weight made from a bottle of water and some cord. The bones had to be gently pulled apart to allow them to knit together neatly and properly. His invention did the trick.

When Bill Griggs turned up at Fakinah on the morning of 4 January to arrange the airlifting of some of the patients to Medan for more comprehensive treatment, he told James, 'I can take about fifteen patients. They need to be stabilised surgical patients, adults only and must not need a relative to accompany them.' He proceeded to go through the ward with Sudhakar to identify suitable patients.

Zahara didn't fit the bill. She was a high-maintenance medical patient, but her chances for survival would improve if she could get some decent, advanced-level medical care. She was sweating profusely, breathing hard, was quite delirious and needed constant monitoring and complex medical attention. She also needed more oxygen than they could spare, and generally more assistance from their minuscule number of staff than they could give her.

James Branley talked to Bill. 'Her chances will be best if she gets out of Banda Aceh to a better-equipped and fully staffed hospital,' he said. After some persuasion, Zahara was added to the magic list, much to the relief of her uncle.

To the world at that moment in time she might have been just one person, but to her uncle she was the world. Her transfer boosted the morale of the team enormously. Her young life now had a chance of being saved.

James had another patient, a policeman, with a degloving injury to his foot—the skin and flesh had been peeled off. He had his young daughter with him. 'Here, sweetie,' said James, giving her a dinosaur. 'This is for you!' She smiled and took it curiously. James had grabbed toys from his own children's toy chest as he had frantically packed for the deployment. They were all boy-oriented, given he had four sons, but this little girl didn't seem to mind at all.

James also gave a small green car and a mouth organ to the little boy on the ward who had stolen everybody's hearts—Zulfahmi. On the day before the team left, James took Australian news reporter Jessica Adamson of Channel Seven aside. She had asked if she could help. 'You can help,' he said, 'you might be able to somehow find this young boy's grandmother. You are possibly the only chance he has of finding her.' He gave Jessica a mission—to find Zulfahmi's sole surviving relative.

James was keen to work well with the Indonesians and to be able to relate to his patients. He hadn't been schooled by the Australian Jesuits for nothing. He had learned that you reached out, to be truly kind. You put others and their needs first. You made an effort. This underlying character is what had brought him to Banda Aceh in the first place. That and an understanding and supportive wife, Valeria, who was a doctor herself—an obstetrician—and was also raising their four boys, Hugo, Jack, Liam and Callum.

James had bought a book on Bahasa in Jakarta, studied it on the plane, and he and Paul tested each other. When James arrived at Fakinah, he wrote a list of commonly used Indonesian words on a cardboard box flap and put it on the dormitory wall above the table where everyone charged their mobile phones. Sudhakar added a few extra words to it.

James worked out a way of doing what he needed to do, without causing waves. He dressed down, in Australian-style board shorts, and was always chuckling, always being happy and light-hearted. James had been to the Bali bombing and was uniformed there. Here, he felt less threatening. The Acehnese patients had lived through war, and they connected fear and suffering with uniforms. He wasn't about to compound their misery; they had been through enough already. The reason for the team attending as civilian rather than military made sense now.

The fact that James was an infectious diseases physician and microbiologist, and the Head of the Department of Microbiology for the Nepean and Blue Mountains Pathology Service in New South Wales was something he subordinated for the cause. He had no ego problem, and he was determined to do what he had come here for.

On the ward rounds, he let the Indonesian doctors take the lead. He would whisper in the ear of the resident (junior) doctor what he thought should be done and let the doctor say it aloud as though it were his own idea. He had a close, cooperative relationship with this young doctor and they both realised it was the way to achieve their common goal.

The police ran Fakinah Hospital. James stood to attention whenever they appeared. If he was using his stethoscope, leaning over examining a patient, he would stop, stand upright and snap to attention. He even saluted them. They loved it.

One day, just when the place was starting to become bearable so far as odour was concerned, about 30 TNI personnel in full military uniform brought the horrifically smelly, rotting corpse of the local police chief through the ward, followed by a fascinated gaggle of press. It was one of the many slightly surreal happenings James and those on the ward would witness.

On the whole he was working well with the second Indonesian medical team. They did not seem threatened at all by the presence of the Australians and were happy to trade professional ideas and treatment regimes. There was Dr Andra, the orthopaedic surgeon, who had a heart of gold according to Sudhakar; Dr Bambang the anaesthetist; and Dr Billi the obstetrician, as well as a few general practice doctors and a number of nurses. There was the urologist in the Emergency Department—and Dr Luhut. It had taken Sudhakar some adjustment to get used to the fact that these last two were police doctors and wore side-arms around the hospital. It was a tribute to the Indonesians who had come from outside Aceh to help that they were there to assist their compatriots, despite having been officially at war with them days before the tsunami hit.

By about day four, James felt the Indonesians were beginning to really relax as they started smiling at this Australian clown of a doctor who wore brightly coloured surf shorts and made the patients laugh. There was one policeman with the job of overseeing the ward; he was so busy he had become extremely frazzled. James spoke to him, 'Go to bed!'

'I cannot! I cannot sleep!' the man replied. He was dozy with fatigue but wanted to keep going.

James prepared him a hot drink with four sachets of coffee, four sugars and some condensed milk. The policeman drank it. It was like a tonic. He pepped up and started buzzing happily around the hospital. Every day after that, he asked James to make him a coffee.

At one particular clinical meeting James was incredulous about certain priorities. The Indonesians were talking about getting a nutritionist. He couldn't quite believe his ears. People talking about the quality of diet when there were people dying of pneumonitis, tetanus, gross infections, severe injuries? Was the nutritionist going to address these people's needs? Fortunately he kept his opinions to himself.

A few days into their deployment, the Australians had finally cleaned the ward to the point where it no longer carried the smell of death and decay. As James was walking through the ward one day, he smelt the most appetising aroma since arriving in the province. Ratpacks were nothing on this, the smell was of freshly sautéed chicken and fragrant steaming rice. Suddenly it became clear to him what had been meant at the meeting—a cook was needed. The patients were starving, some had not eaten for days. Many of them were anaemic and suffering from malnutrition in addition to everything else they were enduring. Now a couple of cooks from the Indonesian island of Kalimantan had arrived. He, like them all, had been concerned with helping the team set up for their own survival, and had concentrated on giving urgent medical care. The patients would eat at last. He offered to swap ratpacks with them; there were plenty of smiles, but no takers.

Lisa and Karyn had made small nursing hats out of face masks and drawn first-aid crosses on them. In the confusion of milling people—staff, media, patients, relatives, friends, students, police and whoever else—there were clearly identifiable nurses to approach with medical problems. The patients were thrilled.

The crowds of people always hanging around the hospital sometimes proved useful. If you needed to move a patient, you only had to point. 'You, you and you, we need you over here.' And suddenly you had ten volunteers lifting the patient with you. There were no hospital porters and no fancy adjustable pneumatic beds on castors. It was all done by the good grace of anyone and everyone.

James noticed that the patients, relatives and visitors did not use a normal greeting with each other. People had all lost family in this tragedy. Instead of 'How are you?' they asked 'How many?'

Taking a patient history was always a challenge because of the language barrier and cultural differences. There were many matters to discuss that would have an impact on their care—the location and nature of their injuries, prospects for recovery, how to take their medicine, any other medical complaints. Prior to surgery, Paul and Annette would point to the place where it looked bad and ask '*Sakit?*' (pain) and where it felt '*Bagus?*' (good). Sudhakar was in a better position as he could speak Bahasa and many Acehnese could speak it also.

Joesra (Yusra) was an interpreter who helped the team considerably. She was a volunteer and she was always at the hospital. Her help and the help of those of the Indonesian doctors who spoke some English was invaluable and helped prevent misunderstandings and misdiagnoses. The Indonesian medical student Marthoenis was also a great help. He could also speak English and would interpret for them, as well as always being on hand to help move a patient, clean something, or hold a piece of dressing.

Apart from injuries and normal non-tsunami-related medical problems, there were many diseases which were caused by the disruption of proper sanitation—from the consumption of affected food, which couldn't be stored properly and festered in the heat, or was not cooked in a clean environment; or from the contaminated water supplies, or the mosquitoes breeding in the many puddles created by the tsunami and the monsoonal rains. James was on the lookout for everything from less commonly known diseases such as shigellosis, meloidosis, amoebiasis and leptospirosis to typhoid, cholera, tetanus, rabies, malaria and dengue fever. He had made the laboratory at Fakinah useful, testing patients' bodily fluids to enable more targeted antibiotics to be prescribed for various infections and lung conditions.

James would draw the drugs he needed from the pharmacy. The Australians had brought these supplies with them, but they diplomatically allowed the Indonesians to be in charge. The pharmacy, run by a Dr Rummer, was on the ground floor, beneath where the team slept.

The Indonesian team was very hard-working. Apart from the specialist doctors and a number of nurses, a band of general helpers had arrived, wearing bright orange-yellow T-shirts. They tidied the hospital grounds, emptied bins, and swept corridors. They used stiff brooms made of twigs tied together. It worked a treat.

The hospital was looking colourful, almost festive, as it was festooned with damp clothing which had been washed and was hanging on lines strung up everywhere.

Relations were now good between the Australians and the Indonesians. The second team which had arrived were keen to work well with the Australians. CASTA, for their part, no longer felt as though they were treading on someone else's turf.

James was usually the only Australian doctor on the ward when the surgeons and anaesthetists were operating at Fakinah and Norm was in the Emergency Department. Alan Garner was the other designated emergency physician in the original Bravo team.

Dr Alan Garner was the Medical Chairman for NRMA CareFlight/New South Wales Medical Retrieval Service and spent about a third of his time at Nepean Hospital as an Emergency Medicine Specialist. He had completed a Masters in Emergency Planning and Disaster Management and had written on the topic. He had been in Brisbane in late December when Dr David Cooper called him. He had had to hastily organise colleagues to cover his work and then he flew down to Sydney to get the CareFlight cache ready and join the team. His wife Marie was very under-standing, as were their children Lucy (six) and Daniel (four). Alan had previously been summoned to the Bali disaster and afterwards he and Marie had discussed the issue of the 'rushed departure'—it went with the territory.

CareFlight is a registered charity which runs an emergency helicopter, road ambulance and fixed-wing medical retrieval service in New South Wales, employing doctors who specialise in anaesthetics, emergency medicine and intensive care. CareFlight has also developed its own disaster cache to support an Urban Search and Rescue (USAR) response.

The cache for the USAR taskforce had been designed to look after the medical team first, then ten critical patients, fifteen moderate patients and 25 patients with minor needs. The underlying principle was that the patients had to be extricated from whatever disaster had befallen them and then, after immediate stabilisation, be handed over for care of a longer term nature.

The CareFlight cache had been packed and ready to go by the Tuesday evening, 28 December. It would not be sufficient on its own, so Emergency Management Australia (EMA), faxed through a 29-page list which would theoretically provide medical care for 500 people for three days.

Alan Garner and Ken Harrison had gone to Westmead Hospital, where the pharmacist and nurses bent over backwards to fulfil the list's requirements. Drugs, bandages, dressings, urinals, bedpans, syringes. The order was huge and filling it took all that night. Supplies were also being flown up pronto from the Commonwealth Serum Laboratory (CSL). Some of the much-needed diagnostic tools, monitoring equipment, surgical equipment and anaesthetic equipment were already in the CareFlight cache, but in the meantime the equipment to outfit the team was being hastily and methodically put together down at Greenacre Fire Station. The fireys there were working solidly, assembling a cache of gear which included everything from tents, sleeping bags, water, rationpacks and eating utensils, to torches, protective clothing, shovels, brooms and electricity generators. Everything the team needed to enable them to live in a 'hostile' environment.

Once they arrived in Aceh, Alan judged that his services would be best utilised working initially with Ken, sorting and managing the cache of equipment. In Bali, he had seen what a shemozzle could result when stores were not managed carefully. You ended up with a bunfight, with people rummaging at random through boxes, and no supplies that you could find.

He was impressed when he later saw how the Fire Brigade managed their stocks. Every item had to be requested and then it was handed over. Whatever came back was cleaned, re-charged or whatever was needed, and then it was returned to the store. He and Ken were not going to let Banda Aceh become a stores debacle. You could use things to their maximum benefit, even if you were short on supplies, if you managed what you had with extreme care. Alan stayed with Ken for the first few days at Banda Aceh until the stores system was humming.

Then he could focus on patient care. One particular patient affected him greatly. This patient was a 28-year-old man, an engineer who spoke English quite well. He was critically ill with aspiration pneumonia, and was becoming more and more short of breath. He was in respiratory distress, sweating profusely and his ability to take in air was severely compromised. Despite his condition, he was determined to give an account of what had happened. His village had less than 2000 people in it. The tsunami had washed him out to sea, where he floated 2 kilometres off the coast, hanging on to a piece of wood. He then managed to work his way back to shore, a slow process which took him over six hours. He found that there was not one building left standing and not a single living person in his village. It was deathly quiet. He walked north along the coast for two days, until a fishing boat picked him up. He had then been flown in from the west coast by the US Navy.

Alan gave him antibiotics and supplemental oxygen, tried to make him as comfortable as possible, and help him rest. This patient really needed around-the-clock intensive care, with three nurses on successive shifts devoted just to him and specialised medical equipment—like ventilators and monitors—which they simply didn't have. He died during the night. This was a very sad outcome for those on the ward. They had tried to save him, and having heard that he had been the last known survivor in his village and had gone through purgatory to reach them made it even harder to take. The media had swooped on this man. A picture of him and Alan appeared in *Who* magazine in Australia, as the story had epitomised the spirit of the survivors of the tsunami.

Alan felt hollow after the man's death. You could rationalise it as an inevitable event all you liked, but you still wanted to have saved that life. Afterwards, he stood in the hallway at Fakinah, feeling the dull weight of the loss. Running over everything he had done, thinking about the hopelessness of unavoidable mortality. Wishing the man could have survived. The man had the spirit and the will to do it—why hadn't he lived? He had made it thus far.

As Alan rested against the wall, James Branley went busily past. James noticed his distressed team-mate—he would never forget that look on his face. James stopped, put his hand on Alan's shoulder, and offered a few words of comfort. They shared a quiet moment. They had all 'been there'. There was nothing you could do about it.

In the last few days in Banda Aceh, the team commandeered the airconditioned offices upstairs at the back of Fakinah Hospital. There was enough sleeping space for six people. To decide who would get a spot, they all went into a ballot.

Ken Harrison told Paul that he had won a spot. Paul asked, 'Who put me into the ballot? I didn't want to go into the ballot!' Ken had put all 28 names into the ballot. It offered respite from sleeping in the crowded, stiflingly warm dormitory, with its nightly nasal orchestra. Paul felt that someone who worked in the heat all day should have the benefit of it. After all, he was working in Fakinah's operating theatre, which was cooler than many other places.

Rosie Clifton had also won a spot upstairs. These were the best of nights for Rosie. She had worked extremely hard and now she could actually sleep properly, out of the oppressive heat.

It was the evening of 6 January and Mike Flynn was pacing like a fractious lion. He had given the Sigli Three—Annette Holian, Brian Pezzutti and Ray Southon—strict instructions: leave at four, so you will be home before night falls and the curfew comes into effect. Travel after dark was forbidden in Aceh province and the UN had required permits for their personnel to travel outside the metropolitan area. The province was controlled strictly; the ceasefire between GAM and TNI was being managed tightly, to be effective. Mike had also heard that there had been another shooting incident out in Aceh province, and he was not taking any chances.

But where were they? Frankly, all in the team were a bit concerned, but couldn't do anything. They knew this one was pretty much completely on Mike's shoulders. Some tried to take his mind off it, discussing the team's departure from Banda Aceh, scheduled for the next day. There were many aircraft movements, particularly as dignitaries and world figures were beginning to arrive. The possibility that the airfield would be closed and no departures permitted when they were due to go was a reality they had to deal with mentally. They wanted to get home to their families—and get there safely. The earth tremors were still a constant variable, which could change anything at a moment's notice. Nothing was guaranteed.

Mike knew the Sigli Three had to get back somehow, they knew the whole CASTA team was about to pull out, and that they were all leaving together at first light. He ran over some scenarios in his mind. If they had broken down on some dodgy road in the dark in strange territory, could he muster the resources at short notice to go and find them, rescue them and return them in time for their flight out? Would he be placing more people at risk? Oh, for a portable NRMA road service! He began the sketch of a backup plan in his mind. The possibility of them being caught up in a hostile situation—a kidnapping or worse—was not something he could seriously dwell on right now.

Meanwhile the three had wrapped up surgery at Sigli Hospital at around 4 p.m., as planned, but had been way-laid by the MSF and their hosts, who invited them to stay for a celebratory champagne. It was Brian's birthday and it seemed boorish to decline. They were also rather wound up after the whole deployment's intensity. It was probably not going to hurt to stay a little longer. There had been a lot to be sad about, now was a chance to lift the spirits with happy human contact and friendship. Ever-conscious of their ambassadorial role, they decided to seize the brief opportunity with both hands.

After an hour or so they set off. Night fell as they drove the couple of hundred kilometres back to Banda Aceh. The mobile phones were not working, but Annette managed to send an SMS to Mike.

He received it anxiously. Let it be good news.

At first he was startled, but then he roared with laughter. In the dark of the vehicle and unable to see the mobile phone buttons, Annette had texted: 'All Ok. Still inbound. Annette, asian and ray.' It broke the tension for Mike. He realised she must have meant Brian, not 'asian'. They were safe. Hallelujah!

When their car finally pulled in, he barely waited for them to alight before enveloping them all in an overjoyed bear hug. They were surprised — Mike was generally not the demonstrative type — but they were pleased. It was heartening to be so cared about. Then they realised how worried he must have been. They headed up to the dormitory to greet their relieved colleagues and to ensure they themselves also had all their things ready for departure the next day.

chapter eighteen

Coming Home

Paul climbed into the tip-truck. There were no supplies this time, just the team and the team's luggage. It was a scary truck ride back to the airfield. He shouted to the others to duck from time to time, as they swept under branches. Everyone was excited to be going home, but at the same time was sad to be leaving the Acehnese, who needed them.

They had all risen at 5 a.m. on Friday, 7 January. The early morning types—the larks—had woken all sprightly as usual. Today Paul felt slightly nauseous. It was the intense fatigue.

The incoming Team Echo had not arrived yet. They were on a commercial aircraft somewhere, flying from place to place. The CASTA team members had listened at their various briefings to the updates on Echo's movements with heavy hearts, realising with each instalment of news that the chances of a handover were becoming slimmer. There were many theories flying about, not the least of which was that the commercial aircraft was the same plane type as the 737 aircraft which had hit the water buffalo and crashed earlier in the week and was therefore considered too much of a risk to land, necessitating their transfer to an Air Force plane.

This morning the CASTA team members despite being dog-tired were in fairly chirpy moods and when they were advised that an Estonian medical team was due to arrive any day at Fakinah, wrote a welcoming message on a whiteboard, underneath a drawing of an Estonian flag. They also messed with the minds of the incoming Echo team, taping up a sign telling them to 'Please keep BBQ plate clean and put the empty beer bottles in the recycling'.

The CASTA team arrived at the airfield early in the morning and found it congested. It had never been designed for this amount of air traffic. Overnight it had become an international airport. Australians were in the tower, helping out with the traffic controls. It was hair-raising work, and needed cool customers.

The airfield was teeming with forklifts and machinery unloading and loading aircraft holds. The team looked on longingly. If only they had had these when they first arrived. The area surrounding the airfield was also unrecognisable. One hundred and thirty aid agencies had arrived, creating a busy tent city.

Kofi Annan, the UN Secretary-General, arrived at the airfield just before 10 a.m. He was surrounded in the heat and noise by a dense media scrum as he walked, looking unusually uncomfortable and harried, to the terminal. After about half an hour, he returned, still followed by the same gaggle of press, to a helicopter waiting to fly over Banda Aceh so he could see the effects of the tsunami.

The visit of the UN dignitary had the same effect that Colin Powell's visit had two days earlier. No aircraft movement was permitted. The team had to wait at the airfield for more than six hours. They would get to Jakarta some twelve hours after leaving Fakinah hospital.

Having no overlap with the incoming Echo team was a considerable downside to the departure of CASTA. A hand-over would have been preferable as nobody wanted to leave the patients without cover. The team had cared for them in their time of need and the Acehnese thought the care had been very special; they had grown attached to each other.

The day before, one of Karyn Boxshall's patients, a young woman named Patria whose husband and child were missing, had cried. She had heard the team was leaving and she said to Karyn, 'I don't know what I will do now. You are like my family. You have to go back to your families, but you take a part of me with you.' Karyn held Patria's hand and squeezed it. Swallowing hard.

Norm had been at a meeting the day before he left. It was the usual morning clinical meeting. Or so he thought. Then the urologist asked to say a few words. 'Thank you very much,' he said in halting English. 'We appreciated your assistance. We could not have done without you. We will miss you. Thank you for working with us. Thank you for coming and helping us.' He choked as he spoke, and Norm felt his own heart lurch. He knew that their rela-tionship had changed during their time together. He also realised that he and the urologist had never learned each other's names. There had never been the need, and yet they had formed a real bond, working together over long hours tending to desperate patients. By the end, they had shared patient care, swapped ideas, traded advice, helped each other out—holding a scalpel here, lifting a limb there, injecting sedation for each other's patients. One day, after he had returned home, he would learn the good doctor's name was Dr Lufti.

The clerical assistant who kept the records in the Emergency Department spoke up too. 'Thank you,' he said. 'We are sad that you have to go. What you did here was very good.' He paused, and his eyes filled with tears. 'We will not forget you.' Norm almost couldn't bear it, it gave him a tight chest, but he thought it was a lovely farewell. The time here had been fraught with emotion, and he wanted to keep it all inside until he got home. Norm and the urologist had graduated from mutual disdain and suspicion to total professional trust and admiration. It was a lesson for life, for both of them.

Norm didn't say goodbye to the patients, even though he had admitted many of them to the ward and to surgery. It was partly self-preservation, and partly a desire to remain strong in their eyes. He felt that they were best supported by him presenting a strong, professional persona. The nurses were saying goodbye to the patients and seemed to do so happily. Norm couldn't risk showing how he felt, so it was better to slip away. He hated the fact that he was leaving—there was still so much to do.

Sudhakar had braced himself and left Fakinah without looking back. He had his own reasons to feel heavy-hearted. He didn't know what would happen to Zulfahmi, and there was nothing more he could do.

The team left everything—stretchers, bedding, supplies. Paul tried to leave his bag of clothes, but some kind soul packed it into the truck. Shmackers finally found his alarm clock when he was assembling all his gear to leave. He found it tucked in his shoe in one of his bags. Funnily enough, the alarm was set. He realised with horror that it was set for 6.30 a.m. east coast of Australia time, which was about 2.30 a.m. Banda Aceh time. The mystery of the annoying middle-of-the-night alarm was finally solved. He would never be able to own up to that one.

One of the most comforting things about leaving was knowing that they had done their best to set it up well for Echo, the incoming team, who would have accommodation, a pharmacy, a functioning operating theatre with anaesthetic machines which actually worked, a thriving ward and Emergency Department, a kitchenette, a more reliably working water supply, toilets and camping showers. It had been a hard slog moving those 17 tonnes of supplies in disgustingly difficult conditions. Any thought that their set-up and supplies might be in jeopardy was totally demoralising. They left Yusra, their kind interpreter, in charge.

Sudhakar was at the airfield, still wondering about Zulfahmi and what fate would befall him, when suddenly he saw Paul Van Buynder walking beside the runway, carrying Zulfahmi in his arms, followed by an entourage of reporters. They had earlier sent an SMS to Sudhakar: 'We have Zulfahmi and Yusra with us. Will be at the airport in 15 mins. Jessica, Ch 7', but René had borrowed his phone to call Switzerland so Sudhakar had never seen this message. It all came as a delightful surprise. Sudhakar was overjoyed to see Zulfahmi. The little boy felt the same way—this kind doctor had made him better. Now they could have a proper goodbye.

As Sudhakar and Zulfahmi were being interviewed, concerned team members questioned Yusra. 'Weren't you taking care of our stuff?' they asked.

'Yes!' she replied. 'But the police told me "Thanks very much, we'll take care of it from here".' Some of the team members were very worried that the supplies might be stolen, but Liz reassured them, reminding them of the police chief who would shoot any would-be thieves. They were later advised by the Echo team that everything was present and accounted for on their arrival.

As Sudhakar hugged Zulfahmi, he saw Paul Dunkin watching and called him over to join in. Paul was watching this happy scene from afar, but he had to protect his own heart here. He had his own life to live after this, and it would have been just one wrench too many. He smiled and waved goodbye from a distance. Sudhakar understood. Zulfahmi smiled.

Sudhakar thought about Zulfahmi on the flight to Jakarta. The last he had heard, Jessica was still trying to track down the boy's grandmother or any other distant, living relatives. Sudhakar was fretful about him—he knew there was a risk that he would never find any family again or that he would be picked up by the Muhammadiyah group, which was an Islamic group operating orphanages.

Sudhakar had approached the Americans at the airfield the morning of the day CASTA was leaving. The Americans were staging retrievals up and down the coast and were in the best position to help. Perhaps one of their helicopters could include this in a mission? He had urged US Lieutenant Lisa Peterson, the US Navy doctor on board the USS *Lincoln*, to: 'Please help find a relative of this child.' He explained his concerns for the child, mentioning his darkest fears—of child abuse, or that the child would be recruited into a terrorist group. 'I will talk to my superiors and get back to you,' Lisa had said. 'I cannot promise anything.' It was an awkward situation. Nobody knew where the grandmother had been left behind, and the language barrier meant that it was hard to work it all out. There were hundreds of people who had been collected, from many places along the coast. There were thousands, in all sorts of different accommodation. Their homes and streets were gone. How were they going to find this child's grandmother?

Sudhakar had taken photographs of Zulfahmi on his digital camera and given his whole camera plus its memory stick to the Americans, so they could show villagers the child and find the one living relative. After farewelling the team out at the airfield in the morning, Yusra went back to Fakinah Hospital with the Americans and Zulfahmi. There they discovered a patient who was a village elder from Zulfahmi's region. Together they pored over a map and obtained detailed information about where best to search. It was like looking for a needle in a haystack.

Some of the team slept on stretchers in a tent at the airfield, waiting for the flight to leave. It was hot and tedious but their weary bodies didn't notice. They were finally allowed to depart. They boarded the plane and Sudhakar turned his phone off. There really was no point in getting your hopes up. It was the end of the deployment and, whilst it would have been very satisfying, it was probably not meant to be. He would get on with life but never forget the small, lonely boy who had embodied the true sorrow of the tsunami. Zulfahmi had affected them all deeply.

Sudhakar told himself that, in the scheme of things, it was just another child's welfare. He rationalised—many had died, this one was lucky to be alive. Who knew where he would end up? The community would surely look out for him. But Sudhakar couldn't help how he felt—he loved his own sons very much and couldn't help feeling anxious for this child who would now have no love in his life, at a time when he needed it most. Zulfahmi was recovering from surgery on his injuries. Sudhakar felt strongly that no child was 'just another child'. Who knew what one particular life was destined for? It was such a shame that this story couldn't end more positively. He would just have to *get over it*.

Leaving the airport in Jakarta that evening was a shemozzle. Some of the team members left the plane, followed by some Acehnese refugees, followed by more team members. The Australians and Acehnese haphazardly filled two buses. Luggage was intermingled even though destinations were different. The two separate groups should have been put on two separate buses, but it hadn't worked out that way.

The team had depleted its reservoir of cheerfulness. All they wanted were showers and sleep. Now that they were close to it, the delay and kerfuffle were torture. It was a slow, irritating trip through many boom-gates. Each stop to let people off meant discussions and raking through bags searching for which belonged to whom. It was tough on everyone. Nobody needed this; they had all been strung out enough.

Sudhakar turned on his mobile when he boarded the bus, on the way to the hotel in Jakarta. It beeped again and again, interrupting his morose reverie. SMS messages from Jessica. 'Chopper due back in halfa. Has 5 evacuees but not sure who. They're going to try again first thing tmrw if they don't get her 2nite.' The very next one read: 'GOT HER! We r on our way to the hospital.'

Sudhakar leapt for joy and ran around the bus, showing the message to members of the team. Everyone was thrilled. Zulfahmi had somehow found his beloved grandmother, with a bit of help from some Australians and Americans.

The team all knew that Sudhakar had grown close to this child and that the rescue had been a long shot.

Marj and Paul chatted excitedly; everyone was beaming. This was great news. This was unbelievable. They were incredulous. Lisa Dillon was thrilled. Zulfahmi had been Karyn's and her patient on the ward, and she too had grown very attached to the plucky little boy. In her eyes, this was the best thing that had happened on the entire trip.

The next SMS beeped. 'Of course . . . we went to 5 villages—she was in the last. Amazing pictures, very sad. When Zulfahmi saw her, reality set in. He says he can now sleep.' Sudhakar punched the air with delight.

The Western Australian contingent did not get to stay overnight in Jakarta despite being bone-weary. The delays had gobbled up any time for relaxing. The next direct flight to Perth took off in a few hours, but then there would not be another until Sunday night, two days away. They desperately wanted to get home and see their families. The other option would have been to go via Sydney the next day, which would add hours and hours of travelling time to their trip. Terry didn't mind leaving now, it would let him attend a motorbike race. They rushed into the hotel, had a shower, ate something and raced out to the airport for a flight to Perth via Darwin.

The goodbyes were rushed. Inadequate. Nothing could be said which really summed up anything. Nobody knew when they would see each other again. They had formed very close bonds and they had been in a surreal environment together. They had laughed, teased, eaten many meals, slept, worked, helped, cut into people, cried together. Now it was over, and they hadn't even thought about what 'over' meant.

Sudhakar looked out from the bus. The Western Australian contingent had been forced to leave in the middle of a wonderful dinner at the Jakarta Hotel, and were now waiting on the bus, ready to move off. It was dark, but one lone figure had left the sumptuous table to see them off outside. The man stood at attention, and then raised his hand in a farewell salute as the bus pulled away from the kerb. It was their tireless leader, Mike Flynn.

It was a strange feeling going home for the Western Australian seven—Sudhakar Rao and René Zellweger, Norm Gray and Paul Van Buynder, Rosie Clifton, Terry Jongen and Karyn Boxshall. They knew they would never be the same again. They had a bond they would share forever.

Sudhakar's wife, Narelle, bundled her three sleepy young boys into her car. It was early morning and still dark as they made their way to the airport. At arrivals, Paul Van Buynder came out before Sudhakar. He walked into his wife Jan's arms and his protective resolve gave way. Good-humoured throughout the whole deployment, the intensity of what he had experienced—and undoubtedly overwhelming fatigue—had finally got to him. He had maintained his cheerfulness the entire time, keeping buried in his heart all that he had seen and been part of. Now that he was home, amid love and safety, it surfaced.

Narelle Rao turned away as she saw Paul's whole body shudder, not wanting to intrude on such an intimate moment. Privately she was concerned about whether Sudhakar would be a complete basketcase. From what she knew of Paul Van Buynder, he had never struck her as a particularly demonstrative person. Sudhakar was more emotional. She worried as she waited. You wanted to support the effort but you didn't want to lose your husband's psychological wellbeing by doing it.

A smiling Sudhakar walked out. He was very happy to see her and his boys. He was fine. He was still Sudhakar, but he carried many stories to share with his wife. One in particular was rather special; it was about a brave little boy called Zulfahmi.

Paul Dunkin, and a few of the others in the team who were still awake following a lengthy after-dinner debrief, remained talking until late in the bar at the hotel in Jakarta. Sherryn Bates had outdone herself again. The best champagne and beers on the house. A well-dressed local Indonesian, sitting with friends, observed them for a time and eventually came over and introduced himself to Paul, as he stood ordering drinks at the bar. 'Where have you come from?' he asked. 'What have you been doing?' The team looked fairly haggard.

Paul explained that they were Australians who had come to help in Banda Aceh after the tsunami. How were they doing up there, the man wanted to know. Paul said they were doing it tough. They talked for a time about the Australian relief effort and the Acehnese people, this man's fellow countrymen. After a while, the Indonesian's friends came over and each of them shook Paul's hand. 'Thank you,' they said. 'Thank you.'

Nobody had said anything like this at this stage. It didn't compute that people would thank him. Paul hadn't even thought about what had been done as something worthy of thanks. He wobbled inside now. This was very special. These thanks were sincere and personal, and they came from Indonesians.

Liz sat next to Paul on the Herc between Banda Aceh and Jakarta. It was noisy, they couldn't hear each other talk, so they all passed around photos of their families instead. Paul sat next to Alan Garner for the Jakarta to Sydney leg. Qantas, of course.

Paul sat in the plane seat and tried to relax, but he was in turmoil. Strangely disturbing thoughts were writhing around his tired brain. Don't go there, Paul told himself, but the thoughts persisted. He had been inexplicably torn inside when he had been told it was time to leave Banda Aceh. He knew that getting a flight in or out of the place was horrendously difficult. The incoming team was going through a tortuous time just getting there. When CASTA managed to tee up the flight out, the team had to seize the opportunity — the next chance might not have been for days. The chaos and uncertainty which always accompanies disasters was multiplied ten-fold for this one.

The fact that the medical team left without a handover of patient care rankled within Paul. More than that, he was consumed with guilt about leaving the patients *at all*. The Acehnese, who had done nothing wrong and did not deserve what had happened to them, were suffering intensely. It was beyond human comprehension what had happened to them, and here he was, *running out on them*. It upset him deeply, but he couldn't express it to anyone. He did not even know where to start. These thoughts and emotions, powerful and distressing as they were, tumbled around in his head. Even as he adjusted his body in the plane seat, feeling his weary muscles ache, he felt angry at himself for having *one thought* about his own, pathetic, bodily comfort.

His head was bursting with the stress of concealed torment. He had no idea that these reactions were normal.

He wanted to crawl into the seat-pocket in front of him and shed all the tears he had kept bottled up in Banda Aceh. The pragmatic side of his brain tried to talk calmly over the screaming emotional side. He tried to listen—he needed to hear it. Needed to hear something *now* which would stop the frenzied self-reproach that had hit him without warning.

The emotional side told him that bodies were still being pulled from the rubble at a rate of a thousand per day when the team left. The garbage mounds throughout Banda Aceh were still there—although they were slowly being moved, cubic metre by cubic metre. The precious few children who survived were being rounded up and questioned by aid agencies in order to establish their identities and histories, with some hope of finding living relatives. The bedrocks of the society—the children and the elderly—had been mostly killed. What was going to fix that? Priceless records and memories had been lost forever. Countless livelihoods had been destroyed. All the institutions which rely on an intact society to function—government, justice, education, security, transport, health—were effectively trashed. These people he was *deserting* were so needy that it defied even broad description, let alone itemisation. In all the tens of thousands of deaths, the team had saved only a relative handful of lives. They had not been able to give the people they had made amputees any paramedical aids such as walking-sticks, wheelchairs, crutches or prosthetic limbs. They knew that the loss of a limb might consign some to a life of poverty and physical incapacitation.

Then the pragmatic side of his mind kicked in. It had to. Paul reminded himself that he and the team had been gathered together in the Christmas holiday season, from all across Australia, and at short notice. Nothing like this had ever been done before. CASTA had been a civilian surgical team, it was a major international disaster, they were the first on the scene to help, and they were completely self-reliant. They had managed to spread their services across three hospitals—Fakinah, Kesdam and Sigli. Mike Flynn had lent himself to the task of coordinating field hospitals arriving subsequently. The team had managed to do their jobs well and stay in good health. Nobody had been injured in the intensely physical, four-fold unloading activity of 17 tonnes of supplies, from plane, to airfield, to trucks, to upstairs at Fakinah Hospital. It was nothing short of miraculous. Dysentery had been kept to a minimum, despite the filthy surrounds and shortage of water for cleaning hands and surfaces. Nobody had gone 'troppo'.

From Paul's own perspective, he had gone there to anaesthetise patients for surgery and had found two dirty operating theatres with two broken anaesthetic machines and no monitoring equipment. Through steady scrounging and tinkering—and the fellow scavenging and fix-it abilities of Watto and Bruce—the three had cobbled together two working machines, and two monitors. He had been able to contribute personally. They all had.

Paul knew that the presence of the team had boosted the morale of the Acehnese. Every life the team had saved was a bonus, when so many had died in that community. More importantly, the team had captured the attention of the world, with the help of the media. The Acehnese would benefit for years from the donations this had triggered.

The team had left a legacy on many levels.

Apart from the surgical contribution, the team had been part of a public health effort which had prevented the possibility of yet another tragic consequence which could have caused further widespread destruction—think cholera, typhoid and other serious, contagious diseases. A measles outbreak was detected and scotched.

They had parted on excellent terms with the Indonesians: with both those in charge and the medical staff. Respect was the cornerstone of every successful relationship. They had managed to find common ground upon which they could respect each other: they were both there to help. They had worked hard and side-by-side. Even with all the language barriers, cultural and religious differences—and the historical and territorial sensitivities—it had somehow worked.

Yes, parting with the patients had been wrenching for the team. The Acehnese were the most stoic and positive people Paul had ever encountered. The memories of their bright faces, their happy greetings each day and their obvious gratitude, would stay with him—stay with them all—forever. The deaths of those they tried so hard to save would be stowed away deep inside, where only such recollections can go.

The team members themselves had done the best that they could. They had all wept at some point—when the raw sadness occasionally engulfed them—but nobody folded. Mike Flynn had briefed them that their aim was to smooth the way for future teams' arrivals and to alleviate suffering, as much as they could. This had been their mission, it had been achieved, and so the mission was then complete. It was time to go. Time to let others take over. It was time, as Paul told himself now, to build a bridge, and *get over it*.

At Sydney airport, I waited with my sister Libby and Liam, Darcy, Francis and baby Pierce. The young lads tore around the private room, which had been thoughtfully set aside for the arrivals from the disaster zone. It was away from the public eye and allowed for distraught reunion scenes to take place without embarrassment. There were friendly personnel from New South Wales Health who gave us a pamphlet about what to expect on Paul's return. Paul had also been given a similar one in Jakarta with a cheery list of medical symptoms to be on the watch for, such as indications of malaria, or something even more dire.

Common reactions described in the pamphlet included feelings of great sadness and grief for what had been witnessed, and for the overwhelming loss of human life and devastation. The traumatic events for which the person had been a participant, even in a saviour role, could leave the person in a state of abnormal alertness, which would prevent them from relaxing and feeling safe again. They might find it difficult to return to normal pursuits and everyday concerns, feeling that they were trivial in comparison to what they had been doing, and because there were people suffering in the disaster zone with incomparably greater needs. It might be hard to under-stand your children squabbling over a toy, when you had seen orphaned children, losing limbs, being strong.

I wondered to myself whether Paul would be okay emotionally as well as physically. I hoped the mission had not been at too high a price. We still had four little boys to raise together. Paul came through the gate and his boys rushed him. He was smiling widely and we all hugged in a writhing family swirl of legs and arms and squeals of delight. Things were looking good.

Paul brought home one souvenir, the little bell he had found on the shore. It had tolled for him and he never questioned it. No man is an island. We are all a part of the human family, the world community. When one part hurts, we all feel it and want to take the pain away. And in one way or another, when this tragedy happened, we showed we would. Quietly and quickly, we did what we could.

Epilogue

CASTA's replacement, Team Echo, left Adelaide on 6 January flying with a commercial airline. Echo expected to arrive in Medan, Sumatra, via Darwin, later that day. They could not obtain air traffic control clearance to land in Medan, so they flew to Batam (an island south of Singapore), Indonesia and then Penang via Kuala Lumpur the next day. Their aircraft was unloaded and the cargo and team transported by truck and bus to Butterworth, Malaysia. They grabbed a few hours' sleep before flying by Herc to Banda Aceh, arriving at dawn on 8 January 2005.

The first operation they performed was emergency surgery for a gunshot wound. They did their first full ward round the following morning. Their role in their time there was to perform reconstructive and restoration surgery — grafts and skin flap operations.

One of the items they brought, in their ten tonnes of supplies, were dog biscuits for the emaciated local dogs.

Echo was headed up by Dr Hugh Grantham.

Epilogue

Team Foxtrot from Queensland, Australia, arrived on the morning of 19 January 2005 and Echo departed a few hours after their arrival. Foxtrot had 25 personnel, with less emphasis on surgical capability and more on public health. Foxtrot was followed by Golf in early February, the last of the acute disaster relief medical teams from Australia. AusAID arrangements are now in place for long-term needs.

The night after Paul and the CASTA team returned home, an international fund-raising cricket match was played at the Melbourne Cricket Ground between teams representing Asia (including Australia!) and the Rest of the World. It was Monday, 10 January 2005. It drew a crowd of around 70 000; Paul watched it on television, as did people in 120 other countries. It raised over $14.5 million for the tsunami relief effort. The CEO of World Vision, Tim Costello, said he was 'blown away' by the level of generosity of contributors. The Packer family gave $3 million. Others gave what they could, and then gave some more, as did many corporations.

Tim Costello gave a run-down of how the money would be spent: 30 per cent on emergency relief, 20 per cent on economic recovery and community rehabilitation, and the remaining half on infrastructure and redevelopment. 'Australia needed to do this. Wanted to do this,' he said, after a charity telethon raised a further $20 million in one night. Generous donations were made continuously over the days and weeks following the tsunami. He reflected the views of many as he went on: 'This is a unity I have never seen in my lifetime.'

A rock concert was held at the Sydney Cricket Ground on Saturday, 29 January to raise money for the tsunami victims. A crowd of 48 000 attended and, by all accounts, it was a knockout success. The money raised, which was estimated at almost $2 million, went to a group of charities including the Australian Red Cross, Oxfam Community Aid Abroad, Unicef and CARE Australia.

MSF was so inundated with donations that they had to begin returning some of it.

Local communities staged their own fundraising activities. Stu Lloyd was the MC at a social night at the West Pymble Bowling Club and raised $46 000. There were countless examples of such activities. One mother started packing boxes in her garage to send overseas. All in all, it has been estimated that over this period the Australian public donated over $200 million to charity. Caritas alone received $21 million.

Although it was never a contest, such generosity inspired other nations and Australia led the field in the amount donated by any government (a $1 billion Australian aid and reconstruction package) until it was announced on Wednesday, 9 February 2005 that the USA was almost trebling its tsunami aid to $US950 million (A$1.2 billion). Germany was incredibly generous, as were Britain, Japan, the Netherlands, Canada and Norway, their donations — both government and private — totalling hundreds of millions of dollars. In addition to funds, many, many countries sent practical aid in the form of surgical teams, NGOs and boxes of aid. Australians also helped in a practical sense elsewhere than Indonesia. In response to Australia's offer of help, the government of the Maldives requested primary care support (general practitioner-style services), Sri Lanka — public health, and Thailand and other places — disaster victim identification services (DVI). Australian teams were sent accordingly.

The Americans' immense practical contribution in Banda Aceh did not go unacknowledged. At the end of January 2005, the Indonesian Army Chief of Staff,

General Ryamizard, made time to visit the USS *Abraham Lincoln* to say a personal thank you to the sailors onboard.

At the request of the Indonesian government, by the end of January 2005, the International Organisation for Migration had agreed to build 11 000 pre-fabricated houses for homeless Acehnese families. Each is to be 36 square metres—not large, but they are only intended for use for up to two years while permanent reconstruction plans are being developed. They will then be able to be dismantled and used elsewhere. Thousands of tents have already been supplied to house some 400 000 families. IOM has a truck fleet which brings in relief and reconstruction loads, requested and co-ordinated with the relief agencies.

By the end of January, approximately 108 000 corpses had been counted in Aceh and another 127 000 people were still declared missing, with at least 400 000 Acehnese refugees needing to be re-located. By April, the Indonesian death toll was 126 915, and 37 063 people were still unaccounted for. The death toll for all eleven affected nations was estimated to be as high as 200 000.

Father Chris Riley, Australian priest and Founder and CEO of Youth Off The Streets, has, together with the State Member for Bankstown, Tony Stewart, founded an orphanage in Aceh. He is working in co-operation with the Indonesian government and with Muhammadiyah, an organisation which represents 40 million Muslims in Indonesia and acts as an aid distributor throughout Aceh Province. They already operate hundreds of orphanages across Indonesia. Sudhakar learned about the aims of this group after his return home and became reassured about their purpose.

Australia sent the ADF (Australian Defence Force), who set up a hospital in Zainal Abidin Hospital, the main hospital of Banda Aceh, cleared out the mud-filled morgue it had become, fixed up the equipment and stayed for ten weeks until it was back on its feet again. HMAS *Kanimbla* arrived on 13 January, fully stocked and full of medical and other personnel.

Prime Minister John Howard visited Banda Aceh on 2 February, and Australia's then Maritime Commander, Rear-Admiral Rowan Moffitt RAN, followed up developments with a visit a month later.

In March 2005, it was announced that President Susilo Bambang Yudhoyono would make an historic visit to Australia. His mission would be an opportunity to thank the Australian people in person for their support during the tsunami crisis. He would attend a meeting of the Australia–Indonesia Partnership for Reconstruction and Development (AIPRD), a joint body formed to administer the aid gift given to the Indonesian people by Australia.

President Yudhoyono's trip, which was planned for Wednesday, 30 March 2005, was postponed when an earthquake measuring 8.7 on the Richter scale rocked Nias, an island off the coast of Sumatra, south-east of Banda Aceh, at 11.10 p.m. on Easter Monday, 28 March, killing an estimated one thousand people and destroying homes and public infrastructure. He visited Australia shortly thereafter, on Sunday, 3 April 2005. In April he signed legislation establishing the Rehabilitation and Reconstruction Agency for Aceh and Nias (BRR). On 18 May, he lifted the state of emergency in Aceh, and on 15 August a peace treaty was signed with GAM.

The New South Wales members of the CASTA team received an award from then New South Wales Premier Bob Carr and Governor Marie Bashir on Thursday, 17 February 2005. The plaque read: 'For a job well and bravely done in responding to the Boxing Day Tsunami,

2004'. The governor told the team that she had received numerous letters and messages from diplomats and envoys of tsunami-affected areas, and also from countries not affected, expressing their gratitude and admiration. On 11 May, team members from all over Australia were awarded recognition certificates from the New South Wales government.

In September 2005, Australia's treasurer Peter Costello, accompanied by his brother Tim, made a goodwill visit to Banda Aceh to witness first-hand how Australian aid was being put to good use. The minister was mobbed by grateful children at a school being re-built with the funds. It was one of numerous such AusAID/AIPRD projects.

There is a gargantuan reconstruction project underway in Aceh, with many contributors including Catholic Relief Services, JRS, World Vision, ACTED, IRC CARDI and many other agencies and governments. It encompasses building thousands of new homes, repairing mosques and setting up community programs for everything from sanitation to education and child protection, to farming and fishing business recovery. UNICEF alone plans to build 230 new schools.

Put simply, the world has rolled its sleeves up for the immense job ahead.

Life has moved on for those who were involved at the outset in this extraordinary humanitarian effort.

Bill Griggs came home and married his fiancée Maree on 4 February 2005. He recovered from a bout of pneumonia which he developed at the end of his strenuous time in Banda Aceh. He continues as the Director of Trauma Services at Royal Adelaide Hospital.

Allan MacKillop was relieved of his Aeromedical Evacuation Operations Officer role in Medan by Squadron Leader Paul McCarthy (since deceased). Alan went back to life as Medical Director of CareFlight Medical Services, on the Gold Coast, where he lives with his wife and three grown children. He remains in the RAAF Specialist Reserve.

Greg Norman left the RAAF on 17 January 2005 and resumed civilian life in Queensland with his wife Sandra and their three young sons. He still serves in the RAAF Specialist Reserve.

Bernard York returned to Sydney from Jakarta on 19 January 2005 and repaired to Naval duties at HMAS *Waterhen*, Waverton.

And as for the CASTA team . . .

Mike Flynn went back to his position as the New South Wales Health Services Functional Area Coordinator for Disasters and Medical Director of the Ambulance Service of New South Wales. He gave a number of talks on the Banda Aceh experience, as did many of the team members.

Paul Shumack went back to RAAF Base, Amberley, and also to building his workshed. He successfully finished it within a couple of months, complete with wiring. He continues to work for the children's charity, Variety Club.

Karyn Boxshall went back to life at the Royal Perth Hospital and her partner Alan, with plans for possible further studies.

James Branley returned to his work as Head of the Department of Microbiology for Nepean and Blue Mountains Pathology Services and gave talks from time to time on Banda Aceh and the medical issues it raised. He and Valeria took their boys north of Forster for some all-important time out.

Bruce Cameron stayed as the Senior Rescue Instructor with the New South Wales Fire Brigades Rescue Section at Greenacre Fire Station. The deployment had not only been relentlessly hard work for the two fireys, it had been unfathomably gruesome. However, along the lines of Paul Hogan's thinking, their view was 'See a shrink? Don't you have any mates?' He and Watto looked out for each other. Bruce painted pictures of what he saw in Banda Aceh, and spoke about some of his experiences at Warrimoo primary school to an enthralled audience of school children.

Rosie Clifton went back to work in nursing and the designing of a new home.

Liz Cloughessy resigned from her post as Clinical Nurse Consultant at Westmead Hospital and began a new career chapter in the New South Wales Health Counter Disaster Unit. She kept in touch with Marthoenis, the young student who had helped CASTA so selflessly at Fakinah. Marthoenis stayed and assisted each Australian team that followed. He was helpful clinically and also as an interpreter. Liz looked for sponsorship for his nursing studies on her return to Australia. She arranged for books to be sent over to him. He chose to write his final year thesis on the psychological effects experienced by people who lost their limbs in the tsunami. In September 2005, Marthoenis graduated with a Bachelor of Nursing.

Rhonda Cowderoy went back to nursing on night shift and to life with husband Bruce.

Lisa Dillon went back to being Nursing Unit Manager at Westmead Hospital Emergency Department. She had made many friends among the team and took time out to catch up with many of them on her return. A highlight of her deployment was being met by her husband at the airport with fresh fruit and much-craved Diet Coke.

Paul Dunkin went back to his work as a cardiac and general anaesthetist at various Sydney hospitals and his role as president of Shore Anaesthetics. The day after he got home, he took his wife and four sons up to a beachside cottage near Forster, close to where James Branley and his wife Valeria and their four boys were holidaying. After an initially hesitant start, James and Paul ended up talking for hours each night about their experience. Paul gave a presentation at the Sydney Adventist Hospital about the relief effort in Banda Aceh. In August he won the *North Shore Times* Father of the Year.

Alan Garner appears on television from time to time, giving the public information about various CareFlight activities. He is endeavouring to gain government and corporate support for a supply cache which would enable the State to respond quickly and capably to a disaster.

Jeff Gilchrist remains a SCAT paramedic with the New South Wales Ambulance Service.

Norm Gray went back to Fremantle Hospital to work and took a month out to travel to New Zealand and then to

Hawaii for a conference. After the fatal SeaKing helicopter crash in Nias, he was asked to replace the late Squadron Leader Paul McCarthy who had been engaged to speak in Fremantle, Western Australia, on the ADF contribution to the tsunami. The talk topic was changed to the Australian civilian contribution, and was made into a memorial occasion to remember and honour Paul McCarthy. Paul McCarthy had replaced Alan MacKillop as the AME receiving officer in Medan in the final days of CASTA's time in Banda Aceh, and then had stayed to work with the ADF in Banda Aceh, before he went to Nias. In August 2005 Norm joined a medical team working in Iraq.

Ken Harrison went back to his multiple roles, which are too many to list, but which include being a consultant to CareFlight and an anaesthetist. He put all the team photographs on CD and made up some T-shirts bearing the logos of the various groups which had contributed people to the effort, such as New South Wales and VicHealth, CareFlight and the New South Wales Fire Brigade, plus the slogan which had made their constant loading, unloading and stacking of boxes bearable — 'Storeman and Doctors Union'.

Annette Holian ended up joining HMAS *Kanimbla* on 1 April 2005, bound for Nias, Indonesia, the island off the coast of Banda Aceh which experienced the earthquake on 28 March. On 2 April, an Australian SeaKing helicopter bringing a medical team from the ship to help in Nias crashed in a field, killing nine service personnel. Annette was on board *Kanimbla* when this happened and was involved in operating on the two crash survivors and also in identifying the deceased crash victims. The ADF Board of Inquiry, before which she would appear, commenced on 6 September.

Adrian Humphrey, SCAT paramedic, on his return went straight into his area office in Wahroonga, New South Wales, where he is currently doing rosters and other bits and pieces of administrative work behind a desk, which is quite foreign to him. He volunteered to do a twelve-month secondment in the office because he needed a shoulder and knee operation this year to restore them after the toll constant action and outdoor activities have taken, all part of the normal hazards of life as a SCAT paramedic.

Terry Jongen went back to his motorcycle racing and to his role as Clinical Nurse Specialist in the Emergency Department of the Royal Perth Hospital. He started his Masters degree in Nurse Practitioner studies.

Paul Luckin went back to work as an anaesthetist in Queensland. He gave many talks to trauma conferences, St John Ambulance, and the local church.

Jeremy McAnulty went back to work as the Director of the Communicable Diseases Branch, New South Wales Public Health. He gave talks on Banda Aceh and sent out a survey to the team to find out what impact the doxycycline had had, and to find out about any other health issues they had experienced.

Brian Pezzutti stayed busy with speaking engagements, emphasising his pride in being Australian. He continues to work as an anaesthetist in Lismore and volunteered for further service following the Nias earthquake, but was not needed at that time. He continues to be very active in New South Wales in improving mental health services. His health test for the needle-stick injury gave him the 100 per cent all-clear.

Marj Raggett returned to work as a nurse at Westmead and travelled to Canada.

Sudhakar Rao went back to being Director of Trauma Surgery at the Royal Perth Hospital, Western Australia, and to life with Narelle and their three boys.

David Scott went back to life as an anaesthetist in Lismore Hospital and his various other roles, including chair of the Anaesthetists Consultative Group to the ADF. It felt strange for him to walk the streets of Lismore and see no piles of rubble, debris and bodies. His brain had normalised the bizarre sights of Banda Aceh.

Peter Sharwood returned from Banda Aceh and started packing almost immediately. He then set out to help in a hospital in Iraq, where insurgents battled for power against the newly elected democratic Iraqi government.

Ray Southon returned to theatre nursing and went to Fiji to build a house for a relative.

Paul Van Buynder resumed his public health role, speaking at various venues about the issues he had been involved in. He spoke as far afield as Alice Springs in the Northern Territory.

Greg Watson (Watto) returned to Greenacre Fire Station too and he and Bruce Cameron continue to work together.

Despite the success of the operation, they analysed it from the perspective of lessons learned and implemented a few changes. The power generators for future deployments will run on diesel, a fuel which can be transported on the aircraft, and collapsible trolleys will be included in the cache. So will more lollies.

René Zellweger returned to his work as a trauma surgeon at the Royal Perth Hospital. His work was greatly appreciated by the team. One day after the team's return, David Scott was talking with Peter Sharwood about the merits of Peter's Swiss army knife. 'We did better than that for Banda Aceh,' David said. 'We took a Swiss Army surgeon (René).'

Normally in a hospital in Australia you have a major, distressing operation sporadically. In Banda Aceh, every case was significant and every case was distressing. The operations were back-to-back and there could be no medical debrief about them—there was no time. While working in the disaster zone, their minds had become so numb that they never really talked about their circumstances. They did not begin to dwell on how it was affecting them. Now, after they had arrived home, gradually, it all came out. How they felt and what they thought of it all. It was cleansing and healthful. And we learned more about our spouses.

What they had witnessed and felt would be a part of them now. Their lives were never going to be the same. Experiences change you. You never view anything the same way again. There was abundance everywhere you looked—robust health, vitality, safe climate, peacetime, sweet air. Comfortable homes, long hot showers, comfy beds with fresh crisp linen, disposable everything, pain relief on demand, bountiful food and, wonder of wonders, fresh drinking water—out of the tap. But best of all was that you had the loves of your life in your arms again.

Some of the Acehnese would never experience that joy again. Their dear ones were gone. Paul just hoped that knowing people cared about them had brought them some comfort. You could bear anything in life if people cared for you, loved you.

Something happened one night at home shortly after Paul's return which meant far more than any public accolade could. Our ten-year-old son Liam asked me and Paul to watch as he rehearsed his homework. The Year Five boys had to give a short talk about what made a hero. Character development was part of their school training; 'People for Others' was the school motto.

Liam held his notes and spoke clearly, earnestly. He was not an ostentatious child. He described certain values and why he thought they were heroic. Then he paused. He obviously wanted to end his talk with conviction. 'Dr Paul Dunkin is an example,' he said. We were speechless.

Paul Luckin perhaps best summed up how many of the team felt on leaving Banda Aceh. He said the team would never forget certain things about the time there: the patients, the enormity of the disaster, the smell. The team had witnessed a desperate need in the local people's eyes for someone to help them, to give them some moral and emotional support and some physical assistance. There was something else. A quiet acceptance. It was the same quiet acceptance some in the team had seen before—after horrific wars, disasters, accidents, terrorist bombings. In Rwanda, Somalia, Bougainville, East Timor, Port Arthur, Bali, Vanimo. After train crashes, police sieges, cave-ins, bushfires, landslides, mountain and cliff rescues. It was a deep sadness, but without despair. Something beyond grief. As though feeling blessed to have survived. It was a reverent, patient and quiet strength. A noble determination. It was the primordial core of all endurance—it was *the human spirit*.

It was breathtaking to witness it. And humbling.

The human spirit is what inspired those who went to help, and motivated those who gave support back home.

Not everyone could be on the ground in Banda Aceh in those early desperate days, but people were still able to help, in very real ways. As the needs continued and grew more complex, Australians continued to help.

Cementing of relationships, building of bridges. A tsunami of death brought an even bigger wave of hope.

Constant kindness can accomplish much. As the sun makes ice melt, kindness causes misunderstanding, mistrust, and hostility to evaporate.

Dr Albert Schweitzer (1875–1965),
1952 Nobel Peace Laureate.

Author's note: On 1 October 2005, a second series of Bali bombings took place. The references in this book refer to the first Bali bombings, which took place on 12 October 2002.

Appendix 1

Dramatis Personae

Combined Australian Surgical Team, Aceh — 'CASTA' Alpha
Team Leader: Dr Michael Flynn (NSW)
Orthopaedics: Dr Annette Holian (VIC)
Surgeon: Dr Sudhakar Rao (WA)
Anaesthetist: Dr Brian Pezzutti (NSW)
Anaesthetist: Dr David Scott (NSW)
Emergency Physician: Dr Alan Garner (Careflight NSW)
Public Health: Dr Jeremy McAnulty (NSW)
SCAT Paramedic: Jeff Gilchrist (NSW)
Emergency Nurse: Liz Cloughessy (NSW)
Emergency Nurse: Lisa Dillon (NSW)
Operating Room Nurse: Marjorie Raggett (NSW)
Operating Room Nurse: Raymond Southon (NSW)
Logistics (Medical): Dr Ken Harrison (NSW)
Logistics (General): Greg Watson (NSW Fire Brigade)

Bravo

Team Leader: Dr Paul Shumack (QLD)
Orthopaedics: Dr Peter Sharwood (QLD)
Surgeon: Dr René Zellweger (WA)
Anaesthetics: Dr Paul Luckin (QLD)
Anaesthetics: Dr Paul Dunkin (NSW)
Emergency Physician: Dr Norman Gray (WA)
Infectious Diseases: Dr James Branley (NSW)
Public Health: Dr Paul Van Buynder (WA)
SCAT Paramedic: Adrian Humphrey (NSW)
Emergency Nurse: Terry Jongen (WA)
Emergency Nurse: Karyn Boxshall (WA)
Operating Room Nurse: Rosemary Clifton (WA)
Operating Room Nurse: Rhonda Cowderoy (NSW)
Logistics and support: Bruce Cameron (NSW Fire Brigade)

Wing Commander Bill Griggs AM RAAF SR: Director Trauma Services, Royal Adelaide Hospital. Recce team member for Australian government. Head of AME at Banda Aceh in the early days after the tsunami.

Wing Commander Allan MacKillop RAAF SR: Medical Director of Careflight Services, Gold Coast. Recce team member for Australian government. AME receiving officer at Medan.

Wing Commander Greg Norman RAAF: (Then) Commanding Officer Richmond Air Base Hospital. Recce team member for Australian government. Worked at Kesdam ED with Army medics in the early days after the tsunami.

Lieutenant Bernard York RAN: Officer-in-Charge, Fleet Logistics Support Element, HMAS *Waterhen* Sydney. Officer interface at Halim Perdanakusuma Air Base Jakarta between NGOs and others and Indonesian government, assisting Australian embassy staff in the early days after the tsunami.

Appendix 2

**Speech At Reception With Premier
For Personnel Involved In The Tsunami Aid Effort**

Government House
Thursday 17th February 2005
Her Excellency Professor Marie Bashir AC
Governor Of New South Wales

Premier, Minister Kelly, Minister Iemma, Distinguished
Guests And Friends

It is with the greatest pleasure that we welcome you all to
Government House today to honour and to express our
gratitude to you—unselfish and committed Australians—
you who responded so speedily and with great skill and
compassion to the victims of the Indian Ocean tsunami.

The United Nations has declared that this was the
greatest human catastrophe which it had faced. And
certainly across our own nation, Australians of all ages and

background reacted with an immediate and extraordinary empathy, an immediate responsiveness from yourselves and other Australians like you, across all the professions and trades, the services, national and international sport, and countless volunteers.

You are the representatives of a good society, renowned for its generosity of spirit and for its capacity to reach out to one another, and to strangers in need.

But these qualities have never been more illuminated than in the weeks following the tsunami, by yourselves and your colleagues which have made your fellow Australians so proud, and the whole world observe with admiration.

Watching the heartbreaking scenes of devastation on the television, we had but a miniscule idea of what awesome challenges confronted you. But I was also deeply aware that your diligence in working together so co-hesively, was miraculously able to prevent a *second* tragic consequence of widespread destruction, that of typhoid, cholera and other potentially lethal infectious diseases.

It is no exaggeration to say that because of your com-mitment, your skills—you have to a considerable extent diminished the attitudes of suspicion and distance in which Australia had erroneously been held for some years.

Indeed you have added valuable diplomatic strength through your genuineness and humanitarian actions which will never be forgotten.

I should tell you that I have received numerous letters and messages from diplomats and envoys of tsunami-affected areas, many also from countries not affected, expressing their gratitude and admiration.

There is still much to do, working together to rebuild shattered communities and lives, and being vigilant scientifically to the possibility of another tsunami.

More than ever before, Australia stands in a strong position to play an increasingly leadership role in the peace and stability of the region.

Your contribution has been immense, —incalculable, — and with the Premier, these sentiments —and our gratitude — are expressed on behalf of all the people of New South Wales.

Thank you all.

Appendix 3

Acronyms, abbreviations and explanations

ACTED   The Agency for Technical Cooperation and Development

ADF   Australian Defence Force

AIPRD   Australia–Indonesia Partnership for Reconstruction and Development

AHDMPC   Australian Health Disasters Management Policy Committee (known colloquially as 'The Alphabet Committee')

AusAID   Australian Agency for International Development

AUSASSISTPLAN   Australian Commonwealth Government Overseas Response Plan

BRR   Baden Rehabilitasi dan Rekonstruksi (Rehabilitation and Reconstruction Agency for Aceh and Nias)

CASTA   Combined Australian Surgical Team, Aceh

CSL   Commonwealth Serum Laboratory

DG	Director-General
DoHA	Commonwealth Department of Health and Ageing
ECG	Electro-cardiogram
EMA	Emergency Management Australia (a Commonwealth body)
EMST	Early Management of Severe Trauma
ERC	Emergency Relief Co-ordinator
Fakinah	Rumah Sakit Teungku Fakinah Hospital, a privately-owned hospital in Banda Aceh secured by the police force after the tsunami
GAM	Free Aceh Movement (Gerakan Aceh Merdeka)
HSW	Health Services Wing
HSFAC	Health Services Functional Area Coordinator for disasters
Herc	RAAF C-130J Hercules, a cargo plane flown by the Air Force
IDPs	Indigenous Displaced Persons
Interfet	International Force for East Timor
IOM	International Organisation for Migration
IRC CARDI	International Rescue Committee Consortium for Assistance to Refugees and the Displaced in Indonesia
JRS	Jesuit Refugee Service
Kesdam	Rumah Sakit Kesdam Hospital formerly military Hospital in Banda Aceh secured by TNI after the tsunami
NUM	Nursing Unit Manager
OCHA	(United Nations') Office for the Co-Ordination of Human Affairs
PAR	Post-Activity Report
PKF	Peace Keeping Force

RAAF	Royal Australian Airforce
RAN	Royal Australian Navy
RNZAF	Royal New Zealand Air Force
SARS	Severe Acute Respiratory Syndrome
SCAT paramedic	Special Casualty Access Team Paramedic
SIM	Sultan Iskandar Muda (Airfield at Banda Aceh)
SMS	Short Message Service—text messages sent via mobile telecommunications network
SNM	Senior Nurse Manager
TNI	Tentara Nasional Indonesia (Indonesian Military)
TVRI complex	The compound surrounding the TV station in Banda Aceh which housed the largest of the displaced persons camps
UN	United Nations
UNIMOG	A commonly used Military 4WD light truck
USAID	United States Agency for International Development
USAR	Urban Search and Rescue
WHO	World Health Organization

Acknowledgments

Thank you to my sister Armelle who encouraged me all my life to write and specifically suggested I write this book 'in my spare time'!

Thank you to my sister Libby who supported me along the way and, best of all, found me my publisher Richard Walsh.

Thank you, Richard, my wonderful publisher. Words are somehow inadequate for what you did. You made the recording of an extraordinary event in history, the tsunami and the initial relief response, a reality. Thank you for your kind and wise input. Thank you Annette Barlow, Karen Gee, Jody Lee and the wonderful team at Allen & Unwin, for bringing this story to the public.

My heartfelt thanks to the CASTA team: Michael Flynn, Paul Shumack, Karyn Boxshall, James Branley, Bruce Cameron, Rosemary Clifton, Liz Cloughessy, Rhonda Cowderoy, Lisa Dillon, Alan Garner, Jeff Gilchrist, Norman Gray, Ken Harrison, Annette Holian, Adrian Humphrey, Terry Jongen, Paul Luckin, Jeremy McAnulty,

Brian Pezzutti, Marjorie Raggett, Sudhakar Rao, David Scott, Peter Sharwood, Raymond Southon, Paul Van Buynder, Greg Watson, and René Zellweger. Without your contributions, loyalty and enthusiasm and generosity of spirit which led you to go to the disaster zone, there would *be* no story. Thanks for entrusting your tale to me. Although reluctant to paint yourselves as heroes, and busily back in your 'normal' demanding jobs, you made the patient effort to meet me, answer my copious questions, telephone calls, SMSs, emails and provide photographs. I will never forget you. It was a complete delight meeting every one of you, and an honour to record your story. I am very proud to know you. Although I was not in Banda Aceh, I hoped to capture some special memories of your work and give a glimpse of what was happening back in Australia. Any virtues to be found in the book are to your credit, any mistakes are mine.

I thank all the team's better-halves, families and colleagues, too. Your support was evident, every member of the team made mention of the fact that they could not do what they did without strong backing from home, and the cover given by their workmates.

Two of the spouses I must mention by name — Narelle, Sudhakar Rao's wife, for having a total stranger stay in her home, waiting on me as I interviewed team members and giving lots of encouragement; and Katrin Heusser, René Zellweger's wife, who sent me information a number of times and gave me strong moral support from the day we first met. Thank you to both of you!

Thank you to Bill Griggs, Alan MacKillop, Greg Norman, Hugh Grantham, and my brother Bernard York for your contributions to the book and for the work you did in Indonesia.

Thank you to others such as Brigadier Ken Brownrigg and Flight Sergeant Michelle Maclachlan, and the many, many people involved in vital roles in the relief effort in Indonesia from the ADF—from aircrew to loadmasters and air-traffic controllers to medical personnel with the ADF field hospital. Without the work of the former, the CASTA team could never had done what they did, and the work of the latter from all accounts helped put Banda Aceh medically back on its feet.

Thank you to all the amazing people behind the scenes who worked around the clock to enable the team to go to Banda Aceh, properly equipped and with the right under-lying plan, and supported their efforts while they were over there.

To my late sister Noelle. Your love of literature, your help with my essays over the years and your positive comments about my letters to you helped me in so many ways. Thanks Nellie.

Thank you to my sister Ingrid for your go-get-'em words and timely copy of *The Alchemist*; Lisa Hill, for ideas, advice, laughs and sharing of ideals and dreams—and fascinating title suggestions; Julie Hatton, who has always set the best example of perseverance and human spirit to me; Pam Hatfield for setting me on the writing path years ago, and Sandy Street for the positive energy and tips.

Thanks to Stu Lloyd for the invaluable eleventh hour boost and advice. Thank you to Dr Nigel Symons and the staff at the Sydney Adventist Hospital ('the San') who treated me to an informative tour of a first-class Australian hospital. Thank you Kylie Saul for helping me with my children whenever you could, what would I do without you? Thank you Dad, for offering to edit, and thanks Mum for correcting my English in my childhood and convincing me that I could do anything I set my mind to (because a young French girl called Joan of Arc had led soldiers into battle).

My thanks to my wonderful extended family and incredible friends for your ideas and friendship. The power of an affirming word should never be underestimated.

Thank you to my beautiful boys: Liam, Darcy, Francis and Pierce. This was definitely a whole-family effort.

Finally, thank you, Paul, for going to Banda Aceh in the first place and for giving so selflessly throughout the entire interviewing and writing process. I could not have done this without your tireless support and love. You are my rock and my inspiration. You have always encouraged me in every endeavour of my life and I can never thank you enough.